THE WORDS OF

ᴇ   4

11/2/05

The Words of Gardner Taylor

(available in both hardcover and paperback)

Volume One
NBC Radio Sermons, 1959–1970

Volume Two
Sermons from the Middle Years, 1970–1980

Volume Three
Quintessential Classics, 1980–Present

Volume Four
Special Occasion and Expository Sermons

Volume Five
Lectures, Essays, and Interviews

Volume Six
50 Years of Timeless Treasures

Available also as a six-volume set.

AUDIO RESOURCES
Essential Taylor and *Essential Taylor II*
    compact disks or audiocassettes
    featuring selections from the multi-volume series

THE WORDS OF GARDNER TAYLOR

VOLUME 4

SPECIAL OCCASION AND EXPOSITORY SERMONS

Gardner C. Taylor

Compiled by Edward L. Taylor

Judson Press
Valley Forge

Delivered as the presidential address at the Progressive National Baptist Convention in September 1968, "The Power of Blackness" was first published in James H. Cone and Gayraud S. Wilmore, eds., *Black Theology: A Documentary History, 1966–1979* (Maryknoll, N.Y.: Orbis Books, 1993).

Delivered at the American Baptist Convention in June 1958, "The Elements of Evangelism" was first published in *The Watchman-Examiner* on August 14, 1958.

Delivered at Harvard University on the occasion of Black Alumni/ae Day in 1993, "Climbing Jacob's Ladder" was first published in *The Harvard Divinity School Bulletin* 22, no. 4 (1993).

"A President of Preaching," the eulogy for Sandy F. Ray, first appeared in *The Amsterdam News*, April 21, 1979. It was later published in *The African American Pulpit* 4, no. 1 (2001): 80, published by Judson Press.

"A Mighty Oak Is Fallen," the eulogy for Samuel DeWitt Proctor, was first published in *The African American Pulpit* 4, no. 1 (2001): 76.

Unless otherwise noted, Bible quotations in this volume are from *The Holy Bible*, King James Version. Other quotations are from the Revised Standard Version of the Bible, copyright © 1946, 1952, 1971, by the Division of Christian Education of the National Council of Churches of Christ in the United States of America. Used by permission.

Library of Congress Cataloging-in-Publication Data
Taylor, Gardner C.
    The words of Gardner Taylor / Gardner C. Taylor ; compiled by Edward L. Taylor.
        p.   cm.
    Includes bibliographical references.
    Contents: v. 1. NBC radio sermons, 1959–1970. ISBN 0-8170-1466-7 (paperback : alk. paper). v. 2. Sermons from the Middle Years, 1970–1980. ISBN 0-8170-1467-5 (paperback : alk. paper). v. 3. Quintessential classics, 1980–Present. ISBN 0-8170-1468-3 (paperback : alk. paper). v. 4 Special occasion and expository sermons. ISBN 0-8170-1469-1 (paperback : alk. paper). v. 5. Lectures, essays, and interviews. ISBN 0-8170-1470-5 (paperback : alk. paper). v. 6. 50 years of timeless treasures. ISBN 0-8170-1471-3 (paperback : alk. paper).
        1. Baptists Sermons. 2. Sermons, American. I. Taylor, Edward L.
II. Title
BX6452.T39   1999
252'.061 – dc21   99-23027

Printed in the U.S.A.
09   08   07   06   05   04
10   9   8   7   6   5   4   3   2   1

To *that splendid, now shining company*
at Mt. Zion, Morning Star, and Ebenezer
— *some of whom knew slavery's dark night* —
a band of believers who gave light and heat,
information and inspiration
to my childhood.

Contents

About the Author

Dr. Gardner Calvin Taylor is presently pastor emeritus of the historic Concord Baptist Church in Brooklyn, New York, where he served as pastor from 1948 to 1990. Dr. Taylor has been widely acclaimed as one of the most outstanding preachers in the nation. He has preached on six continents, delivered the 100th Lyman Beecher Lectures at Yale University, and preached the sermon at the prayer service for the inauguration of President William Jefferson Clinton in 1993.

Now retired from the pastorate, Dr. Taylor continues to be in great demand as a preacher and lecturer. He recently accepted an appointment as distinguished professor of preaching at New York Theological Seminary. Dr. Taylor lives in Brooklyn, New York, with his bride, Phillis Taylor.

About the Compiler

Edward L. Taylor is founding pastor of the New Horizon Baptist Church in Princeton, New Jersey. During his ten years of ordained ministry, he has preached at colleges and universities across America and has ministered in Europe, the Caribbean, and Africa. Rev. Taylor has received numerous citations and awards for preaching and congregational ministry. He presently serves as a dean of Christian education for the General Baptist Convention of New Jersey.

A native of Ville Platte, Louisiana, Rev. Taylor currently resides in New Jersey with his wife, Constance La Trice Taylor, and infant son, Paul Lewis Taylor.

PREFACE

Occasionally I am asked to speak to ministers and students about the life and preaching of Gardner C. Taylor. Almost always someone queries the impossible: "Which of Dr. Taylor's sermons is your favorite?" That is like asking a bear, "What type of honey do you like?" It is inconceivable that I could pick only one. However, I do offer volume 4 of *The Words of Gardner Taylor* in response to these questions. The selections found here are the sweet honey to which I return most often.

This volume represents sermons preached by Gardner Taylor on special occasions as well as a selection of his expository sermons delivered from the Concord pulpit. The special-occasion sermons demonstrate Dr. Taylor's literary genius to an extent that cannot be offered to a Sunday morning congregation populated by people of various backgrounds and ages. The occasions at which Dr. Taylor spoke seem to be a thread running through the quilt of American history. A youthful Taylor, age thirty-two, preached "They Shall Ask the Way" during a main session of the Baptist World Alliance. He would go on to speak at that event on three other occasions. All of those addresses are preserved here.

Dr. Taylor delivered "The Christian Drama" on the anniversary of the Montgomery Bus Boycott at the invitation of an admiring Dr. Martin L. King Jr. In 1972, Dr. Taylor wooed and won the hearts of Harvard in his famed message, "The Strange Ways of God," a memorial sermon in honor of Dr. King. This book would not be complete without Dr. Taylor's eulogies of pulpit giants Samuel Proctor and Sandy Ray. Perhaps most notably, however, Dr. Taylor's sermon "Facing the Facts with Faith," delivered at the Inaugural prayer service for President William Jefferson Clinton, was a landmark for African Americans and all who treasure proclamation in the public arena.

In 1986 Gardner Taylor was taken by the notion of preaching through a book of the Bible. He preached through the book of

Ephesians, concluding the series in 1987. However, as Dr. Taylor pondered those expository sermons from Ephesians, he was soon led to begin preaching though the book of Revelation. Among our many conversations, I recall a particular remark made by Dr. Taylor about his start of this series. He stated, "I knew something special was going to happen." Indeed something did happen. At the conclusion of the series, without contrivance to his schedule, Dr. Taylor concluded his pastorate at Concord with the last book of the Bible, its last chapter, and its last verses.

These expository sermons are a glowing example of Dr. Taylor's willingness to grow beyond the traditional sermonic schemas to which he first became accustomed. His verse-by-verse journeys through each text blend the deep and textual riches of each passage with an oratorical genius. It was not possible to present the series from Revelation in its entirety here. Instead, only Dr. Taylor's sermons on the seven churches of Asia Minor and his final sermon delivered as senior pastor of Concord Church are presented here. In a later volume, sermons from Ephesians and others from the Revelation series will appear.

I wish to extend a special word of thanks to Mrs. Phillis Taylor, who located the remarks Dr. Taylor made at the funeral of Marshall Shepherd, and who discovered in the Schaumburg Museum Dr. Taylor's eulogy of Sandy Ray (as printed by the *Amsterdam News*). In addition, I am grateful to Minister Jacqueline Glass and Sister Donalda Britt, who were tireless in their efforts to bring the manuscript to press. I pray this volume becomes a blessing in the lives of readers, as it has in mine.

EDWARD L. TAYLOR

ACKNOWLEDGMENTS

I would like to extend my heartfelt thanks to Judson Press for the opportunity to bring these sermons, addresses, lectures, and other works by Dr. Gardner C. Taylor to the American public. The publisher's skill and objectivity have made the process of publication a joy. The technical assistance provided by Mrs. Phillis Taylor, Pamela Owens, Gloria Arvie, and my wife, Constance La Trice Taylor, along with the contributions of DBS transcription services of Princeton, were invaluable.

A debt of gratitude is owed to the Chicago Sunday Evening Club and to the libraries of Union Theological Seminary of Virginia, Yale University, Harvard University, Howard University, Southern Baptist Theological Seminary, and Princeton Theological Seminary for the invaluable resources provided to me for the compiling of this work.

In addition, I must acknowledge with appreciation the work of Deacon Bernard Clapp of the Concord Baptist Church of Brooklyn. Deacon Clapp has worked diligently for twenty-five years as head of Dr. Taylor's tape ministry and provided the bulk of the materials found in these volumes.

Most of all I wish to thank Dr. and Mrs. Taylor for their understanding, patience, and cooperation in this project. How grateful I am to have been afforded the opportunity to compile *The Words of Gardner Taylor*. I thank God for having so gifted Dr. Taylor that we should be given this rich corpus of material.

EDWARD L. TAYLOR

Acknowledgments
from the Author

The first portion of this volume contains, primarily, public comment on the Civil Rights Era in American history from a specifically Christian perspective — if that is not too bold a claim to make.

The second portion contains sermons preached from the Book of Revelation, in which I spent the last two years of my preaching in the Concord Church pulpit.

I was privileged to visit the sites of the seven churches of Revelation at the insistence of my late wife, Laura Scott Taylor. At her urging, we undertook the journey, flying from Istanbul to Izmir (formerly Smyrna) to begin the pilgrimage. I salute her memory with lasting and affectionate gratitude.

Gardner C. Taylor

Introduction

GARDNER C. TAYLOR

America's Twentieth-Century Preacher

by Edward L. Taylor

Early in United States history, the names Cotton Mather, Jonathan Edwards, and George Whitfield begin an exclusive list of American preaching legends. Since then, Henry Ward Beecher, John Jasper, Phillips Brooks, Jarena Lee, C. T. Walker, Lacy Kirk Williams, Sojourner Truth, and Harry Emerson Fosdick are among the names to be added to the roster of those who have displayed excellence in preaching. Many others could be included.

One name, however, deserves singular recognition among Americans who have proclaimed the gospel of Jesus Christ. That name is Gardner Calvin Taylor. Rarely do legends live in their own time, but Dr. Taylor has proved to be an exception to the general rule. His preaching stands as an unparalleled model — indeed a lighthouse — for all who would aspire to preach Jesus.

Gardner Taylor was born on June 18, 1918, in Baton Rouge, Louisiana. His father, Washington Monroe Taylor, pastored one of Louisiana's most prestigious churches, the Mt. Zion Baptist Church, which is registered today in the Baton Rouge Courthouse as the First African Baptist Church.

Washington Monroe Taylor, who also served as vice president at large of the National Baptist Convention, U.S.A., died when Gardner was just thirteen years of age. But under the tutelage of his mother, Selina, young Gardner developed into an outstanding student, eventually enrolling at Leland College, a black Baptist college located in Baker, Louisiana, just ten minutes from Baton Rouge.

As a college student, Dr. Taylor displayed a wide range of interests and talents. He was a star center who led his football team to

1

victory against Grambling. He was a serious student who devoted much of his free time to reading books. He excelled in extracurricular activities, especially debate. Among the several classmates he regularly engaged in informal, friendly debates was H. Beecher Hicks Sr. The debates, accounts of which have found their way into Louisiana Baptist lore, typically focused on matters of faith. Dr. Taylor made use of several resources, but his favorite text was Robert Ingersoll's *The Mistakes of Moses*.

During his college years, Dr. Taylor looked to Leland College President Dr. James Allen Bacoats, who succeeded Washington Taylor at Mt. Zion, as his primary mentor. Although surrounded and influenced by ministers his whole life, Dr. Taylor did not at first aspire to become one himself. Instead, he wanted to be a lawyer, and in pursuit of that plan he applied to and was accepted at the University of Michigan School of Law.

A tragic personal experience, however, would change not only his plans for law school but also the entire direction of his life. On a spring night in 1937, Dr. Taylor had taken President Bacoats' car on an errand. On a rural highway, a model-T Ford came out of nowhere and crossed his path. The impact was devastating. Two white men were in the car. One died instantly; the other died later as a result of the crash. In those days, the society's instincts were to regard a black nineteen-year-old participant in such an accident as a murderer.

Thankfully, however, at the court hearing, white Southern Baptist minister Jesse Sharkey, a witness to the accident, testified that young Taylor was innocent of any wrongdoing. Freed from any fear of prosecution, Dr. Taylor put aside his letter of acceptance to law school and began to think about the ministry instead. Out of this tragic experience, he ended up thanking God and offering himself to God for a lifetime of service.

In the fall of 1937, Dr. Taylor enrolled at Oberlin Graduate School of Theology. While there he wooed and later (in 1940) won the hand of Laura Scott, his first wife, who now sits with Jesus. During those years, the soon-to-be Mrs. Taylor began sharing with Dr. Taylor her love for literature, plays, food, and other elements of the larger culture that would go on to inform Dr. Taylor's preaching. She began her helpful critiques of his work, critiques that would continue throughout her life. During a period in which Dr. Taylor was heavily involved in politics, she said to him, "Your preaching is getting a little thin." That was all the counsel he needed to cut back on his political involvement.

At Oberlin, Dr. Taylor began several practices that, through the years, have greatly influenced his preaching. Most significantly, he immersed himself in the study of preaching as an academic discipline. Like Andrew Blackwood, he realized that every master preacher he respected had made a study of admired preachers.[1] He read sermons constantly, especially those of such early legends as Alexander Maclaren, F. W. Robertson, Frederick Norwood, Leslie Weatherhead, Clarence Macartney, and Charles Spurgeon. He read preaching journals such as *Christian Century Pulpit* from cover to cover.

When a student of preaching inquired of the great expositor Stephen Olford what the difference was between the pastor in England and the pastor in the United States, Olford stated in quick retort, "The pastor in America has an office. The pastor in England has a study." Defying that stereotype, Gardner Taylor has always had a study.

While still a student at Oberlin, Dr. Taylor became pastor of Bethany Baptist Church in Elyria, Ohio. His first pastoral experience, which ended upon his graduation in 1940, affected him deeply and helped him mature in many ways. Since then, he has always shown great love and sensitivity toward those who are starting out in pastorates or going through times of trial in churches across America.

Upon graduating, Dr. Taylor returned to Louisiana to become pastor at Beulah Baptist in New Orleans. In 1943 he returned to Baton Rouge to become pastor of his home church, Mt. Zion. Just a few years later, he was presented with two rare opportunities, remarkable for a man of just twenty-nine.

The first consisted of an invitation to speak at the six-thousand-member Concord Baptist Church in Brooklyn, New

York, whose pulpit had been recently vacated by the death of Dr. James Adams. To the astonishment of many, Dr. Taylor declined Concord's invitation to preach because it fell on Communion Sunday at Mt. Zion. (Some would consider it divine providence that on the date on which Dr. Taylor was originally invited to preach, New York City was besieged by a major snowstorm, among its worst ever.) To Dr. Taylor's surprise, he was reinvited to preach at Concord, and this time he accepted. On the Sunday he preached, Concord was filled to capacity. The sermon, "I Must Decrease, and God Must Increase," captivated those in attendance.

The second of twenty-nine-year-old Taylor's remarkable opportunities was the chance to travel to Copenhagen, Denmark, to attend the Baptist World Alliance. On the Sunday morning of the Alliance, he preached at Second Baptist Church of Copenhagen. Upon returning from his six-week trip to Denmark, Taylor was informed that Concord had invited him to become its next pastor.

No one who knew Taylor doubted that he would accept the invitation. They perceived him correctly as a man of vision whose mind was energized with great and inspiring thoughts and who possessed an immeasurable hope and desire to contribute to the advancement of the Christian faith. Many pastors move on because God has placed before them the challenge of a larger church. For Dr. Taylor, it was more than that. His response to this call entailed fulfilling his role in the destiny of the kingdom of God. As Dr. Taylor's friend David Iles put it, "Gardner was big enough for the field, but the field was not big enough for Gardner."

At the 1948 State Convention in Alexandria, Louisiana, Taylor announced his intention to accept the position at Concord. In doing so, he told delegates, "God has called me to preach at the crossroads of the world. I must go." No one in Baton Rouge had to go far to hear Taylor's farewell sermon at Mt. Zion. Radios throughout the black community were tuned to the church's weekly radio program. According to local seniors, it was as if Dr. Taylor were preaching in every home.

At age thirty, Taylor went north, serving the Concord Church from 1948 to 1990, in the process amassing what is among the most respected pastoral records in the twentieth century. Eleven months into his pastorate, Dr. Taylor began serving on a local school board. He went on to become the second African American to serve on the New York City Board of Education.[2] For a short time, he led the Democratic party in Kings County, America's second most powerful political party organization, behind Mayor Daly's Cook County in Chicago.

Nine thousand people were added during Dr. Taylor's tenure at Concord; the church experienced enormous growth. When the building was destroyed by fire in 1952, Dr. Taylor oversaw the building of its present sanctuary, completed in 1956 at a cost of $1.7 million. He presided over the establishment of the Concord Elementary School, where wife Laura served as principal for thirty-two years at no salary; of the Concord Nursing Home, which was founded with 121 beds, along with a seniors residence; and of the Concord Credit Union that went on to amass assets of $1.8 million. He also helped to establish the Christfund, which was endowed with $1 million to support community development, especially in the area of youth.

Despite these accomplishments, however, it is Dr. Taylor's record as a preacher that has distinguished him in American Christianity. The diversity and sheer number of places where he has spoken are a measure of the respect he has earned as a preacher. He has preached before the Baptist World Alliance on six occasions. He followed Harry Emerson Fosdick and Ralph Stockman on NBC *National Radio Vespers Hour,* which was broadcast on some 100 radio stations. National denominations from ten foreign countries, including China, England, and South Africa, have invited him as a special guest. He has also appeared before eleven U.S. denominations.

Even as an octogenarian, Dr. Taylor continues to receive acclaim and honor for his homiletic skills. He has received fifteen honorary degrees. He has served as president of the Progressive National Baptist Convention. A countless number of seminaries and colleges have invited him to preach or lecture. Among them is Yale University, where Dr. Taylor delivered the prestigious Lyman Beecher Lectures. Twice, *Ebony* magazine has honored him as one the greatest preachers in American history. *Newsweek* included an account of Baylor University's distinction of Taylor as one of the twelve greatest preachers in the English-speaking world. In an article on the seven great preachers of the pulpit, *TIME* magazine called him "the Dean of the nation's Black Preachers."[3]

I once asked Dr. Taylor that all-important question, "Are great preachers born or made?" After considering for a brief moment, he remarked, "I think that God gives one natural gifts, but there are some secrets. Those may be learned."

One of the underlying secrets to Dr. Taylor's success is simply hard work. He has read thousands of books, most of which now rest in his own library. Nearly every week he wrote a full sermon manuscript over a period of several days. Typically finishing on Saturday, he would then commit its ideas to memory. Very rarely does he speak without a manuscript of his remarks on file. Given two years' notice before delivering the Lyman Beecher Lectures at Yale University, Dr. Taylor kept up with his regular preaching and writing schedule, teaching appointments, and pastoral and family duties while still finding time to read all of the previously delivered lectures, which numbered about seventy book-length manuscripts.

In Dr. Taylor's preaching can be found a mix that includes a sort of grand nineteenth-century Victorian style, the richness of the African American folk tradition, and a unique interpretation of modern homiletical theory. The richness of his words and sermon design are legendary. Without fail, his introductions whet the listener's appetite. Like an *hors d'oeuvre,* they hold us for a time but make us eager for more. His message moves toward its purpose as a staircase headed to the top floor of a mansion. His rich language and genius for metaphor help to assure listeners that what may appear to be a steep climb is actually an escalator ride.[4] Each message includes thoughtful theological reflection and biblical scholarship, while steering clear of intellectual arrogance and abstraction. To Dr. Taylor, content and delivery are of equal importance. His delivery contributes to his distinctive interpretation of every text, personifying what Phillips Brooks defined as truth through personality.[5] Dr. Taylor embodies the best of what preachers have been and the hope of what preachers should become.[6]

Hearing Dr. Taylor preach opens a window to the essence of his soul. There we gain a glimpse of how his character has been wedded to the text. His legendary marking of the cross with his foot grounds him. His thumbs behind his lapels lift him as he hangs his head in sorrow with Job at his narrow window, enters the dressing room while a freshly bruised Jesus puts on his own clothes, or bathes himself in the blood which is a balm in Gilead. Such skill is unique in preaching. He exhibits his own prescription for sermon building, displaying genuine pathos and ethos through his mastery of African American rhetoric, through eloquence, and by grasping each audience's understanding of the human circumstance.[7] These are the very qualities that endeared Dr. Taylor to Martin Luther King Jr. and that should endear him to us as well.[8]

Dr. Taylor has proven the adage that "diamonds are made under pressure." Many people with similar gifts have faltered at accepting the challenge to greatness in their professions, but Dr. Taylor rose to the occasion. Each invitation became for him an opportunity to be gifted by God for the experience at hand. In part because of who he is as a person, Dr. Taylor is revered as a preacher among preachers. His ministry has never been clouded by personal scandal. He has a unique reputation for not changing his preaching schedule when invited to larger or more prestigious places. All this helps to explain why fellow clergy have granted him the standing he deserves today.

Although retired for nearly a decade, Dr. Taylor still maintains a hectic schedule, spending time with Martha, the daughter of his first marriage, her family, and his new bride, Mrs. Phillis Taylor. Frequently, he crosses the country preaching in pulpits all over the nation and occasionally overseas as well. He recently accepted an appointment as distinguished professor of preaching at New York Theological Seminary.

I am privileged to have had the opportunity to compile *The Words of Gardner C. Taylor* for the American public and, indeed, for all the world. Most of the sermons in these volumes were first preached in the Concord pulpit. Volume One contains sermons preached on the NBC *National Radio Vespers Hour* in 1959, 1969, and 1970. Future volumes will contain additional sermons (many of which have never before been published), lectures, articles, interviews, presentations, and special addresses, including his Baptist World Alliance addresses, the Martin Luther King Jr. memorial sermon, his address at the funeral of Samuel DeWitt Proctor, and the sermon delivered at the inauguration of United States President William Jefferson Clinton. (Readers should note that some editorial revision by Dr. Taylor may give these sermons or lectures a modern touch in style or language, but the content of the messages has not been changed in any substantive way.)

For half a century, God has used the words of Gardner C. Taylor to shape lives and develop faith. The purpose of these volumes is to help preserve his legacy. The sermons, lectures, and other selections included in this series are far from exhaustive, but they are highly representative. They are intended for readers' enjoyment, but they can also teach and inspire. Most importantly, it is Dr. Taylor's hope that those who encounter his words, even many years after they were preached, will be drawn to a closer and more intimate walk with God.

Recommended Readings

Susan Bond, "To Hear the Angel's Wings: Apocalyptic Language and the Formation of Moral Community with Reference to the Sermons of Gardner C. Taylor." Ph.D. diss., Vanderbilt Divinity School, 1996.

Gerald Thomas, *African American Preaching: The Contribution of Gardner C. Taylor* (New York: Peter Lang, in press).

Notes

1. William H. Willimon and Richard Lischer, eds., *The Concise Encyclopedia of Preaching* (Louisville, Ky.: Westminster John Knox, 1995), 37.

2. Clarence Taylor, *The Black Churches of Brooklyn* (New York: Columbia University Press, 1994), 118.

3. These remarks may be found in *Ebony* (Sept. 1984; Nov. 1997); *Newsweek* (Mar. 1996); and *TIME* (Dec. 31, 1979).

4. Brian K. Blount, *Cultural Interpretation* (Minneapolis: Fortress Press, 1995), 72.

5. Phillips Brooks, *Lectures on Preaching* (New York: E. P. Dutton & Co., 1907), 5.

6. For discussion of the style and content of African American preaching, see Albert J. Raboteau, "The Chanted Sermon," in *A Fire in the Bones: Reflections on African-American Religious History* (Boston: Beacon Press, 1995); Henry H. Mitchell, *The Recovery of Preaching* (San Francisco, Harper and Row, 1977), *Black Preaching* (New York: J. B. Lippincott, 1970), and *Celebration and Experience in Preaching* (Nashville: Abingdon Press, 1990); Evans Crawford, *The Hum: Call and Response in African American Preaching* (Nashville: Abingdon Press, 1995); Frank A. Thomas, *They Like to Never Quit Praisin' God* (Cleveland: United Church Press, 1997); Bettye Collier-Thomas, *Daughters of Thunder* (San Francisco: Jossey-Bass, 1998).

7. Gardner C. Taylor, *How Shall They Preach?* (Elgin: Progressive Convention Press, 1977), 65.

8. Richer Lischer, *The Preacher King: Martin Luther King and the Word That Moved America* (New York: Oxford University Press, 1995), 50–51.

Section One

Presidential Addresses

✒ 1 ✒

The Salt of the Earth

Retirement Address as President
of the Protestant Council of Churches of New York City, 1961

I would express to you very earnestly some half-organized but recurring thoughts about our Protestant witness, thoughts which have persisted in haunting me for some time now. As Paul Tillich and others have pointed out with extreme clarity, we are in what might well be called a post-Protestant era in American life. The old assumption of an America basically Anglo-Saxon in national origin and Protestant in religion is now only a national memory. The memory of such a country is still so fresh, the transition so recent, that many do not yet see that, while the melody lingers on, the song is ended.

America today is no longer characterized by Protestant domination of the religious, cultural, and political scene. The regnant moods of the nation are created by communities other than the Protestant one. The recent national election is a major symbol of the shift. The secular community which the Protestant community has spawned is a giant in the new complex of this land. As far as Christian contribution to contemporary society is concerned, the Roman Catholic community, still possessed of the inevitable aggressive compulsions of a minority, is now reaching its rightful place in national influence. The great, darker masses of Protestants coming in on New York City and other cities these days are preoccupied with problems of prejudice and discrimination and so have not come to feel themselves really a part of the Protestant community. The Jewish community, alert and sensitive, finds it necessary to make its alliances and to lend its considerable influence at one time to the Protestants, at another to the Roman Catholics, at another to the secularists, depending on which, at the moment, comes closest to fulfilling the ethical requirements of that ancient faith. All of this means that Protestantism does not enjoy actual, secure majority position in America, and this is most obvious in New York.

I do not enter upon this sketchy analysis in a tone of despair, for I think that the contemporary Protestant plight is not a reason for any dirge of demise but rather warrants sounding drums of destiny. Our brightest days can be ahead. We must discover again and assume anew our historic stance as a "peculiar people." We have become too afraid to be different, too afraid to be the "called out." Many commentators have indicated that our culture's success standards of crowds, wealth, and status are the church's standards, to its hurt. There rings across the silent centuries the voice of Jesus Christ still saying to his people, "Ye are the salt of the earth: but if the salt have lost his savour..." (Matthew 5:13). What point?

The millions of Americans who are only nominally Christian will never be galvanized into active commitment by further coddling in the name of Christ. The hero is not dead in men's souls. They will respond to a way in Christ which offers tears, contempt, and "homelessness" in the present order, which demands abandonment of primary concern for the praise of men and a willingness to lean on God. Not for the sake of angularity but for the sake of faithfulness to Christ, our Protestant community must once again call men to be different, to risk contempt as being "a little off." Until we are again a covenant community, distinguishably committed, caring little for the endorsement and less for the embrace of the culture around us, we shall be disloyal to our Lord and debilitated in our witness.

Along with this, a prophetic note must be more clearly sounded in our witness to this city. I say advisedly, and after considerable reflection, that we need to have our ethical purposes aimed at more startling targets than gambling and liquor and Sunday observance, important as they are — and without, I trust, neglecting them. We individual Protestants stifle and stagnate our churches and councils by forcing them to mute their prophetic note until there is a consensus of conclusion among the constituents. No radical prophetic theme will belong to our churches and councils until it belongs to individual Protestants.

The great business of erasing poverty, supporting just wages for the most menial tasks, alert political aggressiveness in terms of positions in the structure of government for Protestant laymen, coming to grips with the city which will increasingly dominate American political life, wiping out the fatal flaw of disparity and discrimination, challenging the nation to something better than a fat, fatuous, fumbling contentment — this is the job of an alert Protestantism. And this must be understood to be the mandate of God laid upon individual Protestants and the divine mission of our institutions, or we are through, and rightly.

We are now virtually thrust into a new and excellent position for carrying out this role. For all practical purposes, we are a minority community. I say out of long experience that there are certain advantages in a minority status. We are no longer caretaker of this society, in the sense that Protestantism is its quasi-official religion. God has now, by that minority status, put us in a position to speak prophetically to the society, to challenge this city and this nation to its best and fairest possibilities. In this kind of venture, numbers are not crucial. Herbert Butterfield has pointed out that there are remarkable examples in the affairs of men where "a mere handful of men, providing they have faith and a sense of mission, can produce an extraordinary landslide in history." To this we are called to the glory of God.

A people called Protestant, willing to be different, loyal to their Lord, courageous and yet humble, beholders of a vision and at the same time practitioners in the realities of living, can build in the desert of our day "a highway for our God" (Isaiah 40:3).

⌒ 2 ⌒

The Power of Blackness

The President's Message at
The Progressive National Baptist Convention, Inc.,
Washington, D.C., September 1968

Comrades in the cause of Christ, assembled here in Washington, D.C., a number of considerations impress themselves indelibly upon our minds and clamor insistently for our attention. One feels here in Washington that he stands close to the nerve center of the political arrangements of the whole earth. The ancients once said that all roads lead to Rome; so today all roads seem to lead to Washington as the governmental leaders of the world shuttle in and out of this capital of the mightiest land since Rome spread its *Pax Romana* over almost all of the known earth.

One feels immediately here in Washington the memories and influences of the men of our nation's founding who so conceived and so dedicated this land to freedom's purposes, though, like all mortals, they were themselves infected with the foibles and failures which belong to our common humanity. What names out of other eras this city summons to memory — Washington, Jefferson, Lincoln, and Douglas, to name but a few.

Those of us who see the nation as yet unfulfilled in its historic purpose are moved by other memories and thoughts when we come to this city. We think of that historic day in August 1963 when a number which it seemed no man could number gathered beneath the likeness of Lincoln and heard our communal leaders issue to the nation in its very capital the anguished cry of the disinherited, the pained pleading of democracy's forgotten people. Who can ever forget the ringing words of the only authentic spiritual genius America has produced, Martin King, as he thundered a paean of hope in his immortal "I Have a Dream" address? Who

16

can forget the deafening crescendos of assent as they rose up out of the innumerable host of Americans of all races and classes and colors and creeds gathered here?

As we come back to Washington, we of the Progressive National Baptist Convention are poignantly and painfully aware that our brave young standard bearer is no longer among us. His gallant heart, his gifted mind, his eloquent voice are denied us at a time of greatest need. Looking out upon the unfulfilled dream, the wasted years, the broken promises, the moral ambiguity, the puzzled uncertainty of the nation, a memorable apostrophe from literature floods the mind. One thinks of Wordsworth lamenting the passing of the author of *Paradise Lost* from English society at a time of great national crisis:

> Milton! thou should'st be living at this hour:
> England hath need of thee.
>
> Ah, Martin King, we mourn for you, but even more
> We long for your leadership.

As we remember Dr. Martin King's trials and triumphs, we remember our part in them. Progressive Baptists may take justifiable pride in the unassailable fact which must now be forever true, that when he had no spiritual home among black Baptists, cast out from the house of his fathers, Progressive Baptists gave him a black Baptist residence. You provided him with an address in the community of black Baptists. Let angels record that truth, and let succeeding generations bring their gratitude to your tent door.

True to Martin King's labors and hopes, we must face forward. Here in Washington we see more than the shrines of a nation's memories; we remember Resurrection City as the shrine of the nation's shame in its callous disregard of the cries of hunger and deprivation rising from millions of black, brown, Puerto Rican, and white throats. America, what madness is upon you, that hearing the anguished cries of hunger from your own children you could be so unmoved, so insolent, so hard-hearted! You do not remember that Jesus said, "Even evil souls know...how to give good to your own children" (paraphrase of Matthew 7:11). The cry of the poor must not be stifled. The indictment by the disinherited must not be silenced, or else the God of history will act with summary judgments upon a nation which had so much and would do so little.

How long will we persist in our madness in Vietnam? Can you not hear our gallant young leader pleading in that mournful eloquence of his, last year, in Cincinnati, asking the leaders of the nation to confess and repent of our wrong in Vietnam and so to save the nation the judgment of history and history's God? What an amalgam of destructive results has flowed from our futile commitment in that land so far away. Our boys die; our nation is divided; our young people despise us; our poor are unfed; our postal service must be curtailed; the world condemns us; the police are made the suppressors of legitimate protest; and all our instrumentalities of law are made the ugly tools of an evil national policy, thus rendering them enemies of peace, foes of Christian idealism, and servants of sin and wrong. Ah, brash young republic, hear from their graves the pleading of Robert Kennedy and Martin King and thousands of our slain young men begging for the end of war and carnage!

Progressive Baptists, we must ask ourselves where we are going and why. It would be improper for me, as I pass on the standard of this host of the Lord to other hands, to command the direction in which we are to move. However, I make bold to throw out some hints of what it seems to me God is saying to us.

The division of Baptists into so many factions along racial and other lines must shame and pain us all. I know that we Progressive Baptists represent a new aspect of that division. I believe that God has called us out for a purpose. We have already extended a hand to other Baptists. Conversation has begun with American Baptists looking to closer cooperation. National Baptists of America have extended a hand of Christian friendliness to us. I preached for them in February. Through a delay in correspondence, we did not receive their acceptance in time to have one of their preachers open to us here the things of God. I hope that you will see to this another year. Likewise, our outstretched hand must be offered to others. We are sufficiently fluid, sufficiently fresh, sufficiently unencumbered, and, I trust, sufficiently inspired of God to initiate the work of reconciliation which at last will make of our Baptist witness in this land one grand, united fellowship, to the glory of God and to the honor of Christ and to the healing of the nation.

I rejoice that our Christian Education Congress goes forward under the leadership of Dr. William Upshaw of Akron. We all take enormous pleasure in the progress of Progressive Women under the guidance of Mrs. Minnie Bruce, ably aided by our first women's president, Mrs. Uvee Arbouin. I plead for support of our laymen now headed by Mr. Roy Riser. Likewise, our Ushers' Convention merits our interest and encouragement as they move under the presidency of Mrs. Annie M. Serrano. Dr. R. A. Cromwell continues to guide our Foreign Mission Bureau with dedication and discernment. We must enlarge our support of our foreign mission enterprise. We must likewise continue our interest in Christian education.

I shall not dwell upon our desire to secure property. This issue is very much alive, and it may be that God is even now opening before us a fresh possibility. Better to take our time and buy wisely than to rush and purchase blindly and foolishly. We still must secure land, and we will.

I have recently attended the Baptist World Alliance Executive Committee as your representative, along with Dr. L. V. Booth, our executive secretary. You will be gratified to know that Progressive Baptists enjoy a very great regard and confidence in our world Baptist family. Also we have assisted some of our young people in their trip to the World Baptist Youth Conference at Berne, Switzerland.

I do not know how to assess the contribution and consecration of L. V. Booth to our Progressive Baptist work. I have found him thorough and thoughtful, filled with vision and vigor. Indeed, I count the friendship which has grown between us one of the rich rewards of my tenure. He has put aside personal preference and opportunity more than once, as you know, in order to serve our convention. I pray and hope that the convention will remain aware of his spirit of devotion to our cause.

Progressive Baptists cannot live apart from the heady ferment now occurring in the land among our own people. The winds of change are blowing in the thinking of many people about our present stance and future direction in this land. We who minister to people must listen carefully to hear what is being said, to catch the words of truth being uttered in the excessive rhetoric of violence of so many of our best young minds. Those of us who are thirty-five and over came forward in an integrationist generation. We are startled and sometimes angered by younger people as they talk about separatism. Much of this talk is angry, petulant, pointless. We need not abandon the dream of an integrated society, but we need to hear what is real in much current comment.

To the amazement of some and the anger of others young black people have evolved a whole new thing about integration and separatism. At a memorial service at Oberlin College (whose child I proudly am) following Dr. King's martyrdom, white people were shocked to see the first rows of venerable old Finney Chapel reserved for blacks. Preaching in Chicago this past year, I was astonished to learn that black students had demanded segregated housing. At Colgate Rochester Divinity School, I was steered to a separate section of the cafeteria by black students who wanted to be among themselves. In Dearborn, Michigan, a minister announced that he would leave that community, where his is the only black family, to return, he said, "to be with my own people."

I find it illuminating that Jesus called his disciples apart, as it is recorded in the ninth chapter of Luke. Jesus must have seen that every group must at some time or the other get with itself, find itself.

I have come to see that a church needs to separate from the

world every so often. It must carry its own ceremonies of identification, its own acts of worship and praise when and where there are people of the same conviction, who love the same Lord and march under the same banner.

The same applies to a race such as ours. Not in isolation but in retreat and communion among ourselves we must find our true selves in terms of those shaping events which have formed our peculiar and singular historical experience in this land.

The Scriptures suggest that the apartness into which Jesus led his disciples was redemptive, cleansing, creative, restoring, preparatory. He called them apart that they might be empowered. "He gave them power and authority" (Luke 9:1). Is this the valid word in the pained shrieks and the angry screams of the young black power men? He gave them the power. Something must stir inside of us if we are going to be adequate. That theme of power recurs like a symphonic theme through Holy Writ. I count 155 times it is used. The stranger who certified Jacob's new relationship spoke of power: "thy name shall be called no more Jacob, but Israel: for as a prince hast thou power with God and with men" (Genesis 33:28). In the magnificent, singing fortieth chapter of Isaiah his promise about enablement is clear: "He giveth power to the faint.... Even the youths shall faint and be weary, and the young men shall utterly fall: but they that wait upon the Lord shall renew their 'power'; they shall mount up with wings as eagles; they shall run, and not be weary; and they shall walk, and not faint" (Isaiah 40:29–31). Of Jesus it was said, "As many as received him, to them gave he power to become the sons of God" (John 1:12).

There is a power growing out of our experience of blackness in this land. There is much that is wrong, distorted, disfigured, crippled about us, but there are gifts and powers in the very limp which is our history here. There is a quality of rapture among black people which is authentically Christian. There is a sense of optimism which sees the threatening clouds of life but sees them shot through with the light of God. "Over my head I

see trouble in the air, there must be a God somewhere." Black
people have been forced to be three-world people, inhabitants of
white America, inhabitants of black America, inhabitants of that
strange land of the amalgam of their racial dreams and what was
beheld in the haunting report: "Looked over Jordan, and what
did I see? A band of angels coming after me." There is the gift
and power of black people as members of the disestablishment
to see the society in its splendor and in its shame. There is the
power of the rhythmic beat orchestrated by trouble and mourning and hope and which one hears in the strange, sad music of the
black preacher when he moves honestly within the cultic setting.
There is an apocalypticism, a Christian anticipation in vivid im-
agery of new structures produced out of cutting moral judgment,
a beholding born of stillborn societal aspirations and aided by the
bitter midwifery of rejection and scorn.

When Jesus had empowered his disciples, he sent them back
into the world. So finding ourselves as black Christians with a
peculiar experience in this nation, we must return to the nation
bearing in Christ's name the gifts of our blackness.

We must take this stand in this ugly, sorrowing, sinning world.
We must lift the hope of life in the colony of death even as
Moses lifted the serpent in the wilderness. We must tell men and
women that God loves this world — this angry, ailing world —
unto Calvary. We must bear tidings of redemption to earth's
darkest places.

As we serve we must ever tell people who sent us. We are not
among humankind of ourselves, of or by our own choice. We
must tell all who sent us. We are not placed among humankind
as a gimmick or a gesture. We must ever remind those to whom
we bring a cup of cold water, a visit in sickness, a concern in
nakedness and imprisonment as to who sent us.

We bear the crown seal of Jesus Christ. We are sent by One
who loved the world so intensely that hate could not remold his
love into its own likeness. We are sent by One who confronted
evil with a character so clear and a purpose so pure that the

hitherto unconquerable powers of wickedness were powerless before him. We are sent by a God who came where we are in Jesus of Nazareth in order that we might get where he is. He came here, being born in Bethlehem, reared in Nazareth, tempted in the wilderness, preached in Galilee, arrested in Gethsemane, tried in Caesar's court, died on Calvary's cross, and rose from Joseph's tomb. We must tell the world that this God has credentials of identification with us in Christ Jesus.

And now as I prepare to pass the standard of leadership on to other and more capable hands and turn to take my place loyally again in the ranks among Progressive Baptists, "To Jesus Christ be glory and honor and thanksgiving and power and might for ever and ever" (Revelation 4:11; 5:12–13).

Section Two

Sermons and Addresses to the American Baptist Convention

❦ 3 ❧

THERE IS POWER IN THAT CROSS

Denver, Colorado, May 1953

The superintendent said to the Negro principal, "John, I know that for the last six years we have been promising to you and to the Negro people, a school for Negro children. I know that it's awfully difficult to teach knowledge in a church building hardly designed for a schoolroom. And, to tell you the truth," he said, "I want you to know that I've been wanting you to have it. But we've discovered that the ten schools we have for the white children just aren't enough. And while I recognize that there ought to be at least one school for Negroes, I'm afraid we're going to have to postpone it another year and build another school for our white children." To which the principal replied, "I'm very glad to hear that, sir, for if there's anything our country needs, it's more education for our white people."

There are the voices of expediency that say in our land we must stop political corruption in our political subdivisions because the kind of political corruption which robs American citizens of their guarantees does us no good in the forum of the nations of the earth. These advocates of expediency say that because other peoples are watching us, we must stop our quota systems for Jewish medical students when our nation is crying for physicians. These voices of expediency say that because the world is watching us, we must do something for the American Indians, whose prior presence in the land should have given them some kind of moral claim. We appropriated the land in the name of civilization and progress, though atomic death and flame-throwing tanks might

---

The introduction to this address, which was delivered to American Baptists at their annual convention in 1953, has been omitted. What is preserved speaks to a tortured time in American race relations. — GCT

27

not be less barbarous than tribal warfare. There are those in our land who say that these things we must quit, and we must quit them because the nations of the earth have their eyes upon us and because we must prove our right to moral leadership in the world.

And even among racial minorities, there is from leadership the contention that we must reduce the pressures of our struggle in order not to lose the gains we have already made in the American society. These voices of expediency, in other words, say that we must stop these things not because we believe they must be stopped but because it is wise for our own future to do so. I submit to you that these are worthy sentiments, but they hardly spring from worthy motives. These advocates for expediency say that we must believe in democracy in order to convince the world of our right to moral leadership in this seething and turbulent age. I submit to you that if we are going to do anything, if we are going to convince the world, it is because deep in our own hearts and in our own souls we are committed to our democratic faith and not because we are seeking to convince someone of how good we are.

The Christian church is likewise under indictment. Before we left Brooklyn, Harold Manson, officer of this convention, said to me these words. They burn still. He said, "The world does not take us Christians seriously because we do not take our discipleship seriously." And there is, in *Camino Real*, Tennessee Williams's latest play which has just completed its Broadway run, a character who says, "Brother! What is that? It's a word for pulpits and not for life." They have even fashioned poetry about our own impotence as a Christian church. One wit has put it this way: "Outwardly splendid as of old, inwardly sparkless, void and cold. Her force and fire all spent and gone, like the dead moon, she still shines on." That's what a great number of people think about the life and power and vibrancy of the Christian church of which you and I are a part.

And let us confess it openly tonight. The voice of Protestantism, once the directing voice of our nation, has become in many parts of the land a faint and powerless echo in the halls of government which determine the conditions under which Americans live. It has become a faint and feeble voice because, as political leaders say, the people of Protestantism are not found in our major cities in the political clubhouses where the policies of the nation are wrought in miniature. Let us admit it. There are some Congressional committees that are sure that Protestant leaders can be pilloried and held up to public shame because no unequivocal Protestant evangel like a winged thunderbolt will shake the voting places next election.

There are many labor leaders in our country who believe that the Protestant church is a kind of spiritual solarium where tired old spiritual limbs are warmed once a week. And there is a notion abroad in our land that employers with their yearly subscription can keep the church in senile quietness, dim, musty, innocuous, where too much light, so like that of the flaming eighth-century prophets, had better not come. Our American Baptist yearbook lists in at least one state the churches of its constituency according to race, perhaps with good reason. Likewise, it is an open secret that a Christian church can hardly survive in a neighborhood where more than one or two Jewish families move in because Christians cannot live where the population is not white, Gentile, Republican, Protestant, and third generation.

I would not paint too dark a picture. There are hopeful signs. There are signs of the morning; the banners of dawn are in the skies. The signs of a better day are already etched in the hills in the east.

Last October, I and the people of my congregation watched a magnificent old building committed to flames. We stood that crisp October night in a drizzling rain, chilled at the marrow of our bones, and watched it committed to fire. That was on a Friday night. The embers had not stopped smoldering before twenty-two churches of every evangelical persuasion and race had begun their deeds and words of concern about us. On that Sunday morning we gathered in a grand and historic Methodist church, cutting across the lines of denomination and of race, and had a memorable fellowship. Dr. Arthur Bouton, the great-spirited pastor of that church, said to reporters of the New York dailies afterwards, "It's a shame that we've got to burn a church down in order to get Christians together."

But the depths of concern and mutual care were there. And I know a church in the greatest city of our land, located in a rapidly changing population area, which instead of running has decided to stay where it is. An officer of this convention is member of that church. That church has made its membership as wide as the provisions of the gospel of Christ. And it is today one of the strong churches of New York City, and I believe that it is strong because it has been willing to open its doors to all people who come in the name of our sovereign Lord and of his Christ.

I dare not take leave without saying that we who are black who have come to Denver this week have discovered the Christian imperative at work in this city. There has been no hedging about hotel facilities and about restaurant accommodations and about other things that we find so often across the face of America and north of the Mason-Dixon line. But there has, rather, been here a willingness without oversolicitousness, which itself is a subtle expression of a certain uncertainty.

While the morning is coming, there are still voices raised out of the dark night. On the opening day of this convention we were treated to a strange spectacle. In the Denver dailies they carried on their front page, and rightly, the account of a Christian leader in another state, and I blush to say that he was Baptist, who said that if the Supreme Court of the United States finds segregation illegal, 311,000 Baptists are ready to throw the cloak of religion and the sanctity of Christ around the institution of segregation by setting up private schools in order to circumvent the last refuge of the American judicial arena. That, from a Christian leader!

I sat in this auditorium the other night, and I watched the host of young men and women in splendid dedication to the service of Christ in foreign fields. But when I remembered this statement, I saw their final act through a mist of tears. For then and now I shudder to think of what bitter rejoinders will be flung in their teeth if this statement is released in the papers of Asia and Africa. I shudder to think of how the communist evangelists will pick up this, from a Christian leader, the executive secretary of the Baptists of a certain state, and what use they will make of that. What an insuperable burden we put upon the Christian evangel by our reservations and by our bigotries. And let me quickly confess that the suspicion and the resentment and the bitterness in this country are not confined to people of lighter hue.

I stand before you tonight smitten with shame that in my own beloved borough, in Brooklyn, my own church, all black, is less Christian, at least in appearance, than the baseball diamond at Ebbets Field in the same borough. And some of us are saying, as I shall be saying in college commencements across the South this week, how tragic that Negro people who could bring their sorrows and their heartbreak to the American conscience and courts are not addressing America with God's Word in tenderness and humility and in love, but allow bitterness and resentment to so fill their hearts that all of these years of agony and heartbreak are wasted. It is a two-way street.

I do not hold with those people who say that we do not preach human rights, we do not speak of remedies for economic disparity because we do not want them. What use is there to catalogue the almost endless list of our delinquencies both black and white? I am firmly persuaded that many Christian people of all colors kneel in shame every time they bow to pray to the Lord, Father of us all. I am persuaded that thousands of people across this land bow in deep humiliation and in profound sorrow at their failures at the point of class and race to live out the glorious provision of the evangel of grace which has been committed to our hands.

I also do not hold with those people who believe that education alone will solve the problem of our differences, our chasms, many and wide. Laws may come flaming as they did in the fires of Sinai. They may come in holy imperative from the voice of God himself. But there is no guarantee that men who know the right will do the right. We who are Christian have more than such injunctions. Yes, our gospel says to us that every creature, every human soul, is of infinite and endless worth to the heart of God. Our gospel says that the concern of God for every individual is so like that of a shepherd who leaves ninety and nine sheep safely in the fold and goes out into the darkness, braving distance and danger in order to return one lost to the fellowship of the others.

Still, these injunctions alone are not enough. But thanks be to God tonight that we Christians have more than the mere commandments of our gospel. We have a Christ, a person — real, compelling, sustaining, empowering, imbuing, transforming. I am suggesting tonight that fealty to our sovereign King can abolish the harsh reality of differences between us.

The other night during the song period we came to introducing ourselves to each other informally. I was sitting over there. A couple, a Mr. and Mrs. Sherwood from Wyoming, turned to me, and she said to me, "Do you love the Lord?" And I said, "Yes, I love the Lord." And our hands met — from how far apart we had come, not alone from almost the span of the continent. She perhaps was rooted in the Arctic regions of northern Europe, and my background is in the hot heart of Africa. But we shook hands in a warmth of fellowship and devotion because we met in a common loyalty. We have our Christ, and if it is hard to bridge the chasm, if it is hard to cancel the bleak, historical circumstances which brought us to this sorry pass, we have a Christ who gives us the power. It was his wisdom never to give a command without giving the power to accompany that command. Jesus said, and his words were like a trumpet blast arousing the slumbering heroism in the souls of humankind, "Follow me." A glad and happy word, but in it also, racing through it like an undertone, one can almost see the perilous crossing, the cold, bleak moors, the contrary weather, God's stormy north side, as an old Scottish preacher said. Trembling and shivering, they must have received that word, and with what misgivings we receive it. Along with the command goes another word, "Go. And, lo, I am with you."

There is in loyalty to Christ the power to bring the spring-time to our frozen and withered spirits. We have a person real and immediate. Yea, and we have a cross. John Henry Jowett, that inimitable spokesman for heavenly things, from Carrs Lane in England to Fifth Avenue in New York, used to say that when men's hearts are led to that blood-spattered tree, a strange and peculiar awe sweeps across their hearts. We have a person, a son-net of God's mercy deeper than any affirmation of the communist evangelists, who claim a brotherhood without owning a father-hood, setting themselves in an impossible contradiction. We have a cross, and we have a Savior. There is power, I declare unto you, at the place of a hill called Calvary. There is power to change re-sisting hearts and to make them sound again with the anthems of praise and sacrifice and service.

God in heaven knows that the pulpits of this land ought to be done with our pietistic, moralistic exhortations to people to do better. We ought to be through with our Ben Franklin almanac's maxims on common sense, parading as the gospel of light and power and grace and renewal. There is power in the cross of our Christ, if only the pulpits of our land would declare it and the people of Christ who are committed to his way would walk in his steep path. There is power in that cross to take the flinty rock of our selfishness and to turn it into gushing fountains of service and of brotherhood. There is power in that cross to take wet and cold altars and turn them into flaming, searing altars of sacrifice and of service to our Christ. The glory of the New Testament was that the disciples had found in Christ a power. Every word they said was a Gloria, songs from the front trenches of their glad struggle for a new world. Listen to them. Even by the name of Jesus of Nazareth whom God raised from the dead, even by him does this man stand before you whole. But if the world marvels at the sense of freedom the disciples got in performing what they contracted to do, they pointed trembling fingers of faith to a rainbow-circled throne as the place where their power was gained and said that by that throne the creature shall be changed from corruption into the glorious liberty of the sons of God.

There is power in our cross to bridge the chasm between human beings, to bring people of diverse backgrounds together. To unite them on that hill where the manna from eternity falls. There is power in that cross, the sonnet of God's grace, the triumphant act of his mercy, the trumpet blast of his determination, to destroy the bastions and ramparts of evil's dark kingdom. There is power in that cross to turn our land into what its founding fathers intended beyond their ken it should become. Oh, my fellows in our Baptist faith, at the place of the tree we find our deliverance. At the place of the riven feet, and at the place of the torn side, and at the place of the thorn-crowned brow, and at the place of the pierced hand we find our oneness, our oneness in Christ, our sovereign Lord, our gracious King. There yet shall march across this world the day of the coming of the Lord. The power of his church shall yet move to the stately music of the anthem of grace and redemption as revealed on Calvary.

There is a new world a-coming, cleansed of pride and prejudice. New world a-coming, purged of struggles and war's red strife. New world a-coming, a family of God. Christ, the first of many brethren, meriting his primacy in the chant of angels and all humanity, "Thou art worthy...for thou wast slain, and hast redeemed us to God by thy blood out of every kindred, and tongue, and people, and nation; And hast made us unto our God kings and priests" (Revelation 5:9–10).

My own people in a dark day realized somehow that that cross is the place of humanity's glorious meeting. Sweat on black backs sparkling in the moonlight and a plaintive voice mixed with sorrow, the anguish of many years raised in plaintive cries, in poignant pleas that ran through their slave quarters and down through the centuries.

Let us break bread together on our knees.
Let us break bread together on our knees.
When I fall down on my knees,
with my face to the rising sun,
Lord, have mercy on me.

Let us drink wine together on our knees.
Let us drink wine together on our knees.
When I fall down on my knees,
with my face to the rising sun,
Lord, have mercy on me.

Let us praise God together on our knees.
Let us praise God together on our knees.
When we fall down on our knees,
with our faces to the rising sun,
Lord, have mercy on us.

✑ 4 ✑

THE ELEMENTS OF EVANGELISM

Cincinnati, Ohio, June 1958

If we Baptists are not evangelistic, we are not Baptists. The winning of men to the service of our Christ has been the great theme of our history, the North Star by which we have sailed the centuries. We are heirs of a great heritage of outreach, a mighty, pulsing offensive in the name of our God and his Christ. We may have been deficient in ritual, naked of stately pageantry, minus the pomp and circumstance in our expression of the Christian faith, but we have been a people of warm hearts and an enormous missionary outreach. To lose this now, or to allow this emphasis to sink to a minor consideration, would be to violate our lofty and worthy spiritual heritage and to repudiate the throbbing impulse which is our Baptist birthright.

Ours is a generation suffering shock and disenchantment, and this is fertile soil in which we can grow the harvest of Christ. But yesterday we were quite certain that this land was the last and best hope of humankind. Poor Scott Fitzgerald, whose gifts were so towering and whose life was so tragic, was trying to say this when he spoke in these words of the American continent and the dream which came to rest over it as "the last and greatest of all human dreams; for a transitory enchanted moment man must have held his breath in the presence of this continent, compelled into an aesthetic contemplation he neither understood nor desired, face to face for the last time in history with something commensurate to his capacity for wonder." Our republic was held in affection from almost one end of the earth to the other. We were the people of peace, prosperity, and plenty. The inscription on the Statue of Liberty in New York harbor epitomized

36

both our self-assessment and the affectionate regard in which the world held us:

> Give me your tired, your poor,
> your huddled masses yearning to breathe free,
> the wretched refuse of your teeming shore.
> Send these, the homeless, tempest-tossed to me
> I lift my lamp beside the golden door.

Ah, but today we are hated by enemies and suspected by friends. The vice president of the United States goes on a goodwill mission, and the theme becomes ill will and hatred. Of course, we are complimented by some of the hatred which America receives from those who cynically use the phrases of freedom for their own ugly and destructive purposes. At the same time, we should have so borne ourselves in this land that even our enemies would have been unable to hurl the words "Little Rock" in the teeth of the vice president of our republic. We should have so carried ourselves that not even our enemies could have accused us of supporting dictators and taking sides with the fat and rich against the starving and poor in Latin America. We are engulfed by a great, dark tidal wave of black and brown and yellow humanity — the majority peoples of the earth in numbers today, but tomorrow, perhaps, in skills also, and we have not been able to convince them that we are sincere, Christian, democratic. Our deficiency is stark before us.

Certain regions of our own land reflect sharply the pride of race, the arrogance of color, and the unseemly emphasis on national origin which in varying degrees afflict all of our land, to the detriment of our evangelism, both nationwide and worldwide. I dare to assert that we shall never effectively speak a saving word to our world while we are in this lost and tragic plight.

Our human deficiency is so evident on a corporate scale because it is so naked and obvious on the basis of our individual lives. We are a people investing millions of dollars on drugs that give us pep and vitality while investing with equal desperation in drugs that give tranquility and relaxation. We are the most vigor-conscious generation in the history of the world and at the same time are the most relaxation-conscious generation our earth has yet witnessed. This paradoxical design for living is symptomatic of our sickness. Our basic illness is one of uncertainty about the meaningfulness of our origin, vagueness about the purposefulness of our existence, doubt about the nature of our destiny. Minus a basic God experience our generation is minus a sense of mighty origins, tremendous assignment, and titanic fulfillment. We are a tired, spent, rootless, lost, nervous era. Having come upon a day of relentless examination of all things, we make one towering and fatal exception — our religious affirmations must be a gang-typed, reason-drained, mass-engendered, issue-dodging efficiency, all done with the right lighting and the proper smiles. Our very pretense to religious experience is perhaps the deepest, rawest symptoms of our deficiency. The truth of it is that in every city and hamlet in our land the people around us, and perhaps we ourselves, are nervous, worn, jaded, frightened fugitives. Having failed to make this the good earth, we are now surveying outer space, forgetting that geography is not our answer and distance is not our Savior.

We have a great and authentic word of divine sufficiency for our human deficiency. The gospel of redeeming love which by familiarity falls so stolidly on our ears and cuts so superficially into our hearts is a breathtaking and exciting proclamation. It is the account of a God who has made common cause with our humanity, getting into the heat and mud and fever of our little earth to pry us loose from all the traps and snares and to set us free to "mount up with wings as eagles; to run, and not be weary; and to walk, and not faint" (Isaiah 40:31). The gospel is the wild, exultant Word of a God free of guilt, who assumes the shame of the guilty that the convicted one might walk again in the sunlight, bearing the precious document of full pardon and restoration. Here is a gospel to snatch the breath away and to leave a person glad and cleansed and rejoicing each and every day.

Someone was writing the other day of the different ways in which Washington and Lincoln are enshrined in the national memory. The writer pointed out that Washington occupies his own unique place in our history. He stands in our imagination a silent, splendid figure, cold and aloof in a kind of Olympian splendor. We are awed by thoughts of the austere George Washington. But when we think of Lincoln we see a man great, yes, immeasurably great, but so like ourselves, sorrowing his way through tragedy, groping, uncertain, yet with a glint of almost melancholy humor filling his bleakest days. We think of Lincoln as one of us, heartbroken, painfully considerate, treading a wine press alone toward an awful martyrdom for the redemption of the republic.

The difference between Washington and Lincoln illustrates the difference between the way men saw God before Jesus and after. Here is the sufficiency of the gospel. We have a God as we have known him in Christ who has come, as the elders of my race used to say, to our dungeon door and has entered there to sit where the prisoner sits until freedom can be wrought. There is in our gospel a carpenter's shop in Nazareth — God doing the common toil of our days. There are hot, dusty villages in Galilee and a Man from Nazareth who walks their streets — God in community with us. There is a judgment hall — God bearing the pain we know of betrayal and denial and base perversion of truth. There is a cross, a lonely gallows on a lonely hill — God bearing our shame, meeting the onslaught of the tides of hell, an everlastingly valid confrontation of God in Christ with all of the ranks and columns of hell and darkness and death that would snatch us from his grasp — and God holding fast. There is in our gospel a broken, splintered tomb — God victor over all that evil could contrive. Here is God in it with us, for us. He is never again, after Jesus, a far-off figure. He is now, guiding, succoring, challenging, strengthening, healing, helping — our very present help.

Faced with a huge human deficiency and blessed with a vast divine sufficiency there remains for a person so encountered and so won a great and imperative urgency. "Necessity is laid upon me," cries one in the grip of this urgency (1 Corinthians 9:16).

You and I are called upon to give voice and insistent witness to this release and renewal which we have found in Jesus Christ. The great need of our generation is that of a sufficient number of men and women who have had decisive encounter with Christ Jesus and who are so filled and thrilled by that confrontation that witness must be borne to what Christ has done.

Arthur Gossip used to relate the account of a fellow Scot who was preaching in a Welsh mining town. As the preacher sought to amplify his message a rough-hewn fellow stood in the church and started to sing the doxology. At the end of the service this coarse-looking miner said to the preacher, "I hope you will forgive me, but when I hear the name of Jesus, I cannot help crying 'Praise God from whom all blessings flow.' " The preacher asked, "But why are you so articulate in your faith?" The miner replied, "Well, you see, Christ has done so much for my life, and being a rough fellow in the mines what he has done is all the more wonderful. Down there in the mines and up here I have to tell the story." The preacher said, "How do the fellows down there in the mines take it?" "Well," the miner replied, "many are doubters. The other day one said, 'Do you believe that story about the water being turned to wine by Jesus?' And I answered, you see, I have been pretty rough, knocking the wife around and spending all of a week's pay on ale and liquor. Then one day Christ came into this life. Well, I don't know if he can turn water into wine, but I know he turned ale and liquor into furniture for my home and food for the children. So, you see, I can't help crying for all to hear 'Praise God from whom all blessings flow.' That's my story."

Every Christ-changed soul has a story to tell. Our evangelism is not alone, maybe not primarily, in great halls, but in the simple witness, person to person, by men and women who, hurt, have been healed of Christ, by poor lives made rich by his coming. The world waits for people who have felt the life-giving touch of Christ and who are willing to declare that the Lord has been real in their lives, turning their darkness into dawn, healing their hurts, liberating their chained spirits, giving songs to their gloomy estate, turning the captive free, throwing light down their darkened way, lifting dark, heavy clouds from their days. This Good News must be declared to humanity in mass and in solitary meeting.

> Go tell it on the mountain,
> Over the hills and everywhere,
> Go tell it on the mountain,
> That Jesus Christ is born.

～ 5 ～

THE TIMELINESS
OF THE TIMELESS GOSPEL

San Francisco, California, May 1965

In the twenty-sixth chapter of the Gospel of Matthew and at the thirtieth verse, these words stare us in the face and stab us in the heart: "And when they had sung a hymn, they went out into the mount of Olives." It is somebody's garret room, doubtless in a humble home, on some undistinguished back street in the great city of David, Jerusalem. A man, obviously the leader of the rest of the group, is talking to them about vast and mysterious transactions involving suffering and death. It is Jesus, spending the Passover with his disciples. That scene in the upper room is beyond any guess one of the most tender and winsome scenes of the entire Gospel. For these are men gathered around their faith in God. And around their confidence of something huge and decisive which God is about to do.

To catch the sense of the gathering, the atmosphere of it, one needs to turn to that painting in the New Testament, that portrait Gospel, the Gospel according to John. And there one senses the kind of affection in which Jesus holds these men as he talks with them. He speaks to them during that evening of his peace, and says to them, "Peace I leave with you, my peace I give unto you" (John 14:27). He says to them, "Abide in me, and I in you" (John 15:4). And then he speaks, according to John's Gospel, those infinitely rallying words in those hours when death has cast a hush and eerie stillness over our homes. "Let not your heart be troubled" (John 14:27). We like that scene; there is something beautiful about it, there is a lovely intimacy. There is a quietness about it, an air of piety, soft lights. And we would like for that

42

to be the extent of the Gospel. We would like for it to be calm in treatment, quietly spoken. A steadying hand upon the shoulder in hours of trouble. Gentle rebukes, perhaps, but never allowed an embarrassing encounter.

The only trouble is that the Gospel does not end there. The passage clearly states that they sang a hymn, that would be the quietness, the beauty, the intimacy, the mystic fellowship, the loveliness, the winsomeness of our Christian profession. But the Gospel goes on to say that when they had sung a hymn they went out into the Mount of Olives. So that these men getting up from that intimate fellowship after the breaking of the bread, and the pouring of the wine, and these strongly reassuring words, spoken by Jesus, went out into what? They went out into violence, and heartbreak, and sweat, and screams, and curses. For there is no way on earth that that element of the gospel which is our personal reconciliation with God, our quiet individual sustenance by him, can be the exclusive quality of the gospel.

It is this other facet which makes the timeless gospel timely for every generation. For these men went out, as I said, to bloodshed, and screams, and curses, and lies, and bigoted trials. Now, granted that had they not sung the hymn, perhaps they could not have gone out with the same gallantry and sense of honor with which they did. But they did go out to face terror, for already the arresting party had begun its ominous journey by torch light to do its dastardly business in the darkness.

Those of us who are Christians sometimes cringe and draw back, because the commitment of the gospel must sometimes be made in agony, and in the forum of hardship, and difficulty, and blood, and death, and danger. We forget, in our anxiety for respectability, in our desire to keep our gospel conventional and polite, that we are spiritual heirs of a people who knew intimately, and firsthand, and repeatedly, bloodshed, and curses, and screams, and sweat and tears and danger. And indeed we are the spiritual heirs of a society which was illegal and which was declared by the empire to be a society illicit. These were individuals who broke the laws as they knew them in the interest of a higher law. And there is no way that we can disassociate ourselves from that except by disassociating ourselves from Jesus Christ.

When they came out from singing that hymn into the Mount of Olives, they went out and by his deed at Calvary established forever a new standard of judgment in the earth. If Calvary is anything, it is the declaration that in our kind of universe, material power and physical strength are not ultimate. It is hard for us to understand that. But if Calvary means anything at all, it means that he has in very fact raided the kingdoms of material power and of physical strength. His deed at Calvary, in which he snatched victory from what seemed to be surest defeat forever, establishes a standard of judgment in the earth. That judgment being that nothing material is ultimate.

We had best learn this is our country. The accidents of history have rendered us in an awkward posture of power, and with it too often an arrogance which leaves this nation one of the most hated political entities on the face of the earth. And we are likely to put our confidence in our chariots and in our armies and in our instrumentalities of warfare. The deed at Calvary is declaration of a judgment abroad in the universe which declares that physical power is not ultimate and not even decisive. For by a strange thrust of history, this cross at last conquered all of the imperial power of Rome.

The president of the United States speaking one night in an evening loaded with hope and promise, and against a background of barbarity seldom equaled in the oft-bloody history of our republic, made this trenchant comment relevant to this judgment which is in history. He said, if you will remember on that fateful evening, that if our nation was to defeat every enemy and to conquer the stars, and yet remain unequal to this issue, the issue of the guarantee of democracy to all of our people, then the citizens of this nation will have failed. For with a nation, as with an individual, what profit it a man if he shall gain the whole world and lose his own soul? We had better learn that lesson, and quickly! For there is a conspiracy in history, a divine conspiracy which renders naught all material power, all physical splendor that is not brought to the service of God. "Not by might, nor by power, but by my spirit," saith the Lord (Zechariah 4:6).

The deed at Calvary to which those men went out singing a hymn has established that principle in the earth forever. Then they went out to begin at the levelness of Calvary a new fellowship. When that awful business on the bleakest of Fridays was done there was hardly a single one of them that stood fast by their commitment, so that years ago Paul Scherer commented that on the day of his crucifixion not a single vote was cast for Jesus. I once reminded him there was one, one vote. It was that of Pilate's wife. But by that time the ballot boxes had been closed, Scherer said.

But the truth of the matter is that even though there was flight, that place of Calvary became the rallying point of a new fellowship, sufficiently broad, inclusive. Our tragedy has been that we have tried to build our fellowships upon far too constricted dimensions. Always we have fashioned our community upon something partial, inadequate, fragmentary. We have built our communities upon the extent of our geography, those areas of the earth in which we live. And we have built our communities upon our creeds and our sex, in terms of those professions we make and those rituals through which we go. And we have built our creeds upon our economic circumstance, making the amounts of our holding and the extent of our property the terms of our eligibility. Or we have built our community upon some external accident, upon color, or accent, or what have you. The tragedy of it is not that we have built a community; the tragedy of it has been that our community has been insufficient for the breadth of our humanity and for the glory and splendor of our destiny.

As the sons and daughters of God, it is at Calvary that a new, and broader, and sufficient fellowship is begun. For where men and women stand in the levelness of Calvary, better still, kneel, they kneel with all of these externals dropping away; they kneel as equals. Equal in guilt, equal in the sufficiency of the transactions there for their redemption. Equal in their destiny. As the sons and daughters of God, equal.

There is at Calvary the beginning of a new fellowship. It is not confined to any one creed. I have stood with men of many creeds who somehow have been influenced by that act at Calvary. I have ridden in police vans with them. I have been detained in jail cells with them, more than once. What was the charge against them? It was that they were protesting, not in the most benighted and backward regions of the South but what is called the most enlightened city of our land, the city of New York.

They were protesting the systematic exclusion of a whole section of the population from the total building industry. And that enlightened city could arrest seven hundred of them. But not one time did it invoke a single penalty against a single builder or a single contractor, though the laws of that city clearly delineate such discrimination as a crime. And indeed across the face of this country, not one time has it happened. But these people were gathered in a fellowship. Some of them, two or three of them, were participants in the life of this convention — people who believe, because of Calvary, that they must commit themselves to the causes which God supports. People who believe, because of Calvary, that they have come to this august stage of human existence to declare the acceptable year of the Lord.

These are people who believe that every valley must be exalted, every mountain brought low, every crooked way made straight, every rough place plain. And the glory of the Lord must be revealed. And all flesh must see it together. Some of them are not a part of any church. They are, as Jesus called them, other sheep. But they are under the influence of Calvary, this fellowship. As Paul Tillich says, in that massive and monumental production of his systematic theology, they are outside the organized church. But they are people who show the power of the new being. There are youth alliances, secular friendship groups, educational, artistic, and political movements, and, even more obviously, individuals without any visible relationship to each other. In them the spiritual presence is felt, although they are indifferent or even hostile to any open expressions of religion. They are the people truly of Calvary, who have caught the spirit of the Lord. These men, who went out from singing that hymn and from that quiet and intimate fellowship, went out under the fellowship of their master and under the event of Calvary to introduce into the world a new radiance and a new power for living life gloriously and triumphantly.

Nowhere in the New Testament does one come across a note of defeat. Always there is an exultant shout, a glad hosanna, a brave and glorious alleluia. These are men and women marching forth under a splendor, under an assurance that they have come to the kingdom for such a time as this. They are the people who go forth strong in the confidence that theirs is a mission and theirs is a purpose — the mission of God and the purpose of Jesus Christ.

Our nation is being changed today, not by cynics. Thanks be to God, it is being changed by a valiant coalition of men and women who march forth in the glorious confidence that no center of power, that no systemic bigotry, that no fortress of reaction, that no long endured institution of oppression can stop the mighty thrust of the purposes of God. It is that glow and that radiance which fills the New Testament. It is that power which belongs to all who truly come to that cross and who have become a part of that timeless gospel. Sometimes that power breathes upon us in ways that lie beyond our power to understand what the end will be. For the glory of the gospel is that we are committed to things so vast, so stupendous, so significant, so incalculably splendid, that they lie beyond our capacity to interpret or understand.

And so it happened with a man at the turn of the century ministering to a congregation in the ghetto of Philadelphia. It was a dark night for his people and indeed for the land. The city of Philadelphia was fastening unwritten codes of oppression upon a large portion of its population. The lynch rope was seen dangling from trees throughout the land with sickening regularity. The codes of segregation were being written across the South and much of the North. Thirty years before this event about which I speak, the whole Northern area of this country had entered one of our history's most abominable and contemptible political arrangements, the Hayes-Tilden decision of the 1870s. It lifted the hand of federal authority from the domestic affairs of recently rebel states and turned from the aspirations and hopes of freedom in order to secure political office and political power for the North. It was a dark night. In the midst of it, this glorious gospel inspired a man ministering, as I said, in the ghettos of Philadelphia, at Broad and Fitzwater streets.

In 1901 Charles Tindley wrote words that have rung across the length and breadth of the nation. They have become the marching song for the liberation of the republic, words that have been now upon the lips of the chief executive of the nation. In that dark night but with a confidence born of the gospel of hope, he wrote, "If in my heart, I do not yield, I'll overcome someday. I'll overcome someday. I'll overcome someday. If in my heart, I do not yield, I'll overcome someday." They went out from singing a hymn to bring to pass these things.

Let us bow our heads together. Gracious God, thou hast thrown down blessed hints of thyself in countless ways, but shown clearest to us in Jesus Christ. We come now before thee. See how we cringe, how craven we are before thy will and thy way. Imbue thy people with thy power that we might go forth to the things that thou would have us to do, because we have become the people that thou would have us become. Arm us with that strength; make us careless of the world's judgment. Teach us our commitment as Christians and make us hopeful of that day when the kingdoms of this world become the kingdom of our Lord and of his Christ. For we ask it in his name and for his sake. Amen.

ᖂ 6 ᖂ

CIVIL RIGHTS EVENTS OF THE 1960s

A Retrospective and Forward Look

Portland, Oregon, June 1985

I suppose the argument will never be settled as to whether great men make moments in history great or whether great moments in history make great men. Perhaps there is no way to separate this, but the appearance of Martin Luther King Jr. at the time when he appeared on the American and international scene certainly gave impetus — and an almost immeasurable impetus — to the whole cause of civil rights in the United States. Indeed, he came for many people to be the symbol and the personification, for that matter, of the civil rights undertaking in this country.

The measure of his greatness may be gauged in part by the fact that the nation, overcoming all of its hesitancies and the blockages of its history, elevated him but a short time ago to a level enjoyed by only one other American, that is, a truly national holiday around his name. Given the spiritual informing, the Hebrew-Christian motivation, which lay at the back of all that Martin King was and all that he did, the holiday around his name might well bring the observance back to the original meaning of holiday as a holy day. That would mean that the annual observance of his birthday will have about it a quality denied even to the father of the country, George Washington. The designation of Martin Luther King's birthday as a day of national observance shows something resident in the soul and character of America, in spite of all the contradictions of our conduct and the presuppositions of our national ways of doing things. There is a grandeur in the national character when the grandson of slaves could be so elevated. Not even the one whom many people would look upon as the greatest of our presidents, Abraham Lincoln, enjoys such

49

a national holiday. He had to be lumped together with another so that we have Presidents' Day. What Dr. King and those who were associated with him did was to heave the nation forward — sometimes against its will — toward the fulfillment of its national purpose and of its historical destiny.

Now there are cynics here and there who seek to minimize what happened in the civil rights revolution — the March on Selma — and all of the things that occurred at that time. The truth of the matter is, with all that did *not* happen, much did happen, and the United States' society was radically altered, irrevocably altered.

To take but one slice of the nation's life, there are more non-white people today on American television than one would have thought, according to the news industry prior to the civil rights revolution, existed altogether in the entire country. One taking that narrow paradigm could well trace area after area in which our country found a decency it had never known before. The civil rights revolution was real, and it was profound. Its effect was shattering to so many mores and practices of this nation, and it set our society on a new course, delivered it from its own destruction, from some of its own guilt, and enabled the nation with less soiled credentials to assert itself as a leader of the world.

Prior to the civil rights revolution, Channing Tobias, the black YMCA executive, after he had served for a while as one of the delegates to the United Nations, once said to President Truman in regard to the Third World: "It may well be, Mr. President, that the black American community, having endured the America we have known for so long, may well be able to bear segregation for another generation or two, but can America stand another generation pretending to be a leader of the world while constantly having to pull down the curtains to try to keep the world from viewing what is inside our domestic scene?" Martin Luther King and the civil rights revolution did deliver the nation from that embarrassment, that national shame, that international placarding of our own gross racism.

At the same time, one remembers that sunlit summer afternoon in Washington when Dr. King spoke about his hopes for the United States, his "I Have A Dream" speech. That address must certainly rank among the supreme statements in all of human history about hope for a society of equality and opportunity.

I preached in South India three or four years ago. I was carried out to a remote Indian village miles from any other community — out in the rice paddies of South India — and there on the wall of the little community settlement center was the likeness of Martin Luther King. And people were talking then about how President Carter had stood before the Indian parliament and had said that Martin Luther King freed him to become president of the United States of America, for no child of the true Confederacy (Texas not qualifying) for generations had until his time been able to be elected president.

At the same time when one thinks of the noble optimism, the magnitude of the vision that Dr. King uttered at the March on Washington, one has to wonder whether, out of the grandeur of his soul and the nobility of his own spirit and faith, he made a miscalculation about the depth of racism; how deeply textured it was and is, and how inextricably scored its consequences are in the whole national disposition. That is the major question before us now. Too, he could not know then and the jury is still out now as to whether, for instance, the black American community has the stamina to sustain over a long period of time its determination to enter fully into the American scene. I think one would have to say that in the name of some kind of tolerance there is a cravenness in the black community which allows it to tolerate, and sometimes to honor, people who betray its aspirations and its desires. There are pathologies in the black community with which blacks have not been able to deal. There is still a question as to whether Dr. King's optimism about our national willingness to make and sustain change in the area of race was a miscalculation. On the other hand, considering where we are, we may have gone farther than any of us realize, for in the American South of my childhood — and not merely confined to the South — the United

States was then what South Africa is today. I have preached in South Africa, in Johannesburg and in Cape Town, and what I saw in South Africa was a replica of what I grew up with in Louisiana.

Our protestations of democratic virtue may have so obscured the depth of racism that Dr. King may have been overconfident about our desire truly to be a democracy. When we realize that in the 1930s and 1940s the United States Senate, mind you, was debating whether there should be, or could be, anti-lynching legislation in the United States of America, we begin to understand who and what we were as a country. All of the people who were cool toward anti-lynching legislation were not confined to the Bilbos and the Eastlands and the Talmadges from Mississippi and Georgia and the other states of the old Confederacy.

There was a man named McNary and a man named Guy Cordon, senators from the state of Oregon. There were William Borah, senator from Idaho, Irving Ives from New York, Arthur Vandenberg from Michigan, and others who, if they did not support the filibusters, certainly acquiesced to them. It was only later we discovered that there were resources in the parliamentary procedures of the United States Senate to block filibuster. The failure to get anti-lynching legislation was more a matter of national will. This is to say how deeply scored and etched into the whole American personality has been the question of race. It is what Gunnar Myrdal called a generation ago "a preoccupation with our internal proletariat."

If Dr. King made a miscalculation, it was in his optimism about the nation's willingness, once it had placed on its agenda a question which had embarrassed it and from which it suffered untold psychic damage and which it had sought to sweep under the rug. Countless conversations with Dr. King left no doubt in my mind that he was beyond question a Christian realist about human nature, but his faith in America was bright enough to persuade him that it would purge itself of its deepest evil. Some attempt has been made, but you and I know that in no part of the country has Dr. King's vision at Washington been fulfilled, and it hardly bids fair to be fulfilled in our generation.

There is something else to be said today about our present position on race. Notwithstanding our enthusiasm and determination during the late 1960s and 1970s to right a longstanding and wrong preoccupation with race and all of the implications of race, we have come now upon a day when America apparently has grown weary of the struggle. I do not now make a political statement; I have no competence in that area. I do now make a statement about the mood of the nation. Dr. King could not anticipate, and those who worked with him could not anticipate, that there would be brought forward by the people of this country, with many other reasons, of course, a national administration whose head had openly opposed the 1965 civil rights legislation and which administration has sought systematically, with the most polite phrase, an engaging toss of the head, and a practiced tremor in the voice, to chip away day after day, year after year, at all of the hard-won gains of our whole civil rights struggle. One listened in vain at the Bitburg cemetery litany to hear some word which spoke of justice where black and white are concerned. One heard, "I am a Jew because anti-Semitism still threatens the world. I am an Afghan; I am a prisoner of the Gulag; I am a Vietnamese in a boat off shore; I am a Cambodian; I am a Cuban; I am an Indian in Nicaragua." One listened to hear, "I am a South African black," but it never came forth.

Here is what faces us in America today. Our problem is still deep. Our journey is still a long one. And let us be honest, my American brothers and sisters, our nation is soft on fascism, defined in part as racism, or else there would have been a greater outcry when the president of the United States said recently in Europe that the people who fought in the Spanish Brigade of the Loyalists were wrong a generation ago and, by implication, Franco, one of the goriest dictators of the first half of the twentieth century, was right. As for the Bitburg cemetery, the truth of the matter is that in sections of this country where there were no large Jewish populations, the appearance at Bitburg, as far as I could tell from the national press, drew little sharp criticism.

There is another development which now faces our civil rights struggle and our Christian witness. We have seen in recent years a joining of the political right to the Christian right, along with slick television packaging of religious pitchmen for greed and for self-indulgence. I do not find it at all surprising that the two supremely popular televisions series in America today deal with admiringly conspicuous consumption. Self-indulgence and greed are now lifted by polite phrase and by practiced, artistic oratory, both from the pulpit and from the public platform, into something not only to be tolerated but into something to be desired. I had started to say that it is a marriage of the religious right and political conservatism at the altar of greed and power. It is rather an immoral liaison of the worst impulses in the American psyche, and in it we see another threat to our whole civil rights struggle.

Denominations, great denominations that have been historically committed to human rights — and I do not merely speak of black/white human rights but of all human rights and of the fulfillment of the Christian gospel in its unmistakable mandate in the area of the liberation of humanity — have been *cowed* by national television and by folksy American magazines filled with sentimentality and with periodic doses of rightist poison, so that allies of the cause of civil rights, some of the great denominations of America, have been neutralized and immobilized and driven back into privatism, into a retreat into a pious, noncontroversial Christianity, whatever that is.

Some years ago at a moment of fearful black denominational struggle, Martin Luther King Sr. called out to some of us a term from the old South, "Hold your holt." There are times and seasons when people of decent impulse can only hold their "holt." These are moments of pause, but as surely as I stand here and as surely as God lives this season will pass in the nation's life. We are in the movies now, led by mediocre screen actors, and we have lost touch with reality, but sooner or later we must come out into the sunlight.

And so I throw out that word to those of you who believe in the great dreams of American liberation and of America's destiny as an exemplar of freedom and hope and opportunity: "Hold your holt!" This sad time will pass. Light a candle in the darkness and the darkness will not put it out, and all the while, "hold your holt."

I grieve that the distance between black and white people and our morbid preoccupation with race have prevented so many of you from knowing the music of Charles Albert Tindley, Methodist preacher in the Philadelphia ghetto in the early decades of this century. Tindley wrote the battle hymn of the civil rights struggle, "We Shall Overcome." There was another hymn he wrote which I do wish more of us knew and had at hand and at heart. He wrote it out of a bitter personal disappointment. He was denied the honor of the Episcopal bench through chicanery of some of his contemporaries, one or two of whom I knew in my own early years. He had the grave disappointment of an embarrassment brought on his family by his favorite daughter, and all of the while the terrorists of America were burning and lynching and driving out of their communities people very close to the heart of Charles Albert Tindley. In that darkest time, far more Stygian even than our own hour, Tindley wrote a hymn, and with it I bid you good day. One of the verses runs:

> Harder yet may be the fight
> Right may often yield to might,
> Wickedness a while may reign,
> Satan's cause may seem to gain,
> There is a God who rules above
> With hand of power and heart of love.

Let me paraphrase what Tindley wrote next: "If I join myself to what is right, he'll fight my battle. I shall have peace some day." Hold your holt.

Section Three

Sermons and Addresses
to the Baptist World Alliance

THEY SHALL ASK THE WAY

Cleveland, Ohio, July 1950

There is a question on the lips of our times, a poignant, desperate, haunting question. A question which arises because our old confidence is gone. We were sure yesterday that we had the future neatly folded, wrapped, and ready for delivery. Utopia was in our hands — our chromium-plated, push-button conveniences told us so. A swaggering age was ready to wave a jaunty farewell to God, for we had outgrown him — our streamlined gadgets were the credentials of our adulthood, our bypass of the old verities. We were quite certain that any further truck with God would be on our own terms — all in the frame of our new science.

"Glory to man in the highest. For man is the master of all things." We granted, with a bit of impatience, that everything was not completely perfected: here and there could be seen man's brutality to man. Education was the answer to such brutality, and since we were not the victims, the length of time it would take was not so critical a matter. In the meantime, those who were suffering the indignities ought to be patient. However, we forgot that history and history's God would not wait on our disposition. Education was the answer, until along came the Nazi horror, established in the best-educated land on earth. Along it came, breathing its threatenings, opening its gas chambers, multiplying the horrors of its concentration camps, venting demonic violence on the basis of race, which was but the elaboration of what other parts of the world had done — some not too far from this pleasant lakefront. An uncertainty leapt to the countenance of our generation.

With a shrug of our shoulders, in the days of our self-confidence, our age confessed that in a world of plenty there were millions who

59

went to bed each night without sufficient food, shivered in the blasts of winter without sufficient shelter. Such conditions men dismissed with catchphrases — the enlightened self-interest of free enterprise would take care of all that. Only it didn't.

With an arrogant twist of the head, a confident age agreed that there were sections of the world where people were denied access to public places, equal wages, and self-government in lands where their fathers had lived for centuries. After all, they were backward peoples who probably did not want anything better. They were the "white man's burden." The mutterings have mounted to thunder in Asia and Africa, and storm clouds hang over lands long smoldering in virtual bondage. The thunders from the East have put a question on the lips of our generation. Our streamlined gadgets, graphs, charts, and scientific knowledge before which we genuflected in worship as to a new god somehow lacked the answer to our haunting uncertainties.

We knew that churches divided along the lines of race, class, and section were mockeries — but were sure that a more feverish campaign for numbers, a new educational building, larger budgets, and well-worded resolutions when we sat in solemn conclave would more than atone for what we lacked of the inclusive spirit of Christ. The only trouble is that the world scorns our preaching of Christ, in whom there is neither east nor west, when we give such poor witness to him in our actions. There is a question on the lips of our generation.

Our gadgets have turned now into threats; our push buttons now contain cosmic death. The voice of judgment is raised to tones of thunder in our day. Over us the clouds of war hang low: our confidence is shattered. Men ask a repentant church to show the way to the world's great dreams of peace and harmony.

In their question is our opportunity. Our situation calls to mind the words set in the fiftieth chapter of the Book of Jeremiah at the fifth verse, "They shall ask the way to Zion with their faces thitherward." These words come at the close of a bewildering experience of slavery, hard by the low canals and willow trees in Babylon. For years, Zion, City of God set on a hill, beautiful for situation, has been to these poor exiles but a dream, a hope long deferred. But now the long night of captivity is past; the purpling dawn of a people's hope brightens the horizon. The children of captivity are free to go home. History's God has given to them a new national opportunity. Alas! the road across the desert is unknown to them; there are no way markers on their journey, but their hopes and hearts are turned toward the city of their dreams. If they can find their way, they will come to its heights, walk in ways which have been hallowed by prophets' tread, and build again on Mt. Zion a sanctuary for their dearest hopes. Thus the word, "They shall inquire the way to Zion with their faces turned thitherward." From the New Testament, as though the question were raised to cosmic proportions, there is bold answer in the fourteenth chapter of John and the sixth verse, "I am the way."

On the lips of our generation, weary and sick, overtaken by uncertainty, desperate, afraid, lonely, and sick, there is the same question. Our age is asking the way: everywhere there is recognition that we are lost.

War after war has been fought with the hope that each is the last one. Alas! the crimson harvest of each succeeding conflict has seemed to bear the seed of the next. Some deep awareness tells us that human life is too precious in the gaze of God to be wasted in the sudden destruction of battlefields and as targets for bombsights. War is immoral, some deep instinct makes us know. It is not our destined way. We inquire the way to that height where they shall neither hurt nor kill in all God's holy hill. Our faces are turned in the direction of peace; our hearts yearn for it. We ask the way to Zion.

Our question is made the more desperate because we are faced with the old mandate of God underscored with atomic power. "This do, and thou shalt live. This do, and thou shalt surely die" (based on Deuteronomy 30:16). Holding in our hands the cosmic flame, we inquire for the cosmic wisdom to use it aright. But how? Larger armies have not protected us against war; greater navies are no guarantee against bloodshed. The centuries speak with one voice at that point. From sea to shining sea, men inquire the way to Zion.

We who name the name of Jesus as Lord proclaim that in his spirit is the way to the world's long-hoped-for Zion of peace. He has plumbed the depths of our universe and come aloft bearing in his spirit the way to peace, the only way honored by the very structure of our universe. It was his faith that a band of committed men and women, partakers of his spirit and consecrated to his will, would be a saving leaven in the world loaf. At a certain point in his ministry, he waited for the return of his disciples he had sent out. When they reported to him their success, his word was "I saw Satan fall from heaven like lightning" (paraphrase of Luke 10:18) — as if their experiences ratified a deep conviction of his. Men and women aflame with his purposes can storm the ramparts of this world's disharmonies, can bring a new earth wherein dwelleth righteousness and peace. Our world's greatest need is men and women in every land, of every kindred, and in every language committed to our oneness in Christ. That oneness is deeper than any national difference — our common faith leaping iron curtains, bridging oceans, uniting continents, abolishing borders, bringing to pass that anguished prayer fashioned in his spirit: "Holy Father, keep through thine own name those whom thou hast given me, that they may be one, as we are" (John 17:11). Enough men and women committed to oneness in Christ can break the evil spell of our recurring slaughters, pull down flags of national pride, and raise the blood-stained banner of Calvary's kingdom in their stead. "I am the way" is his unequivocal word flung back to our desperate questioning. Deeper than all differences of nation or language or culture is oneness in Christ who hath broken down the middle wall of partition. Committed Christians of every language, of every kindred, of every tribe shall make the earth hear echo of heaven's theme:

Jesus shall reign where'er the sun
Does his successive journeys run,
His kingdom stretch from shore to shore
Till moons shall wax and wane no more.

People and realms of every tongue
Dwell on his love with sweetest song,
And infant voices shall proclaim
Their early blessings on his name.

We are beginning to recognize that the problem of race sorely vexes our Christian witness as it does our world's peace. There was a day when men boldly proclaimed the superiority of race, even supported it by spurious interpretation of Scripture, a reflection on the integrity of God and the justice of the Eternal. The day is far spent when men can believe that souls can be evangelized with a Bible in one hand and a whip in the other. Brave voices in Christ are standing up everywhere to declare such doctrines contrary to the spirit of him who made a mercy seat on the ledge of a well in Samaria and who gave his pronouncement on the oneness of humanity in a parable about a dangerous curve on the road that led from Jerusalem to Jericho. There was a time when men sought to bypass the ultimatum of the gospel for one humanity by a frenzied emphasis on individual salvation, thus bringing a shadow on that fundamental truth. Surely the claim of God is laid in sovereign demand at each human heart. An individual and God are the crucial figures in the drama of redemption — but the stage for that tender drama is history, a social contract. Surely the brave shepherd goes a-questing through the night for one sheep — but goes that he may lay it across his shoulder and come home, to put it back in the fold. No doctrine of race can be made to fit in the frame of the gospel of Christ. We shall be Christian at the point of race or be forced to confess we are not Christian at all. We cannot be strong on faith and weak on work without being contradictory. How tragic that within the body of Christ there is such mutual enmity and suspicion. Churches all black are no less guilty of racial sins than are churches all white. I blush still at memory of the words of a friend who a few days ago said in my hearing, "There is no more segregation at eleven o'clock on Sunday morning when we stand to sing 'In Christ There Is No East or West' than at any time in the week in the market place, sports arena, or stadium or gaming casino."

We are realizing that ill will begets ill will. Antipathy is not one-sided. Majorities and minorities share the same hatred which is death to both. The same poison is discovered at the bottom of the heap which is so evident at the top.

Thank God for courageous voices in the most difficult places inquiring the way to Zion from this captivity of racial hatred. Thank God for a growing awareness that we are all one race — the human race. In the midst of our asking the way, we hear a voice, stronger than the iron mountains, more winsome than the sound of many waters, "I am the way."

The glory of the early church, feeling the fresh breezes of his spirit, was in the abolition of the problem of race. Here men of diverse backgrounds, proud friends and kinsmen of the Caesars and humble denizens of the back alleys of the cities of the empire, found in Christ a common gathering place which raised them to the level of a new, blessed, releasing relationship. Perhaps some poor slave in Philippi picked up a letter one night to read it to a gathering of the disinherited of the city.

By the flickering light of a humble room he came to the close of the letter, sealed in an affection of brotherhood. These were the words that humble assembly heard, "All the saints salute you, chiefly they that are of Caesar's household" (Philippians 4:22). They found their answer to the problem of race in him who says, "I am the way." In the beleaguered catacombs, in a humble upper room, during the treasured hour around a table of the Lord, the early Christians wiped away their early differences of race, awed a world with their devotion to all men, snapped the fascination which old Rome held over them, drew gasps of wonder from their generation, raised the banner of a new kingdom, and made the name of Christ a household word in homes around the Mediterranean.

The world looked at them, as it can look at us, asking the way. "What makes you so happy?" said a cynical age to them. They answered saying, "We have come unto life. There is a new dimension to our existence. We were dead behind our crisis event. Our signal that we have passed from death unto life is 'We love the brethren.' Love has given us new life, immune to even the threat of death."

His way of a new brotherhood deeper than race is the only way. In a daring parable he sketched the conditions of admission to see the King eternal. The lines we make he abolishes; the conditions we raise, he wipes out. How shall we see the King? Deeds of kindness, thoughtless incidents of brotherhood are our passports, so said Jesus. A cup of cold water to a thirsting friend, never mind who he is; a visit to a lonely place, never mind who is there. "Inasmuch as ye have done it unto one of the least of these — come, ye blessed of my Father, inherit the kingdom prepared for you" (Matthew 25:40,34).

Do we ask the way to Zion? We hear the question framed in the crash of empires, the deep uncertainty which has gripped our times. Agonized, the days of our years seem to wait for some answer. Around us is a world desperate for a new world wherein dwelleth righteousness and peace. "They shall ask the way to Zion with their faces turned thitherward."

Do we ask the way to Zion? Across the centuries his clear voice declares, "I am the way" — a family in God, a brotherhood originating in me, a comradeship beginning at Calvary, a community in love, a colony of heaven on earth, a blessed fellowship, the closed ranks of a marching army moving to the music of God's stirring act in Christ — "I am the way."

Are we sure our universe will support our way? Are the tides of eternity on our side? Is there some sovereign who guarantees our way is right? In other words, is our gospel underwritten by the ultimate nature of our universe? Can we be sure?

Quickly we move to an event inserted by God's love in the centuries. God has set authentic evidence for the validity of our way in history. He has given sign and token that he will at all hazards stand fast by our way, will not forsake our way, will not abandon it, though the iniquities of hell spill over the earth. At the place of a skull he left the signature of his power on the side of our way. Dramatic words accompany the event. The sun, as hell and earth do their worst, fades in mourning folds of embarrassment as our Way is tested before the blasphemous eyes of irreverent men. The earth quivers on its axis, as if shocked by the severity of the test to which our Way is subjected. There is a hint that the music of the spheres is suddenly silent in the strain of the test to which our Way is put. For a brief, blinding moment our Way seems abandoned. A bleak cry shudders up from the hill, "My God, My God, why?" (Matthew 27:46). Thanks be to God! the last cry is that heaven will not forsake our Way. Up through the pain a cry of tender vindication shatters the darkness. As he reaches for the scepter, we hear a cry that God is holding on, validating our Way. Hands, he says, strong like the fashioners of creation, reach down to vindicate him by holding him fast! Hands, great like those that have measured the waters in their hollows, firm like those that give power to the faint, reach down — the cry of validation of our Way is like some anthem as the morning breaks, "into thy hands I commend my spirit" (Luke 23:46).

◆ 8 ◆

THE MINISTER IN TODAY'S WORLD

Rio de Janeiro, Brazil, June 1960

I

Ministers today must face a world fraught with difficulty. We must minister unto a generation which is faced with odds so huge that they seem insuperable. We are told that no other era in the history of the world has been face to face with terrors so stark as those with which we live day after day and with which we seem destined to live for some unforeseeable length of time, stretching into what looks like a grim and forbidding future. We might well amplify Hamlet's words, "The time is out of joint."

It should be said at the outset that all times are out of joint. The periods of the world's most horrible bloodbaths are times out of joint; the periods of the earth's deep moral ambiguities and startling mental lapses are times out of joint; the times, even, of men's shallow optimism and vain illusions of progress based on human ingenuity and mortal resourcefulness are out of joint. All times are out of joint, since the "whole creation groaneth and travaileth in pain together until now" (Romans 8:22).

When all of this is said, we still sense that the world we know today is thrice cursed. It is bedeviled by the primitive moods and ancient methods we have brought forward to deal with deadly instruments, wrought by contemporary skills. Our earth is a tortured sphere because our nerves have shattered and our spiritual reserves have been dissipated by wild excursions into sophisticated godlessness. These flights have brought us at last to famine in a far country — and at the precise time when spirituality, for so many people around the earth, means the "fig tree shall not blossom, neither shall fruit be in the vines; the labour of the olive shall fail, and the fields shall yield no meat; the flock shall be cut off from the fold" (Habakkuk 3:17). Against these horrible colors is the age-old background of sin, sickness, loneliness, and death!

To this ghastly arena, wet still with the blood of two wars and their resultant fears, to this ghastly arena, crazed by the jerks and twitches of men whose emotional and mental derangement leaves them sad and mad, to this ghastly arena frozen by the winter of men's fear of the age-old terrors of the human heart, the minister of Jesus Christ comes, a lonely knight, to face what looks like the overwhelming odds of multiplied dragons. What shall we say to these Galahads of the cross who must face our fallen, frightened, fugitive generation? Is ours a lost cause, a glorious but dated function, outworn by the massive issues of our times? Or do we hold in our hands the gospel which shall be for the healing of all nations, which shall be the means by which lost men are to be found and thus to find themselves, and which shall give us the power to overpass the ultimate terrors of life?

Our earth is in a life and death grapple with the perils around us. " ... without are fightings.... " Twice we have marched forth to wipe the earth clean of injustice and to destroy war and its causes. Twice we have seen the fearful seed of another war conceived in the womb of the current conflict. Today one-third of the earth's population is hungry. Vast sections of the earth writhe in restless and angry impatience at the oppression by some of the world's most "enlightened" nations. Within a matter of months, we have seen at Bandung the drama of the majority of the earth's population coming together on the basis of geography and color, calling themselves "The Community of the Hurt." We may yet see in our time millions of oppressed and scorned enter into a political and military entity which shall become, ironically enough, the most formidable and overpowering military and political giant the world has yet seen. It may be the tragedy of our time that, standing in the bright light of the greatest evidence of men's determined resistance to slavery and oppression in history, we shall still turn back to a dark abyss of old, dead policies of race and class. We have brought first-century attitudes to deal with twentieth-century instruments and insistences.

II

To such a generation, the minister of Jesus our Lord comes, declaring that in our Lord Christ we have an answer in word and in spirit to the deep, angry hurts of our world — a world which cannot survive fractured by enmities of color, class, creed, or geography. It is now too small a world to sustain huge cleavages of "inferior" and "superior." We who preach Christ and who minister in his name bring to our world a meeting place, level enough, as W. L. Jarvis of Australia said in my pulpit, that all men might stand there as equals; broad enough that all men might gather there in peace; high enough that all men, looking up at its height, might together see a throne set in the heavens over our earth. At this meeting place called Golgotha all men are summoned to see God's offered, God's given event. What choice does the minister of Jesus Christ have but to declare the cross as the earth's sovereign symbol, the place of a new beginning for our tired, cleft earth? In the oblation of service, in unwearied patience, in acts of reconciliation, in deeds of selfless devotion, we are commissioned to live our days, holding before our people this judgment and mercy of God which is Calvary. Foolishness? 'Tis God's!

As our world is scarred by perils around us, our time is characterized also by perils within us " ...within are fears.... " Walter Lippmann writes in a searching book, *The Public Philosophy,* that we are "not wounded, but sick." There is an emotional malady among so many of those to whom we minister. Nerves are raw; emotions are shocked; and many people are living lives of quiet desperation. Something has happened to our emotional equipment. Alcoholism, psychosomatic illness, and sexual aberrations are indicative of our emotional insecurity. The very fact that in so many of our countries the new religion, thinly veiled in Christian garments, of "adjustment," "peace of mind," and "happiness" is symptomatic of the shock and collapse that have gone on inside great numbers of people. The deepest tragedy of it all is that we seem unable to diagnose the cause of our malady or unwilling to admit that the cause is spiritual. A distinguished Baptist,

Dr. V. E. Devadutt of India, told an American audience not long ago of a young college student who paraphrased a part of the Twenty-third Psalm to read, "The psychoanalyst is my shepherd. He maketh me to lie down on green couches." One sees in congregations, along city streets, and on subway trains people in whose eyes there is written anxiety, fear.

There are patent reasons, of course, why nervous collapse and emotional fatigue characterize so many of us in our generation. Two of the reasons given are that the pace of contemporary life is maddening and that we know so much about which to be anxious. Clovis Chappell said, while we shared a preaching mission in a Southern United States city, "Those who are ignorant worry because they do not know any better; those who are educated worry because they know so much about which to worry." Is this vast knowledge and vaster insecurity another area to which we have brought giant minds linked to pigmy spirits?

Surely the spiritual malaise of our time is at the root of our fright and anxiety. We have great mental capital, but we are spiritually bankrupt. People are brought to emotional exhaustion because they do not know who they are or where they are going. Nameless and lost, they panic, and the mental institutions become too crowded to contain the patients. This lostness is a spiritual matter. Joseph Wood Krutch, in a profoundly disturbing book, *The Measure of Man,* reminds us that we are the end products of a debilitating process. He points out that roughly within one half of the nineteenth century Karl Marx, Charles Darwin, and Sigmund Freud published their claims. Darwin insisted that natural selection, operating with mechanical inevitability, had caused man to evolve from other forms of life. Marx asserted that we are the product of a society which is in turn produced by the dialectic processes of matter. Freud insisted that what we call our unique self is the result of the way in which our fixed drives have been modified by our experiences. These high priests of the secular spirit have helped to bring us to the loss of our sense of relationship to eternity. If Darwin deprived man of all credit for his upward surge toward the stature of sonship to God, Marx and

Freud appeared to absolve him of all blame for his crimes and his follies. The spiritual disease of our time, issuing in nervous collapse and emotional fatigue, results from our not knowing who we are. And we do not know who we are because we do not know *whose* we are. We have lost the awareness that we are the children of God.

III

The minister in such a tortured generation, by the proclaimed gospel in its purity and in its passion and by his ministry of conversation and counsel, must offer God's reconciling words to men's lostness. It is the burden of the gospel that we are not far off from God, aliens — or worse, orphans beneath a leaden sky. We are listed as individual and precious assets on the ledgers of God. "He knoweth the way that I take: when he hath tried me, I shall come forth as gold" (Job 23:10). A soul believing that, sure that his or her life is ordered of God, is restored to a peace that the world can neither give nor take away. Wasn't this one of the repeated assurances of Jesus? "But the very hairs of your head are all numbered"; "Ye are of more value than many sparrows" (Matthew 10:30,31). Again, at Calvary a higher light breaks from a loftier sky on our darkened valley of lonely mortality. There God, once and for all, has assessed our value to his heart. There in one huge, eternally valid act God has thrown in for us and our salvation is what God's heart considers to be our worth to him. The word *whosoever* in that great passage which begins "God so loved the world" (John 3:16) is aimed not alone at humanity *en masse* but primarily at every human being. It is no wonder that standing in the pure light of Calvary, New Testament Christians were found crying, "Behold, what manner of love the Father hath bestowed upon us" — of all people — "that we should be called the sons of God.... Beloved, now are we the sons of God, and it doth not yet appear what we shall be" (1 John 3:1–2). But we have a destiny; we do not wander aimlessly! For "we know that, when he shall appear, we shall be like him; for we shall see him

as he is" (1 John 3:2). This is rescue from the status of spiritually displaced persons upon which our generation has fallen to its
anguish.

A part of, and yet above and beyond, these nameless fears
we have mentioned are the ultimate dreads of the human spirit.
No one would be fair in describing the issues of our times who
did not write largest the timeless dreads and needs of this generation and all generations. I speak now of the great universals.
Whether in ox carts or jet-propulsion planes, we are still mortal.
Whether in the darkest jungle, humblest hamlet, or along London's West End or New York's Broadway, humanity must still
face the ultimates. Our generation does not like to mention these
age-old dreads of the human spirit. The very sound of the words
strikes terror in the hearts of humankind. We pull the curtains
and talk small talk, we rush from entertainment to entertainment,
but there is still sin, there is still sickness, there is still loneliness,
and there is still death. Nor will our flippant banter or heroic
stoicism banish their presence. As the tender spiritual had it:

> You got to stand your test in judgment,
> You got to stand it for yourself.
> There is nobody else can stand it for you,
> You got to stand it for yourself.

If we do not dread these final frontiers of the human spirit
for ourselves, there are still those whom God has given us to
love. Our love for them makes us care about these inevitable ultimates. What shall we say to men and women who must face
these terrors?

It all goes back to whether far off yonder there is any empty
throne, or is there someone whose heart can be shaped by his
love into the likeness of a cross? Far across the waters and down
in the swamp country by the Mississippi where I was reared, I
used to hear the people sing:

> Does Jesus care when my way is dark
> With a nameless dread and fear?
> And the daylight fades into deep night shades
> Does he care enough to be near?

It is this simple question which is humanity's immemorial query. Yonder where the chasm stretches, is there a bridge? "If a man die, shall he live again?" (Job 14:14). "O wretched man that I am! Who shall deliver me?" (Romans 7:24). The minister of Jesus Christ faces a terrified world with the gospel of Jesus Christ — glorious, glad tidings of redemption and release. We have the cross to proclaim as God's promise for all our loneliness, loneliness caused by the separation and alienation which sin levies from our soul. We have a sundered tomb, heaven's pledge that God's people have a bridge where the chasm widens. Life is not insane. Our poor mortal souls need not whimper before the gathering clouds. We have a Friend, and our Friend is King, and he does make of us children of his royal house and ministers *all* at the everlasting altars. This is our gospel of deliverance to enslaved souls. This is our gospel of healing to sick souls. This is the gospel of the acceptable year of the Son of God. We have Good News, for our wounded, worried, frightened world — "and they sang a new song, saying, Thou art worthy to take the book, and to open the seals thereof: for thou wast slain, and hast redeemed us to God by thy blood out of every kindred, and tongue and people and nation; and hast made us unto our God kings and priests" (Revelation 5:9–10).

FREEDOM AND RESPONSIBILITY

Miami, Florida, June 1965

As Paul Tillich moves toward the end of his superb triad on systematic theology, he suggests that there are what he calls "history-bearing groups" who from time to time by their aim and dedication give for a while to history its direction. Such a group, he says, has a "vocational consciousness." They believe that they and the fullness of time are met to bring to pass some radical shift in the way human beings look at themselves and the way they look at their fellows. Thus the vocational consciousness of Greece was expressed in the distinction between Greek and barbarian; that of Rome was based on the superiority of Roman law. The vocational consciousness of Italy was expressed in the rebirth of civilization in the Renaissance, that of France in its leadership in intellectual culture. Tillich says that the vocational consciousness of England has been seen in that nation's desire to win all people to a Christian humanism; that of contemporary Russia has been in seeking to make supreme the Marxist prophecy; that of the United States has been in the belief in a new beginning in which the curses of the Old World are overcome and the democratic missionary task fulfilled.

True or not, there is noticeable in the earth today a community of people committed to the proposition that freedom shall cover the earth "as the waters cover the sea" (Isaiah 11:9). This history-bearing group is not defined by geography. They are found on Commonwealth Avenue in Boston and on Sixteenth Street in Birmingham. Their battle cry is heard on Notting Hill in London and on George Street in Sydney. They register their impatience and signal their determination on Kingston Street in Toronto and on Broad Street in Lagos, on Adderly Street in Cape Town and

74

on Alipore Road in Delhi. This history-bearing group in its dedication to freedom is not of one color or of one sect. They are black and white, Jew and Gentile, Catholic and Protestant. They move under an imperious faith that this is freedom's hour on history's clock and that they are the chosen of God to proclaim the fullness of time. Because of their commitment, even unto death, our tortured generation may yet be known as the Age of Freedom. This nameless legion cries out for freedom and reaches forth for responsibility.

Freedom is responsibility. There was a day when in many lands people tried by every ingenious argument to justify human slavery. The idea was advanced that slaves do not have to take the hazards of free persons who must fend for themselves, making decisions, reaching conclusions, committing themselves to a course of action. It remained for Avery Craven, the Indiana University historian, to point out that what is wrong with human slavery, whatever its extent and wherever it exists and with whatever benevolence and sensitivity it may be administered, is that it is wrong for one human to own another, in any measure. It is wrong, Craven implied, because all human beings will be free and yearn to fulfill some purpose. They will court whatever hazards there may be. They will confront whatever responsibilities may exist.

Freedom is responsibility. Freedom is the responsibility of choice. In essence, this right to choose, this responsibility of freedom, is not a right granted by Parliament or enacted by Congress. This right of humanity to the responsibility of choice is a grant of a loftier tribunal than ever sat on earth. God in his wisdom endowed humankind with that precious and perilous gift. One hears the evidence of that gift honored in Israel's history by Joshua. He stands before the assembled congregation and sets before the people their responsibility to decide their course, "Choose ye this day whom ye will serve" (Joshua 24:15). Again and again the Lord Christ honored that freedom which is found in the responsibility of choice. His huge "if" rings with the thunder of a mighty option before which men and women stand and about which they in their freedom must make decision. "If any man will come after me, let him deny himself, and take up his cross, and follow me" (Matthew 16:24).

One of the precious founding documents of my land states the case clearly and translates into political reality the great spiritual affirmation of humanity's right to freedom. The Declaration of Independence states,

> When, in the course of human events, it becomes necessary for one people to dissolve the political bands which have connected them to another, and to assume among the powers of the earth the separate and equal station to which the laws of nature and of nature's God entitle them, a decent respect to the opinions of mankind requires that they should declare the causes which impel them to the separation. We hold these truths to be self-evident; that all men are created equal; that they are endowed by their Creator with certain unalienable rights; that among these are life, liberty, and the pursuit of happiness.

So humanity's right to freedom predates all human institutions. Freedom is the bright responsibility of choice, the competence for which God in his wisdom has given to men and women everywhere and of every estate.

Freedom is prerogative and hazard to choose the wrong, but freedom involves responsibility to choose the right. God has granted us equipment and example. We have the equipment of minds created so that they are able to grasp ideas and to sift alternate possibilities. The gift of mind is one of the loftiest and holiest endowments which God has bestowed upon human beings. Persons so endowed are under responsibility to think beyond slogans, to reason beyond the indigenous prejudices of region or race or religion. No individual granted a sound mind by a gracious God can take sanctuary in the claim that one is conditioned and determined in one's thinking by one's background. A human mind is designed to bring an individual to truth which lies beyond personal background. A human being has a gift which drew from the English tongue's most gifted craftsman, Shakespeare, those memorable lines:

What a piece of work is a man! How noble in reason! how infinite in faculty! in form, in moving, how express and admirable! in action how like an angel! in apprehension how like a god!

Every person has more than mental equipment by which to reach right decisions regarding the sacred rights of all men and women. We are endowed with moral equipment compounded of conscience and the long example of tyranny's failure and freedom's determination. We may engage in all kinds of evasions of language and distortions of truth, but deep in the secret places of our consciences we know that whatever freedom we have, whatever authority of choice we have, mandates us to use our freedom to open the gates of new life to all humankind.

This responsibility to commit our freedom on the side of truth and justice is enlightened and empowered by those examples which God has given us. He has not left himself without witnesses in this anguished area of humanity's common life. One can trace the judgment of God, and his will, in the tragic failure and crashing fall of nations once mighty who would not heed the cry of justice and whose houses are now left unto them desolate. One can hear the sovereign will and determination of the God of the nations echoing in the cry of Amos, "Let judgment run down as waters, and righteousness as a mighty stream" (Amos 5:24). In our inmost selves we know that we are listening to the authentic accents of the Eternal when Micah's voice thunders in the land, "What doth the Lord require of thee, but to do justly, and to love mercy, and to walk humbly with thy God?" (Micah 6:8). This is the age-old will and yearning of God which haunts our history on this planet.

Freedom is responsibility, and without freedom responsibility is a mockery of mind and a blasphemy against God. Can any nation hope to build an enduring and worthy society while rejecting the great foundation stones of religious faith? Can a negative assumption about the sacredness of life establish a society of justice? Is there any greater assault on justice than to hold a human soul responsible while withholding the exercise of that freedom in which alone men and women can act responsibly? Is there any greater affront to the God of justice than to hold persons responsible for civilized conduct while denying to them those communal institutions by which individuals come to understand how one acts civilized? Is there a larger sin against God than to hold persons responsible for the drudgery involved in building a community while denying to them the freedom of participation in that community into whose building their blood and toil have been poured? To refuse human beings the liberating experience of schooling and then to hold those persons responsible as intellectually unfit; to sentence souls to the bondage of living in a filthy ghetto and then to brand them as irresponsible because they are dirty; to deny persons the freedom of employment and then to hold them responsible for not being ambitious; to degrade human souls by epithet and systematic scorn and then to demand of them dignity and to hold them responsible for breaches of personhood is a brutal violation of one's own moral apparatus and an insult to the God whose dignifying stamp is in every human soul.

We who stand on the awesome levelness of Calvary stand in sublime emancipation, the glorious liberty of the sons and daughters of God. That person to whom the cross has truly spoken is free, free from the claim of preference, since "all have sinned, and come short of the glory of God" (Romans 3:23). A person so touched by Christ and his cross is free from the limitations of geography and old parochialisms of class and color, for "if any man be in Christ he is a new creature: old things are passed away; behold, all things are become new" (2 Corinthians 5:17). A person to whom Christ is truly real is free from poisonous divisions that separate human souls punitively and arbitrarily according to skill or sex or skin. For those who have put on Christ, "there is neither Jew nor Greek, there is neither bond nor free, there is neither male nor female: for ye are all one in Christ Jesus" (Galatians 3:28). Such a Christ-touched life is free from paralyzing fear of the disapproval of those in the world around, for with such a person "it is a very small thing to be judged of man's judgment.... He that judgeth is the Lord" (1 Corinthians 4:3–4, paraphrased). A person so confronted, convicted, converted, and confirmed of Jesus Christ is free from the edict of any demonic order, for that person is given "a new commandment...that ye love one another" (John 13:34).

We who know Jesus Christ as Lord and Savior are likewise responsible, for we are sent of him as he was sent of the Father; responsible — for we are summoned to be the light of the world; responsible — to men and women everywhere and of every estate, for our "God so loved the world, that he gave his only begotten Son, that whosoever believeth in him should not perish" (John 3:16). We are the community of the responsible, for we are under imperious orders to commit ourselves to his purposes until "the kingdoms of this world are become" — every bastion of bigotry, every installation of pride, every pocket of rebellion, every rebel frontier, every castle of pretension, every region of false servility must become — "the kingdoms of our Lord, and of his Christ; and he shall reign for ever and ever" (Revelation 11:15).

To be short of this bright glory, as surely we are, is to need desperately to seek God's grace, to be headed toward it is the luster of our destiny, to reach it is to come at last to "a perfect man, unto the measure of the stature of the fullness of Christ" (Ephesians 4:13).

✑ 10 ✑

GOALS OF SOCIAL CHANGE

Tokyo, Japan, July 1970

The rehumanization of human beings is the goal of social change. Structures of government which oppress, or allow oppression, crush out of persons the sense of their personhood which Christian faith believes to be of infinite worth. Customs which deny to any men or women the fulfillment of their capacities and the expression of their talents maim and disfigure human personality, the most precious commodity in the earth. Institutions of religion which disallow any human being's full dignity and status as a child of God blaspheme their faith and rebuke God for the creation in diversity in which he chose to fashion his sons and daughters.

The person who cooperates in individual or institutional injustice seeks to dehumanize the victim. Such a person must rob the oppressed of human status by labels and name calling, in order to make the act of oppression tolerable to his or her own conscience. Those who sought to persecute the early disciples of Jesus Christ employed the word *Christian*, which they considered a label of shame and reduction and which they spat out of clenched teeth in tones loaded with all of the scorn and loathing their diseased minds could communicate. Following this attempt to reduce the human status of the victim, all manner of outrages can be practiced against another person, even to wanton destruction of human life.

Victims may accept the judgment of the oppressor that they are less than human or less human than those who oppress them. It is an epic of singular power and beauty when any people, so oppressed and so outraged, out of the depth of their own reservoir of courage and wellsprings of faith refuse to accept in their own souls the assessment and value which their oppressors seek to place upon them. I am proud to be of the lineage of such a people who looked the worst threats to their personhood in the face, in the form of a brutal form of slavery, and refused to bow their heads or to lower their self-assessment as children of a high and honored destiny. One hears such refusal in that militant old sorrow song of my own people:

> O freedom! O freedom!
> O freedom! O freedom!
> And before I'll be a slave
> I'll be buried in my grave
> And go home to my Lord and be free.

Nevertheless, the repeated assertions, some overt, many subtle, of inferiority and hatred are likely to have a disastrous effect on the victim. Any soul abused by war or racism or poverty or any of the other social ills so prevalent on our planet is a probable candidate for insecurity, anxiety, and, maybe, an abrasive aggressiveness.

Social change which removes the yoke of injustice or the blinding, crimson terror of war or opens long-denied opportunity for the full development of gifts and talents aims at the rehumanization of the victim. As the weight of disparity and disallowance is lifted from burdened shoulders, a person's frame lifts, so to speak, toward that posture which belongs to and which becomes human beings. As the poison of racism is drained from a society, those at whom it has been aimed feel a cleansing of the mind and sense a far healthier climate of life. Such social change in a very real sense means the healing of "the brokenhearted, . . . deliverance to the captives, and recovering of sight to the blind, to set at liberty them that are bruised" (Luke 4:18).

Social change which removes injustice of whatever kind liberates and rehumanizes the offender, also. Those persons who oppress others sever and splinter the bundle of life, thereby fragmenting themselves from their own whole personhood, which is found only in identification with all fellow human beings. The oppressor's conscience is outraged; the warmonger's guilt, however masked, is pervasive and painful; the profiteer who squeezes the life out of the poor finds his or her own life maimed and brutalized. The supporter of doctrines of racial superiority builds a fool's paradise founded upon a lie whose fall must, again and again, leave the bigot angry, frustrated, frightened, and frantic.

Social change gives the oppressor a chance to return to the whole ground of his being as a member of the human family. Indeed, one may raise the question as to who is more benefited in salutary social change, the oppressed or the oppressor. For the individual who has been guilty of committing wrong, social change surely gives that person a chance to hear those words, which once so gladdened another offender's heart (Zacchaeus): "This day is salvation come to this house, forasmuch as he also is a son of Abraham" (Luke 19:9).

Above and beyond these considerations, the goal of social change for the Christian is to honor God. It was he who commanded humankind to have dominion over the earth, not over each other. It was God who willed that all men and women should come of one man in the first Adam and all twice-born men and women should come of one man in the second Adam. To deny our oneness through war or racism or poverty, or any other fragmentation of humanity, is to cast doubt upon God's wisdom in creating "of one blood all nations of men" (Acts 17:26). To affirm our oneness is to see again what God first saw at his creation — that it was and is good.

Section Four

Special Occasions

↜ 11 ↝

THE CHRISTIAN DRAMA

*The Anniversary Sermon for
the Montgomery Improvement Association's Bus Boycott,
December 6, 1956*

If we have been planted together in the likeness of his death, we shall be also in the likeness of his resurrection. (Romans 6:5)

Sitting in a telephone booth in New York City, I heard a man's voice in the next booth. The drift of his conversation indicated that he was talking to his girlfriend. Finally this graphic sentence came through the thin walls of the adjoining booth, "Honey, the merry-go-round done broke down."

Is that a description of our Western civilization? Has the bright dream of human dignity for all humanity now been dissipated by the rapacity and sinfulness of our society's standards? Are we in the twilight of a day that dawned bright and hopeful for the sons of men — a day whose glistening sunrise brought promise of liberty and equality, the family of humankind? Has the old Western ideal of integrity and honor now been laid by the acids of modernity, the brittle creed that a person does not matter in terms of what one is but in terms of what one has or what the color of one's skin is?

Ills of Western Society

Walter Lippmann says that our society here in the Western world is not wounded, not battered under the assault of its enemies from without. He says our society is sick, suffering with internal diseases. Instead of recognizing the Old Testament assertion that all of life is "bound in the bundle of life" (1 Samuel 25:29), we have separated humanity according to crass human standards, for the

85

satisfaction of our pride and prejudice. Bereft of a master sense of God in our lives, we have forgotten who we are because we have forgotten whose we are.

Our society — sore, stricken, separated — needs the infusion of a new sense of spirituality, of the authentic word and will and way of God. We are far-country prodigals, starving beside pigsties and destined never to be whole again until we are back at our Father's house, remembering that the Lord has been "our dwelling place to all generations" (Psalm 49:11), setting ourselves to his will and his way, obedient to his impulses, thinking his thoughts after him, dreaming of a fairer, more just world as our rightful heritage and our obvious birthright.

The New Testament, face to face with a hard-bitten, metallic culture such as ours, confronted the world with an almost unbelievable, radiant faith. If Rome was the society of the crown, the early Christians were the society of the cross. It was the meeting of two mutually contradictory ways of life. One, Rome's, was haughty; the other, Christ's, was humble. Rome's society was founded on success; Christ's way was built on service. The followers of Rome believed in the power of arms and sword; the followers of Christ believed in the power of the spirit of righteousness. One was power-centered; the other was personality-centered.

Commitment to Moral Integrity

The writer of Romans set down in brief compass the faith of true Christians in the way which Christ chose. In one startling sentence that reverses the verdict of the world, this believer declared, "If we have been planted together in the likeness of his death, we shall be also in the likeness of his resurrection." The "death like his" describes the way of his life, the nature of his earthly end. It is a summation of the central commitment of the life of Jesus which has thrilled and haunted twenty centuries.

The "death like his" represents, surely, Christ's refusal to rely on any earthly weapon; the apparent shame and disgrace with which his career ended. That unknown lyricist whom we call the Second Isaiah (Isaiah 53:1–4, 7–8, RSV) was true to the spirit of Christ.

> Who has believed what we have heard?
>   And to whom has the arm of the LORD been revealed?
> For he grew up before him like a young plant,
>   and like a root out of dry ground;
> he had no form or comeliness that we should look at him,
>   and no beauty that we should desire him.
> He was despised and rejected by men;
>   a man of sorrows, and acquainted with grief;
> and as one from whom men hide their faces
>   he was despised, and we esteemed him not.
>
> Surely he has borne our griefs
>   and carried our sorrows;
> yet we esteemed him stricken,
>   smitten by God, and afflicted.
>
> He was oppressed, and he was afflicted,
>   yet he opened not his mouth;
> like a lamb that is led to the slaughter,
>   and like a sheep that before its shearers is dumb,
>   so he opened not his mouth.
> By oppression and judgment he was taken away;
>   and as for his generation, who considered
> that he was cut off out of the land of the living,
>   stricken for the transgression of my people?

Thus the poetry of Calvary's stark shame and fatal bruise. The likeness of his death represents the way of commitment of a life to faith in the moral integrity of the universe. Jesus went to his Calvary believing that his way would be certified and guaranteed by God.

The Cry Heard in the Land

Such must be the faith of Christians! The moment we stop believing that there is a power not our own which makes for righteousness we have suspended our participation in the life of Christ. What else has kept us firm against overwhelming odds?

Far back in the slave quarters our fathers and mothers hummed softly in the twilight the words, "I'm so glad trouble don't last always. O my Lord, what shall I do?" The wail of Israel's ancient cry was on their hearts, "Let my people go." The cry is still heard in the land.

We are committed in Montgomery to the faith that righteousness finds its way to resurrection by facing Calvary. Here some people, "not many mighty, not many noble" (1 Corinthians 1:26), have entrusted their lives and their fortunes and their honor not to the arms of men but to the sword of the spirit. Here a man and men and women with giant souls in youthful bodies have led some people toward the way of Calvary, for the justification of many. Here some people of humble origin, but with a sense of high destiny, have challenged the conscience of the world.

The likeness of his death, the way of commitment to the moral sanity of the universe, the way of reliance upon God's word and God's promises is never a way of particularism for the special benefits of any one segment of the society. Jesus did not go to his Calvary for his disciples alone. He died as surely for Pilate as he died for Peter. He died as surely for the centurion who plunged the spear in his side as he did for Mary Magdalene, who poured her gratitude at his feet. Jesus died as surely for Rome as he died for Galilee and Judea. Jesus died as surely for those who jammed the reed in mockery of a scepter in his hand, as surely for those who threw an old barracks blanket around his shoulder to mock a regal robe, as he did for those simple souls who filled the air with their hosannas and his path with their palms. The word is writ as large as the gospel, "God so loved the world, that he gave his only Son, that whosoever believeth in him should not perish, but have eternal life" (John 3:16).

Seedtime and Harvest

It behooved some gallant souls to take the cross for the redemption of our republic and this Southland to its true dignity, destiny, and decency. We would read wrong the Christian way were we to believe or so to bear ourselves as to give the impression that we sorrow for ourselves alone. Someone must save the nation, someone or some people of vision whose hearts are open to the winds of God's will, whose eyes are open to the beckonings of God's hand, must suffer for the nation's salvation. All the people of this city and section and nation are God's people. Who else could travel the steep, red way of Calvary but those who by bitter plight of circumstance have not known the sins which are nigh inevitable in any majority people?

> And they made his grave with the wicked
> and with a rich man in his death,
> although he had done no violence,
> and there was no deceit in his mouth.
>
> Yet it was the will of the Lord to bruise him;
> he has put him to grief; . . .
>
> and was numbered with the transgressors;
> yet he bore the sin of many,
> and made intercession for the transgressors.
> (Isaiah 53:9–10,12, rsv)

There is in the Christian drama the downward plunge, to apparent defeat, and the pained period of waiting to see the result of it all. We must never forget that our Lord Jesus Christ did not on Friday die and find victory on the same day. At least the victory was not placarded before the world, or for even the eyes of faith to see. The church rightly shrouds its altar in black during the period between the bleak Friday of crucifixion and the bright Sunday of resurrection. There is a spiritual which runs, "You can't hurry God. Why don't you wait, my brother." The commitment must be made, and we must leave the rest to God. The seed must be planted, and though we till the soil, we must wait in that agony of suspense between seedtime and harvest.

Redemption Is Costly

I do not know why truth and righteousness are not immediately vindicated and justified. It may well be that the powers of darkness are not routed with the snapping of a finger. Jesus gave full allowance for the strength of wrong, the power of entrenched evil, as soldiers laid their hands on his innocent person, to lead him away. Said he, "This is your hour, and the power of darkness" (Luke 22:53). I do not know why redemption costs so much — in blood and sweat and shame and suspense — unless it be that evil is a mighty foe, "a strong man armed who keepeth his goods" (based on Matthew 12:29). I know only that when God got ready, as Arthur Gossip says, to turn a world free from sin's awful bondage, it took God giving all of God's all. I do not know why the way of humankind's social redemption must be lined in blood and sorrow. I only know that there is no other way. No cross, no crown. No pain, no birth. No suffering, no salvation. No pain, no peace. Such is the law of our universe, or Christ would not have died.

Those across this land who have made their commitment to the Christian way of sacrifice and hazard for the saving of the nation are going through a dark and fearful night of waiting and uncertainty and horror — here and yonder. To some it must appear unbearable, the burden insuperable. And yet, peering through the tortured night waiting for the morning to come, searching the skies for some sign of approaching dawn, we are confident that God makes his universe to turn on axles of justice.

But it would be vain to imagine, even in the period of waiting and suspense, that the tides of the universe ceased to flow, that God was absent, silent, or inactive. Even though the Scriptures pull a veil over much of Calvary and the interval of our Lord's time in the grave and shut it from human gaze, as if it was too reverent for human view, still the Scriptures suggest that the Father was at work. Judas flinging his silver and his life away bore tragic testimony in his death to the power of God to work in human situations. Simon, whose base denial had added to the weight of Calvary, was likewise plastic to the workings of God's grace. His bitter tears dropped as testimony that the Father who worked hitherto works still. The valiant commitment of Jesus' life wrung from unbelieving lips, even while he died, the blurted cry of the centurion: "Truly this was the Son of God" (Matthew 27:54).

The World's Conscience

If no other words of committal were uttered over the Lord's life-less body, then let the centurion's words be his well-earned eulogy. Many that day, we can safely believe, saw and believed; and, while they were afraid to speak, their hearts were turned toward God's throne. Surely as Friday's lights go out, humble men and plain women standing near the silent hill searched their souls and were touched by this deed of sacrifice.

Make no mistake! Beyond your ken of understanding, even while you wait for the resurrection faith to be reasserted, things are happening. By what has happened here, the world's con-science is a little more sensitive to the whispers of God. Here in Montgomery, behind shutters and in rooms of which you know not, and in houses you would not dream, and among people you would not imagine, soul searching has doubtless taken place. Men and women who want to love the Lord must have asked themselves if they are among those who in your crucifixion help crucify the Lord afresh. Your gallantry and your faith and God's goodness have staved off violence. In distant lands and on lonely islands men have prayed and pray for you. By your Calvary, Montgomery has become a central item on the prayer agenda of the world. Take heart then; even now things of which you and I do not dream are taking place through God's providence and by your commitment.

There is a faith — it is founded in God — that he will bring to pass what he has begun. It is the faith that no life commit-ted to him can fall beyond his grasp. The central drama of the Christian faith is the death of our Lord, the anguished waiting, the glorious denouement on Easter Sunday, the coming forth of the conquering Lord. Christians believe that the resurrection of the Lord Christ was the reversal of all the world's verdicts, the annulment of all claims of evil, the repudiation of the supposed

power of expediency and sin. The coming forth of the reigning
Lord represents for Christians the denial of all the charges of injustice, the disavowal of all the libels that wickedness can impose,
the vindication of the sanity of the universe. The trumpets at the
end of the drama are no longer muted; they blare the coronation;
the banners are lifted to full mast. Christ leads captivity captive
and puts to rout the armies of the aliens.

Here we stake our faith. As surely as God lives, his way must
triumph. God will not leave our souls in hell. "He which hath
begun a good work in you will perform it until the day of Jesus
Christ" (Philippians 1:6). Galling may be our cross, steep may be
our way, long may be our journey, dark may be our night, cold
may be our way, hard may be our lot, heavy may be our hearts,
sore may be our spirits, slow may be our dawn, but if we are
"planted together in the likeness of his death, we shall also be in
the likeness of his resurrection."

One of our ancestors has written, in years now gone, the
heart of our faith as we struggle for a free America and for
our citizenship:

> Harder yet may be the fight,
> Right may often yield to might.
> Wickedness a while may reign,
> Satan's cause may seem to gain.
>
> There is a God who rules above,
> With hand of power and heart of love.
> If I am right, he'll fight my battle.
> I shall have peace some day.

～ 12 ～

THE HAZARD OF THE UNCOMMITTED

A Sermon Delivered to the Chicago Sunday Evening Club,
November 9, 1969

So many of us feel that we can live life on dead center — in equipoise, that we will neither be too much for or against. Some perverse instinct in us tells us that by not committing ourselves we can spare ourselves stress and strain. The only trouble about it is that it won't jell. Again and again Jesus confronts us with this assertion that life, in order to have the benefits it is meant to have, must be a life committed. For instance, that word which he speaks and which is so widely known: He who seeks to save his life — clutch it, to palm it as if it is too precious to be laid down upon any counter — he who seeks to save his life shall lose it. And, conversely, he who is willing to throw it down in the good fight — he who is willing to lose it for a good cause — Jesus said, "he who loseth his life for my sake shall find it" (Matthew 10:39).

There was another instance in which our Lord shows the fallacy of this notion of noncommitment, of neutrality, in a deathless picture. Dr. George Buttrick, who has been so widely and tellingly heard in the pulpits of this land and this generation, once detailed the picture which Jesus drew. Yonder is an empty house. Its owner has been for some purpose on a long journey. The house has been unoccupied by human tenants. Silvery cobwebs have crossed the threshold of the doors, sparkling in the sunlight. The stairway creaks. The shutters are awry. Thick layers of dust cover the woodwork. An evil spirit — using the thought term of his time, our Lord said — an evil spirit comes and occupies the house.

The owner returns from his long journey and to his dismay finds his house in such disrepair. He spruces it up. The cobwebs are all taken away. The thick layers of dust are cleaned. The

93

shutters are restored to their proper angle at the windows. The stairway is strengthened. The windowpanes are polished, and, in the language of the New Testament, the house is "swept and garnished," trimmed and decorated. When the sunlight comes in upon the house and the broom has begun to do its work, the evil spirit discovers that his tenancy is no longer convenient, and so he leaves the house, but as the telling language of the New Testament has it, having wandered in dry places, he finds no other residence. Furtively he comes back to the house. By that time the owner has had to go away on another long journey. The house — swept, polished, cleaned, decorated, trim, tidy — is still empty. Imagination can picture the evil spirit coming again to the house and peering furtively in to the windows to see what has happened to his former place of occupancy. Upon finding it empty, he not only comes back himself, but he goes and finds seven of his fellows, and not one devil, not one evil spirit at last occupies the house, but a horde of them set up residence in the house.

And so the last state of that man — for Jesus was not really talking about houses but about people — the last state of that man is worse than the first. Why? Because a life in neutrality, a life uncommitted, is a life failing its purpose and therefore an easy prey for the very worst instincts that can occur and assert themselves.

This is one of the great problems of our land. One does not have to look long at this country's history to reach the conclusion that here is represented in this land something fresh in history, something bright and hopeful, a new start, a fresh beginning, for never before in the sweep of human history did people from so many varying backgrounds and of so many differing political creeds come together to contract a society, minus the old shibboleths and slogans and assumptions of class and of preference of other continents. And as someone has said, this was a land cross-ventilated by two oceans. Mr. Lincoln, of this state of Illinois, sorrowing his way to his own martyrdom and balking his way to immortality, caught something of the grandeur of what this country meant in history as he spoke of it as a nation — you remember the words — "conceived in liberty and dedicated to the proposition that all men are created equal."

And yet, with all of the grand beginning, the enormous representation in history of a new idea, a people holding the most precious notion of government which has ever been committed to human hands, the one great flaw of our nation seems to be that the nation lacks the capacity to commit itself in a long, steadfast offering of itself to whatever it believes is its destiny and its purpose.

I do not mean now any jerky, episodic, temporary kind of convulsive gift of self. I mean that sustained, steady commitment to what belongs to God and to truth and to right. And if indeed this land with all of its incalculable blessings declines in influence, historians will one day say perhaps — God forbid that it should be — that it was because, with all of the other enormous gifts, this nation lacked the gift of steadfast purpose!

One sees it again and again in our history. The founders of this country recognized that the nation was brought into history for some grand purpose. They spoke words that still out of the very print almost make the heart leap. You remember how our great founding document begins: "When, in the course of human events, it becomes necessary for one people to dissolve the political bands which have connected them with another, and to assume among the powers of the earth the separate and equal station to which the laws of nature and of nature's God entitle them, a decent respect to the opinions of mankind requires that they should declare the causes which impel them to the separation." And then these words: "We hold these truths to be self-evident; that all men are created equal; that they are endowed" — not by any parliament or by any legislative assembly or by any judicial assembly — "by their Creator." There was inevitably a certain embarrassment among the founders, and yet here was a nation with a chance to start afresh, and so they wrote those deathless words. The embarrassment was occasioned over and over again. Mr. Washington's moral hesitation about his own holding of human property, and Mr. Jefferson writing somewhere that "when I think of the institution of slavery in this country and I remember that God is just, I tremble for the future of the Republic." Well, having set down those gallant words, and with a chance to begin something really fresh in history, the nation stammered and stuttered!

Later we came to that fateful engagement of our civil conflict, when once again the nation had another chance to set itself, without compromise, with determination, with a kind of sacred consecration, to that purpose for which it was summoned into history. The nation was called upon in a baptism of blood to cleanse itself and to purge itself of that old sense of disparity and that old institution of inequity and inequality. One hears the names of the battlefields of our civil conflict, and those names still echo with a kind of endless pathos, and they haunt the memory: Antietam, Gettysburg, Spotsylvania, and in my own native state of Louisiana, Port Hudson.

And for a bit, for a while, for one glowing, bright, iridescent moment, it seemed as if the nation was about to throw off its old disabilities and to set out with determination, having cleansed itself in its own blood. But then something happened again, and the nation fell back. There was the old stammering, the old hesitation, and for a hundred years we went on with that heartbreak with which we in our generation are all too familiar.

In 1954 the Supreme Court, usurping that responsibility which should have belonged to the religious conscience of the land, spoke again to the nation's soul and decreed that this must be a nation, at least in education, a nation of one people. And for one splendid bright moment, it seemed that the nation was about to rise up to meet at whatever cost that destiny to which the God of history had summoned it.

But then something hesitant, some stammer, some stutter in our character held us back. It just will not work. And within the last fortnight we have seen that hesitation, that reluctance to commit ourselves steadfastly and painfully to what God bids us do. For we have seen trustees of this precious idea of our United States government and of the highest halls of justice of this land, arm in arm with one of the most repressive political subdivisions in the land, asking that there be a postponement now in our becoming a democracy.

Noncommitment will not work. It does not belong to us, and whenever we try, heartbreak is our inevitable and invariable and inescapable harvest.

As with the broad corporate life, so with the individual, for you and I were not born to live at dead center, in equipoise. We were born for commitment. We are commitment creatures. We were born for a purpose, to throw ourselves in on the side of something which in our souls we know is right. To offer ourselves to God, if you please, to be used in the worthiest sense of the word.

Again and again through the Bible one hears that word. Israel in the early morning of its emancipation is confronted by Joshua with the word "Choose you this day whom you will serve" (Joshua 24:15) — make a commitment! And again and again Jesus was saying that if man (or woman) will be his disciple, let him commit himself.

Underneath a great deal of the rhetoric of violence and the strategy of confrontation by our young people in this generation, there is something else to be said. For there is about so many of them a sense of commitment so tragically and pathetically lacking in their elders, and if anyone listens, underneath the oratory of confrontation, one hears that in them. They weary of the casual and sometimes hypocritical use which their elders have made of precious words like "love" and "justice" and "peace." And indeed those of us over forty have lived for so long so easily and so comfortably with things which so deeply assaulted and corroded the human spirit — poverty and hunger and racism and war — that we have about forfeited our right, really, to bring moral judgment upon young people, for they are committed!

This is why we are here. Any other style of life is a perversion of our creation, for we are created to be committed, to throw ourselves in, to be used to the hilt. Now we may try to hold ourselves off and remain neutral, but to remain neutral is not to be neutral, for if some worthy purpose does not claim us then some unworthy purpose will claim us. If some bright crusade does not win our allegiance and our loyalty, then some small and parochial purpose will claim us. If we have no better master than our own animal impulses, they will claim us, and we will be slave to them because we will be owned. We will be possessed.

I suppose that there is a way in which a person can somehow get through it all and bring one's life to some kind of fairly decent close, if this is what you call living. You will remember how Homer sings of Ulysses in the *Odyssey*, and of how, when Ulysses came from Troy to his home kingdom at Ithaca, he and his fellows had to pass the isle of the sirens whose music was so seductive that sailors had been known to forsake their ships and to break their bodies upon the rocks surrounding the island of the sirens in an attempt to get to the source of such irresistible music. Ulysses, so Homer sings, knowing that they had to pass the isle of the sirens, devised a plan. When they came near, he had his men plug their ears with wax that they might not hear the winsome melodies of the sirens, and he had them lash him to the prow of the ship, that no matter how he strained to be clear and to try to get to the source of that music, he would be unable to do so. And so, with their ears filled with wax and Ulysses himself lashed to the prow of the ship, somehow they passed the isle of the sirens.

Well, there is another story that does not belong to classic Greek mythology. It is the account of Jason and his quest for the golden fleece. These sailors, too, had to pass the isle of the sirens, but when they passed, Jason did not have his men lash him to the prow of the ship, nor did he have them fill their ears with wax. But aboard Jason's ship was Orpheus, whose music was so sweet, as Pope later put it in his poetry, that "it did make hell grant what love did seek." When they came near the isle of the sirens, instead of being lashed to the prow of the ship or having his men fill their ears with wax, Jason commanded Orpheus to play. And as the first, faint lovely strains of the music of the sirens came out to the ship, the soft melodies of Orpheus's harp began to sound through the ship, and the sweeter the sirens sang, the sweeter Orpheus played his harp. The more winsome and irresistible became the melodies of the sirens, the lovelier still became the music of Orpheus, until at last the music of the sirens was drowned in the still lovelier music of Orpheus, and so they passed by the island safe.

That's what life is all about. You may get through in some kind of decency and some kind of dull honor, but there is another way. The world sings its vain songs of pride and prejudice, of pomp and circumstance, of vain ambition, of empty and tawdry prize, and a man, I suppose, may lash himself to the prow of his ship, so to speak, or fill his ears with wax, and somehow get through it neutrally, noncommitted. But there is a lovelier way, a far lovelier way. It is the song of Christ, for his music, the music of commitment, the music of offering one's self to God and those things for which God stands, is a lovelier melody than the world can ever sing. And here you and I are tonight, with whatever years we have left, with the chance to take them and use them, or else to clutch them and to palm them, and to keep them from their commitment. Well, that's one way, but hear the music of Christ, lovelier than all the seductive music of the sirens of this world's vain offerings. Herein is our destiny and our privilege, not to get through dully but to offer ourselves gloriously, gladly, to him, and to find in that offering, true life.

⌒ 13 ⌒

THE STRANGE WAYS OF GOD

Martin Luther King Jr. Memorial Service,
Harvard University, Cambridge, Massachusetts,
January 1972

Father Robinson, Pastor Cooper, reverend clergy, my brothers and sisters. How strange it is that, all across this land tonight as we come to the second week of this second year of the seventh decade of the twentieth century, a kind of shiver would pass through the land. A benign shadow seems to rest upon this country. It is a shiver of memory and of hope. How strange that it would be occasioned by the life of a man who did not live to see the fulfillment of his normal span. How strange that this whole land would be affected so deeply and people of so many diverse beliefs and outlooks could come together in some deeply solemn and profoundly religious atmosphere. How strange that it would occur around the life of a man who did not come of a majority people but who came of the loins of a disinherited and disallowed people. And yet this is the strange and anomalous actuality. From one end of this country to the other beginning tonight, a strange shiver passes through the land, and from one end of the country to the other people begin coming together, warmed by a memory and lighted by a hope. Four springs and summers have come and gone, and yet this shadow looms larger and more blessed upon the country. His widow in her own queenly manner said but within the last few days that it will be fifty years before the full assessment of the life of Martin King can begin to be made in this country, and it will be.

For here was a life of such broad grandeur, of such passion and commitment and dedication and discernment and insight that we stand too close to it to really gauge it. But we do know, though

100

we cannot assess it and we cannot establish the true and precise meaning of this life, we know this: that it has affected each of us, and that life has affected this land indelibly and ineradicably. And whatever attempts there are may be made in this nation to obviate and to obliterate and whatever neglect of accident or design may be perpetuated against this life, its glow will not go out, and its impact will not lessen, and its force will not dim and will not become vague. How strange!

What is the clue to this? God comes at us in strange ways and from such unexpected and, to many of us, apparently awkward angles. What is the clue to this? Well, let me cite another example which may help to set this in its proper context. That is this word recorded in the Gospel of Luke: "In the fifteenth year of the reign of Tiberius Caesar, Pontius Pilate being governor of Judea, and Herod being tetrarch of Galilee, and his brother Philip tetrarch of Ituraea and of the region of Trachonitis, and Lysanias the tetrarch of Abilene, Annas and Caiaphas being the high priests, the word of God came unto John the son of Zacharias in the wilderness" (Luke 3:1–2).

When you start calling these names, it sounds like a roll call of the people who really mattered and on whose side the future lay and to whom the coming generations belonged. Tiberius Caesar, and one thinks of purple and high-ceilinged palaces. Courtiers, screaming eagles of the legions, standing sentinels at the farthest outposts of empire, at the very extreme borders which civilized men counted it worthy to rule. Tiberius Caesar, successor to Augustus, with the Forum in Rome there at one end and over at the other the Coliseum. All roads leading to and from Rome with its seven hills of imperial glory. "In the fifteenth year of the reign of Tiberius Caesar, Pontius Pilate being governor of Judea" — and one thinks of the second line of command, prouder usually in the colonies than even at home, the representation of all the grandeur and glory of Rome. "Pontius Pilate, being governor of Judea, and Herod being tetrarch of Galilee," — the splendor of the court of an oriental monarch — "Annas and Caiaphas...." Annas,

banished in the intricacies and turbulence of Judean politics from
his own place as high priest, but having had the resourcefulness
and shrewdness to introduce his son-in-law, Joseph Caiaphas,
as chief priest. The glory of ecclesiastical authority, "Annas and
Caiaphas being the high priests," and you begin to think that
all that can be said about where power was and where influence
lay had already been uttered. "In the fifteenth year of the reign
of Tiberius Caesar, Pontius Pilate being governor of Judea, and
Herod the tetrarch of Galilee,...Annas and Caiaphas being the
high priests" — and what is really happening is that the man is
establishing some background and setting the stage and describing the scenery for something really important. "In the fifteenth
year of the reign of Tiberius Caesar, Pontius Pilate being governor of Judea, and Herod being tetrarch of Galilee,...Annas
and Caiaphas being the high priests, the word of God came unto
John...in the wilderness."

Does that explain it? God comes at us at strange angles and
from unexpected sources, establishing new bridgeheads in history,
in places where we scarcely expect them. John did not fit the bill
of somebody as a deliverer. He had an awkward, angular personality. His diet was the wrong diet. He ate the old desert food
of the poor — locusts and wild honey. He dressed not in the re-
fined cloth that we call camel's hair but in the roughly textured
hair of the camel. And there were strange wheels in his head;
somewhere in the crooning of the desert winds he believed that
he had heard the voice of God. There was a strange light in his
eyes and a frown on his countenance. His words were cutting
and sharp. They were not compromising, they were not honeyed,
but "in the fifteenth year of the reign of Tiberius Caesar, Pontius Pilate being governor of Judea, and Herod being tetrarch of
Galilee,...Annas and Caiaphas being the high priests, the word
of God came unto John...in the wilderness." Dwight B. Eisen-
hower, being president of the United States, and John Patterson,
the governor of Alabama, J. Edgar Hoover, the omnipotent auto-
crat of the FBI, Billy Graham and Norman Peale, the high priests

of middle America. The Word of God came to Martin King in the wilderness of America.

It was not a kind word that John spoke, because the cutting truth of God is never initially kind; it is only ultimately kind. It is a mercy that comes by way of judgment. It is a healing that comes by way of hurting. It is a making whole by wounding. And so, John spoke of an axe laid at the root of a tree, ready to bring down an old and decaying tree. He spoke of a filtering of the wheat from the chaff. You almost hear a kind of incredulity upon the lips of John.

How could a nation with the heritage and lineage of Israel become so dead and so cold and so hardened and so fit for a cutting and a reducing judgment. Here was a nation which had heard the lyrics of that strange prophet of the exile, the Second Isaiah, "Speak ye comfortably to Jerusalem, and cry unto her that her warfare is accomplished" (Isaiah 40:2). Or that other word, "Arise, shine, for thy light is come, and the glory of the Lord is risen upon thee" (Isaiah 60:1). These were people who had heard the sighs and laments of Jeremiah, the almost unbearable tenderness of Hosea, the raw cutting words, as we have heard tonight, of Amos. Now here was a nation with all of that which had come in John's time to a cold, dead, heavy formalism. And so "in the fifteenth year of the reign of Tiberius Caesar, Pontius Pilate being governor of Judea, and Herod being tetrarch of Galilee, . . . Annas and Caiaphas being the high priests, the word of God came unto John . . . in the wilderness."

How strange that out of a minority people there should come the true spiritual genius, the one true spiritual genius which this land has produced. He did not fit even the notion of black people as to where Messiah should come. For he came from a lineage of preachers, maligned and caricatured as merchants of escapism, unrealistic, not really discerning the signs of the times. And he came with a word of judgment. It was about a nation with incalculable opportunity. You could almost hear in his voice something that bordered on unbelief that this nation could have come to so sorry a pass and could have allowed its racism to become so ingrained and so rigid that it threatened the very future of the republic. Again and again and again, as he spoke up and down the land from one end of it to the other, he said it. There was that strong note, always asserting that the sharp cutting judgment of the God of history will not forever tolerate our delinquencies and dereliction One heard repeatedly that half note of unbelief. Of all the nations, how could this one risk its destiny, given all of the privileges and all of the prerogatives that belong to it? This was a nation incalculably rich in its natural resources. How could it starve its poor and waste a million dollars a day on the other side of the earth? How could it? How could a nation, trustee of the most precious words known to the human heart — liberty, freedom, equality, opportunity, brotherhood — words that make the heart skip beats and for which men have walked willingly into the yawning jaws of death — become so ensnared in Nazi-like doctrines? This nation, with a people gathered from the ends of the earth with all of their diverse gifts brought to the service of the republic, ought to have found higher ground than primitive racism.

Martin King saw a strange apocalypse about the God of history who had, so to speak, in mercy winked at the failures of this nation, through nearly two hundred years. As it came close to two centuries of its apprenticeship in freedom, the nation could no longer hope that the God of history would exempt it from that judgment which has fallen upon every other civilization and nation.

Martin King saw it with a startling clarity. I heard him one night in Cincinnati talking to Progressive Baptists. It was when he first began to utter his cry about Vietnam. There was anger, but there was an unspeakable pathos as he spoke that day and called the land to remember our beginnings, even though those who wrote the great works of our liberation were themselves compromised personalities. To remember the destiny to which the God of history had called this land. And what incredible and incalculable riches God had given to this country, both natural and human, a nation without the old presuppositions of other lands. A nation with a chance to begin afresh, and, if it had had the heart to incorporate those who were already here with those who came, with a chance out of many to produce one people. And yet he saw that after so long of the nation's apprenticeship, it was decision time. Either the nation would stand up and face its God and its destiny or it would be punished.

This was the word he spoke. "In the fifteenth year of the reign of Tiberius Caesar, Pontius Pilate being governor of Judea, and Herod being tetrarch of Galilee,... Annas and Caiaphas being the high priests, the word of God came to John." And so the word of God came to Martin King. But it came to him also in terms of black people, for there was something he saw, something grand, with all that was debased and dehumanized in black people. He saw a grandeur about us. It was a lineage from a long past, forged on the African heath. It was an internal courage, some basic splendor, some strength, some resiliency that would not bow in the face of oppression and would not die in the face of death. Martin King spoke of such grandeur in black people, saw something splendid about our possibilities. It was the heroic lineage of a people who were cast upon a strange and hostile shore. Family life discouraged, parents and children sold up and down the rivers of this land as chattel slavery. And yet a people who looked hatred in the face and would not crumble. With all of their faults and failures, they still believed and still walked toward some bright tomorrow. He spoke of that tomorrow.

This was the grandeur of Martin Luther King, but there was something else about him. He not only spoke judgment about the nation and he not only spoke to our hopes, but he believed that the destiny of history lies above and beyond, partly within, but ultimately above and beyond, the will of human beings. There is a purpose marching through history that will not be turned back and will not be denied and which humankind can frustrate but which they cannot destroy. Martin King said again and again that

God cannot be stopped. As the spiritual had it, God is "so wide you can't get around him, and so high you can't get over him, and so low you can't get under him. You've got to come in at the gate." This is what he said again and again and now what have we seen? The nation has refused his vision, turned away from his dream, and we have seen our country turn upon its young. This land has become the first child-hating nation in history. Failing his vision and refusing his dream and so sunk and so cold and so committed to our own ugly purposes and our own dark ambitions, America has turned on its young. At Kent State and elsewhere, the nation has turned on its young.

Not another winter had come after Martin King fell before, at Chicago at a national political convention, America turned loose its fury upon its young, who, however distorted their vision might have been, saw something terribly wrong about our country. They saw something awfully immoral about the increasing numbers of white crosses in those distant cemeteries in the rice fields of Vietnam. They saw, did young people, something deeply wrong about napalm gas being dropped by a people calling themselves deliverers. Martin King said it loud and clear. He called upon the president of the United States and upon the Secretary of State to lead us out of Vietnam. He said, and I quote his words, "Mr. Johnson, Mr. Rusk, say we made a mistake and let's come out." The nation turning from its vision will now come out, with fifty-three thousand of its best young people sleeping forever on a purposeless battlefield. "In the fifteenth year of the reign of Tiberius Caesar, Pontius Pilate being governor of Judea, and Herod being tetrarch of Galilee,... Annas and Caiaphas being the high priests, the word of God came unto John... in the wilderness."

But what could people do? What can we do now? Who knows whether already the purposes of God have turned from this land? Maybe, maybe not. John spoke it, and so did Martin King. He said that human beings could not bring to pass the purposes of God, that there is a march down the centuries, a sovereign purpose that refuses to be turned around and refuses to be stopped, a footfall, sure and purposeful and steady like the coming of morning, that cannot be restrained, like the dawning of the springtime upon a cold and dead land. Men and women cannot bring it, but they can throw up a highway in the desert and they can make straight in the desert a highway for the purposes of God.

We in this land, black and white, cannot save the land, but we can make straight in the desert a highway. Every valley shall be exalted. We cannot bring the purposes of God to pass, but we can renounce our meanness and our malice. Every mountain shall be brought low. We cannot bring the purposes of God to pass, but we can bring down our mountains of pride and prejudice and pretension. We cannot bring the purposes of God to pass, but we can give up our deceit and our disassembling one with another and make the crooked ways straight. This was what Martin King said over and over and over again. And there that last night while the fiery chariot waited for him, he spoke of hope and of the coming of the dawn and of the breaking of the day. "We shall get to the Promised Land."

Was it a wild notion woven of gossamer? No, it was something deep in Martin King's own background. It came out of that long lineage of his very own people who by the power of God were told one thing and heard another. Martin King spoke out of that long background of the people who sat in the slave galleries of the churches of the North and South. They heard preachers say to them one thing, but they heard something else. It was said to them, You are ordained of God to be slaves, but they heard, "Before I'd be a slave, I'd be buried in my grave and go home to my Lord and be free."

The preachers said to them it will forever be the same, but they heard, "There's a bright side somewhere. Don't you rest until you find it." As they sat in those galleries the preachers said to them that it will never be different, but they heard, "Walk together, children, don't you get weary, there's a great camp meeting in the

Promised Land." Martin King was heir to that vision — and he was its most eloquent spokesman.

And so that night in the mountain in Memphis, he spoke immortal words. I stood there in that pulpit, but three days after he had gone. What an awesome experience! He had stood there with that chariot of fire waiting for him. He looked out and saw it and spoke then about the march of God: "Mine eyes have seen the glory of the coming of the Lord. He is trampling out the vintage where the grapes of wrath are stored. He hath loosed the fateful lightning of his terrible swift sword, his truth...." Then upon tiptoe he said, "Glory, hallelujah!"

⌒ 14 ⌒

PARTING WORDS

Final Sermon as Pastor of Concord Baptist Church,
Brooklyn, New York, June 24, 1990

What does one say at the last when there is so much left to be said? Here or wherever young men and women of ministry may hear about this hour, I will pass on to them a legacy which is a promise. Have no anxiety about what you will preach to the people Sunday after Sunday, year after year, decade after decade. This can be a daunting question. The story is told that Reinhold Niebuhr, that rarest of thinkers about the things of God and the human situation, was asked, "Dr. Niebuhr, were you scared when you preached your first sermon?" "Not at all," came back the answer. "It was the second sermon, since I felt I had preached all I knew in the first one." I can truthfully say to any who hear this as I finish forty-two years of preaching here and fifty-one of preaching here and yonder that I have scarcely touched the edge of the riches of the word of God. Indeed, having started in this Book of Revelation in October 1987, I can see now that at least another three years of preaching are demanded by this book for completion. I have but skimmed the surface.

What can I say to you, my dearly beloved Concord people, now as we part? One thing I must say that whatever reputation has come to me in our country and beyond as a preacher is owed to three sources, after God who called me to this work. I am thankful that I was born into the home of those whose name I bear. They gave to me a sense of the excitement which dwells in Holy Scripture, a feeling for the music in the English language and a mode of reasoning and expression which combined to en- able my preaching to be welcomed into so many human hearts the earth around. That is a mystery which, apart from the old promise of the sent Comforter, I do not understand at all. Second, my preaching, for whatever it has been worth, owes an incalculable debt to the woman I wooed and won as bride fifty years ago come August. That dear heart has been both chief cheerleader and first critic, whose judgment about preaching and preachers astonishes me. Third, and not at all the least, is the debt my years of preaching owe to you. I think it more than my fancy that, having preached in so many nooks and crannies of the world and to so many races and cultures, I find in the taut, eager expectancy, the close, careful listening, the warm, surging tides of deep emotion that roll through here from time to time the supreme challenge to test any preacher and an invitation to whatever even latent gifts a preacher may have. I lay my record at your feet, for you have made me a better preacher than I would have ever been.

How strange that after two years in the Book of Revelation, the last book of Scripture, we would come on this last Sunday to the last part of the last chapter of this last book which seals and concludes the canon, the body of Christian Scripture.

This final scene in the book sounds a note of the utmost gravity and seriousness. Now at the end, with everything that has gone before, we are told, as by a heavenly creature, not to tamper with the Word of God. Is it the angel speaking or is it the Lord Jesus? Whichever, the commandment has a note of stern warning to it. "For I testify unto every man that heareth the words of the prophecy of this book, If any man shall add unto these things, God shall add unto him the plagues that are written in this book: And if any man shall take away from the words of the book of this prophecy, God shall take his part out of the book of life" (Revelation 22:18–19).

Such is the grave seriousness of God's Word. I shudder when I read these words. Everyone who preaches and everyone who teaches and everyone who reads God's Word ought to feel struck to the quick here. And, yes, everyone who ignores the Word of God for whatever reason ought to feel a sharp sting here.

God's Word does not need to be added to. I look back on my responsibility as a preacher called of God and ask myself if ever I tried to make the Word of God mean what I wanted it to mean. I pray not. Our guidebook is not a partial report. It has everything in it God wanted to say to us. Human documents need amendment and adjustment. The original Constitution of the United States identified you and me as three-fifths of a citizen. That needed to be changed, and the cost in blood and money and human anguish is still being paid. The coming of our distinguished visitor from South Africa this week has reminded us that people can write the loftiest language and hide in it deadly poison and the ugliest oppression. Nelson Mandela said that there is a whole body of law in South Africa which must be changed.

God's Word is not so. I look on this with fear and trembling. I have preached up and down the world for forty-two years. I pray God this morning that I have not added anything to this Word because I am male or because I am black or because I am Baptist or because I am American. All that we need is here.

Nor are we to take anything away from this book. A reduced gospel will not save us. Some of us want the Bible cut down so that we can handle it; but it is meant to handle us. Some of us want the gospel of the Son of God scaled down so that our minds with their vanity of a little learning can surround the gospel. The gospel was meant to surround our minds and carry them captive, and it will if we open ourselves to its searching and its tenderness and accept it.

All who do this work in which my life has been spent must come to terms with the truth that the world of human affairs gives very little credit and pays scant attention to this work of preaching and teaching and studying God's Word. I knew that when I said yes to the Lord what it would be like. I know what gets secular acclaim and how one becomes big in this world. I will state it clearly. No one who takes God and his truth seriously can long enjoy this world's applause. Divine communion crucifies the self and robs personality of that aggressiveness which the world honors — for a little while. I know, also, that though I disappear, little noticed, little mourned, and little wept, I have a hope brighter than all of the tawdry, perishing prizes of public honor and favor. If one soul one day before Christ can say that I helped him or her on to God, I shall be satisfied. If some soul can say one day that what I tried to preach here stayed the tempter's power, rescued someone perishing in alcoholism or drugs, inspired a young girl to clean womanhood, I shall be satisfied. If some soul among the hundreds of thousands to whom I have preached can rise up now and in the judgment to say, "That man pointed me on to God, swept cobwebs of doubt from my view, directed me to the healing fountains and told me that Jesus said, 'Behold, I freely give the living water. Thirsty one, stoop down, and drink and live.' " I shall be satisfied. And I shall be forever satisfied if that soul says,

> I came to Jesus, and I drank
> Of that life-giving stream;
> My thirst was quenched, my soul revived,
> And now I live in him.

> I shall be satisfied.

The last words of the Bible are an earnest wish and a fervent prayer, and I give them now to you in parting. The Bible starts with "In the beginning, God." It ends appropriately with "The grace of our Lord Jesus Christ be with you all." It was what John left as his great vision ended, a kind of last will and testament.

And so, my people, I have little of this world's honor or goods to give you now at evening. As I surrender this command, I do not have highly acclaimed position to leave to you. As I take my departure and go out of this pulpit for the last time as pastor, I cannot leave to you pride of place, nor do I have the applause of the world to give you as my legacy.

I do offer something by God's grace. I leave to my successor, the Reverend Gary Simpson, the promise of his Savior, "I will be with you." And may our pastor know a long, bright joy here. The grace of the Lord Jesus Christ be with him.

I leave to all who long to know God better the precious promise: "Blessed are they which hunger and thirst after righteousness: for they shall be filled" (Matthew 5:5). The grace of the Lord Jesus Christ be with you all. I leave to any who are sad the ancient promise that God will "give the garment of praise for the spirit of heaviness" (Isaiah 61:3). The grace of our Lord Jesus Christ be with you all. I leave to all who feel weary on the way the word from on high, "They that wait upon the Lord shall renew their strength" (Isaiah 40:31). The grace of the Lord Jesus Christ be with you all. I leave to all who with me grow old and feel the mist of Jordan spraying on wrinkled brows "When thou passest through the waters, I will be with thee" (Isaiah 43:2). The grace of our Lord Jesus Christ be with you all.

One by one we drop out of the line of march, but let old Concord Church march on. March on through the rain and through the cold. March on through sunshine and storm. March on, and we shall all meet again where God the Son forever reigns and scatters night away. March on, and we shall all be together again in the sweet fields of Eden. March on, and we shall sing the Savior's praise in a fairer world than this. You pray for me, and I'll pray for you. If I get home before you do, I will be leaning over the balcony rail of glory looking to see old Concord marching on up to bright glory.

✍ 15 ✍

FACING FACTS WITH FAITH

Prayer Service for the Inauguration of William Jefferson Clinton,
Washington, D.C., January 20, 1993

President-elect Clinton, President Clinton. It's already past 12:00
p.m. in West Africa. Mrs. Clinton, Vice President Gore, for the
same reason, Mrs. Gore, members of your families. It seems thor-
oughly in order that we should come together in this shrine of
African Methodism which stands as testament to one stream of
determination in this country which found its fount in Richard
Allen, that there should be religious liberty and that there should
be civic dignity. Bishop Brookins, who carries episcopal responsibility for Metropolitan A.M.E. Church, I would have you know
that in Los Angeles two weeks ago I was told that you have
not relinquished your influence in the West. Though you have
presided a long time in Washington, you are a bicoastal bishop.
And Reverend Dr. Deveaux, the word is that some day we will be
calling you bishop. We poor Baptists cannot vote, but we can lean
in the hope that the boat will tilt a little. Reverend clergy, it is also
fitting that we would be in this church, one of whose members is
one of the most distinguished children of African Methodism and
one of the first citizens of this republic, Vernon Jordan.

In the years long ago, when I grew up in the Louisiana swamp
country, my elders talked with almost bated breath about something which had happened, oh, eighteen, twenty years earlier.
They spoke about it hardly with full belief, for many of them
had known the dark night of slavery. And others had been born
when, as my father used to say, you could almost still hear the
echo sound of hounds baying on the trail of runaway slaves. They
spoke of how Theodore Roosevelt, President Roosevelt, had invited Booker Washington, our Mr. Washington, they said how

proudly, to dine at the White House. I would that I could tell them that our friend, Vernon Jordan, invited President Clinton to have food at his house. No, I don't think I would tell them that, I don't think they could stand that.

This has been declared an ecumenical service. I heard a definition years ago defining some of the denominations. It said that a Baptist is a Christian who has learned to wash, a Methodist is a Baptist who has learned to read, a Presbyterian is a Methodist who has been to college, and an Episcopalian is a Presbyterian whose investments turned out well. It may be of some interest to you that nothing was said about our Catholic brethren or our Jewish friends or our Muslim people or Lutherans, and the explanation was that, as the Scriptures say, all of these things had already been added unto them. Let me seek briefly now my footing in the Word of God.

In the Gospel according to Luke, one comes upon these words. "And, behold, a certain lawyer stood up, and tempted him, saying, Master, what shall I do to inherit eternal life? He said unto him, What is written in the law? how readest thou? And he answering said, Thou shalt love the Lord thy God with all thy heart, and with all thy soul, and with all thy strength, and with all thy mind; and thy neighbour as thyself. And he said unto him, Thou hast answered right: this do, and thou shalt live" (Luke 10:25–28).

Across the broad face of this land there is a sense today, and beyond this land, I am sure, of a new energy and vigor being turned loose affirmatively in the coming to incumbency of our new president and vice president. It is as if we have come again to Camelot, but this time with the atmosphere of the Ozarks and in the accents of the great Southern American heartland, and we rejoice in that meeting. A lawyer meets a savior.

This parable Jesus relates at this meeting has come to be called the parable of the good Samaritan. How strange that an itinerant preacher without possessions in a third-rate province off what looked like the beaten path of history, in one of the backwaters of the empire, should have told a story, and the title for it has passed into the verbiage of two millennia. How strange, unless he was something more than human.

A lawyer, appropriately enough, asked the question, and I take it that that craft is not underrepresented here today, "What shall I do to inherit eternal life?" Whether capriciously or sincerely, this lawyer had touched the raw nerve of our human existence. Why are we here? What is our purpose? We come out of a darkness into this lighted room. We stay here for a while; we depart again in the darkness. What is the significance of it? What is the meaning of the high hope that lifts in our hearts and the dreams that people our days and the sense of purpose? What does it all mean?

A choreographer and dancer, lamenting the death by this awful new plague of so many in our national artistic community, said the other day, "It makes one raise new questions about the relationship of life and creativity and death." Well, all of us question that. And we might well ask that about our nation. Why are we here? What is its purpose in history? Here we are protected by the crosswinds of two oceans. Did ever in the history of the world so many people of such diverse backgrounds, of such varying religious beliefs, of such differing political creeds, come together under such a range of circumstances, all of the way from slavery to high privilege? And we have been given the mandate, to contract a society of mutuality and harmony, across the lines of region and race and class. Do you sense, as I do quite often, that this nation represents something new and promising and purposeful in history? I would not want to claim for one moment on this fateful day that the nation is divine. That is an idolatry. Divinity belongs only to God. But I cannot believe that this country would have come into existence without the purposes of Almighty God attending it.

We are here to establish before the world that people can be brought together. And that highest and most difficult undertaking that can be known to the community of men and women can take place, that people can govern themselves. This is the American proposition in history. I need nobody to tell me what the original intent of this land was. It was that there should be an open democracy with liberty and justice for all. Argue as you will, but that is the purpose of America. I know because in our founding doctrines, those who set them down refused to admit anything less, however short were our actualities.

You remember how the Declaration begins? "When, in the course of human events, it becomes necessary for one people to dissolve their political bands that have connected them with another, and to assume among the powers of the earth the separate and equal station which the laws of nature and of nature's God entitle them, a decent respect for the opinions of humankind requires that they should declare the causes which impel them to the separation." And then these words, "we hold these truths to be self-evident, that all" — *people*, they really should have said — "are created equal." That they are endowed, not by any legislative act, not by any parliament, not by any royal edict, but are "endowed by their Creator with certain unalienable rights."

How tempted they must have been to file exceptions. All except, all except Southern Europeans, all except Catholics, all except Jews. I will not use any more glaring examples. But they dared to placard before history "all people." They were not dissemblers, and they were not ignorant of the circumstance. They believed that time and God and the intent of the nation would erase the stain in which they lived and about which a man said that that issue of race, of slavery, lay like a sleeping serpent coiled beneath the table of the constitutional convention. If you come down to our earthier document, our Preamble puts it — was it by accident? — "to establish justice" and then, "to ensure domestic tranquility." That was the order.

They refused to put the hated word *slavery*, the shameful word, in our Constitution. Over and over again the reference is made to persons, even when the reference is made to three-fifths of a person, which I have never quite understood. I know who they were, but I don't know what they were. Three-fifths! They believed, under God, that history and time and justice would erase those stains. This leads me to the belief that this nation, though not divine, is divinely appointed. And I say to you solemnly today, that anybody who speaks or acts against that purpose or acts against the original intent that this shall be an open democracy with liberty and justice to all, comes close to committing treason against the idea of America.

And so this lawyer answered when he was asked by Jesus, "What does your law say?" The questioner goes back into the long, bright engagement of Israel with divine truth, to the sixth chapter of the Book of Deuteronomy and then to the nineteenth chapter of the Book of Leviticus, "Thou shalt love the Lord thy God with all thy heart and with all thy mind." Don't take a breath. "And thy neighbor as thyself." To pause there, "Thou shalt love the Lord thy God with all thy heart," to pause is to miss the meaning of religion. "And thy neighbor as thyself." The great question, though, is how do we know how, for there's a catch here, to deal with "as thyself"? We do not know how to love ourselves. This is the problem in loving our neighbor. And the only place where we can find this out is when we can discover our true creaturehood as we appear before God as individuals and as a nation. It is only in our creatureliness before our Creator that we are able to understand the splendor and the squalor, the grandeur and the grime, the everlastingness and the temporality in our humanity, all brought together. So that it is really a triangle: "thou shalt love the Lord thy God, and thy neighbor as thyself," but you've got to move that last angle back up, "as thyself," *thyself* being understood only *sub specie aeternitatis,* "under the light of eternity."

"This do," said Jesus, "and thou shalt live." It's unequivocal, straightforward, unmistakable. "This do, and thou shalt live." On this fateful day, we enter a springtime, we believe, of new beginnings. There may be spring rains and storms, but it is springtime in America. And as we enter this new era, standing in this assurance, "This do, and thou shalt live," we may confidently look to some bright tomorrow when the hyphens will drop out of our references to Americans and when truth and justice shall remove the dash between whatever we are and "American," and we shall be solely, purely, only, proudly, gloriously American.

Standing under this clear word, "This do, and thou shalt live," we may have confidence in some bright tomorrow in this land, that the things that unite us will obliterate the things that divide us. Standing in the light of that promise, we may believe in some clear day, unclouded by pride and prejudice, when every valley of disparity will be lifted up, when every mountain of obstacle will be brought down, when every crooked way of deception will be straightened out, when every rough place of delay will be removed, and all flesh shall see it, to the glory of God. We see a better, a brighter, a more glorious day in this land which God has given us all. "Mine eyes have seen the glory of the coming of the Lord. Glory, glory, hallelujah, his truth is marching on."

✌ 16 ✍

CLIMBING JACOB'S LADDER

Black Alumni/ae Day,
Harvard University,
Cambridge, Massachusetts, 1993

As Bishop College came to the end of its long years of educational leadership in Texas and beyond, George Clark, one of the outstanding citizens of Texas, said, "Colored people established our schools, and black African Americans are losing them." It is an oversimplification, as all such comments are, but it contains an element of truth that I think we need to take into account.

Black and white Americans have made a major and unconscionable error in not using the Civil War — what Ken Burns called "the defining event of American history" — to delineate who we are as Americans. It is a tragedy. Six hundred thousand lives were lost in the Civil War. In 1866, one-fifth of the state budget of Mississippi was spent on artificial limbs. It is heart-rending to reflect upon women in the South and the North who lost their husbands and sons and brothers. Of those who survived, so many came back maimed and disfigured. If as Americans, black and white, we had taken the Civil War as the defining experience of our national life, as an indication of who we are and what price we have paid for being Americans, the nation might be far, far different.

African Americans ought never to forget that twice in history our relatively small community has been the test of the American undertaking. We became the test of whether there would be a Union, and we have continued to serve as the supreme test of whether there shall be a democratic America. For us to have failed as a community to look back upon that civil conflict and how it came forth is tragic.

Frederick Douglass once contemplated, with great eloquence, the physical features of America: its mighty lakes, its clear sky, its broad rivers, its "star-crowned mountains." When he contemplated, on the other hand, that its rivers bore the tears of his brothers to the ocean and that its fertile fields were watered with the blood of his sisters, that admiration turned to loathing. It is out of this amalgam that we have come.

I was born fifty-five years after slavery. In my childhood in the Louisiana swamp country, I knew people who had endured the harsh, dark night of slavery as children. Mr. Ike Johnson, who had been a slave, used to tell how slave children were fed on the plantation: corn mash was poured by buckets into a trough, and then buckets of milk were poured in. These children would gouge out their food, with the dirt from their hands making colored rivulets in the trough. By the time a black child went to the field at age twelve or thirteen, very likely the teeth were already rotted and the body threatened by dysentery, cholera, pneumonia, and that dread disease, pellagra — listlessness and unbelievable thinness of the body. Scarcely four out of one hundred slaves would live to be sixty. Daniel Mannix in *Black Cargoes* (Viking, 1962) estimated that in the Atlantic passage, twenty-five million people were lost.

What came out of the slave experience? One of the most gallant leaps of the human spirit: being crushed but refusing to collapse, being destroyed but not disappearing.

I say all of that not because you do not know it, but to remind you that the people who came out of that experience established little one-room churches. I have preached in some of them. There were schools in those churches on Monday through Friday. The ex-slaves started grocery stores and began burial societies which became insurance companies. They forged their way through impossible circumstances. That is the heritage out of which we have come.

Early in our years on this continent a dichotomy grew up between those who sought to become a part of the American society and those who refused. The difference is seen in the contrast between Malcolm X and Martin Luther King. These strands and movements have been necessary. Many people wished that they could have been joined. I am not sure that this would have represented wisdom at all; perhaps both would have been compromised. One position left inspiration; the other left institutions. People can hardly get along without both.

Society is held together by those who carry on "resistance within accommodation," as historian Eugene Genovese says. A deprived community is enlivened and animated by those who refuse to accommodate at all and who stand prophetically against society. But it is terribly wrong to disparage either.

Where do we stand today? I am convinced that the day of the dramatic, eloquent national utterance is gone. We will very likely not see it again in our lifetimes. It was necessary. It defined the circumstance. It presented to the American agenda an indispensable item for consideration: whether or not this was going to be a democracy. It gave access to some avenues. The problem was that we were not prepared at local levels to take full advantage of the changed circumstance.

That brings us to where we are now. Whatever is going to be done in our communities will have to be done at the local level: each church, each minister carving out an area of responsibility, accepting an assignment from God to which you will give the very best of that which God has given you. I know a church that has transformed an entire community in terms of housing. It can be done, and it has been done at the local level — not without problems, but it is the responsibility of each of us to see to it that the very best comes out of this kind of undertaking.

I know a congregation that purchased a magnificent dining facility for small banquets. I know another church in Brooklyn that has supported a school to train young black people for leadership roles in society, a school that refuses to accept students whose parents are able to pay the fees of the so-called better schools in New York City. By subsidizing the seven-hundred-dollar tuition, the congregation has been able to pour the richest kind of experiences into these young people's lives. I know a church that uses its assets for lending at rates that are neither prohibitive nor corrupt. It can be done.

In a capitalist society, the only secret is that "money makes money." Every black congregation in America ought to develop a fund for community strengthening and learn to put interest from that money to work in the redemption of our communities. Each of our churches must decide what it will do to redeem that particular community in which God has set it.

What was the glue that kept the slaves together and gave them their sense of worth? I don't want to romanticize; there have always been many African Americans who were never a part of any church. The glue that held the slaves together was their vision of who they were, not in society but in Jesus Christ. Nat Turner's rebellion demonstrated this.

On May 12, 1828, Nat Turner had a vision that the yoke of Christ had passed on to him and that he had to go to Jerusalem, to Southampton County, Virginia, to make his protest. In many ways what he did was futile. He was captured, as were all of his people, and hanged. But his rebellion sent a tremor of fear through the South and gave new impetus to the abolitionist movement. Abolitionists were able to say that obviously slaves were not comfortable in the throes of slavery. *No* slave was comfortable. Nat Turner provided a picture of that discomfort. It is a tragedy of American life that where the African American community is concerned, from Southampton County, Virginia, to Los Angeles, California, the larger society sees only a caricature and hears only a voice raised to hysterical proportions.

Other slaves believed that deliverance belonged to them because of what they heard preached. Years ago I preached in the First Baptist Church in Columbia, South Carolina, the church in which the Articles of Secession were signed and the Confederacy was begun. I stood in that pulpit and looked into the balcony, which must have been the slave gallery. The preacher would turn to the slaves in the balcony and say, "There's a place in heaven for you, too." And in what I call the "slave glossolalia" that came upon our forebears, a translation would occur somewhere between the preacher's utterance and the slaves' hearing. (When does preaching occur? Does it occur when the preacher speaks or when the listener hears? It occurs somewhere in midair.) This "slave glossolalia" is one of the grandest flights of the human spirit in all of human history. The preacher would say, "You will have your own place," and the slaves heard something else: "I got shoes, you got shoes, all of God's children got shoes. When I get to heaven, gonna put on my shoes, and gonna shout all over God's heaven." That glossolalia happened over and over again. It was the mystery of the Holy Spirit at work.

I remember how the thinning ranks of African Americans who had fought in the Civil War, including my own grandfather, would don their old blue uniforms with G.A.R. — Grand Army of the Republic — on the shoulders, and go to the national cemetery in Port Hudson on Decoration Day to remember and thank God. I can still see them — the Reverend Henry Rivers, the Reverend W. M. Spooner, and one or two others. I wish you could have known some of them. Sometimes their likenesses pass before me in the still watches of the night, and their memories touch me so deeply that I can scarcely bear to reflect upon them. I wish you could have heard them in their churches. Their hands were gnarled from labor in the brickyards, the oil refineries, and the cane fields, and their faces were wrinkled. They were denigrated as "niggers," and they were pushed back and pushed down. But one thought redeemed them — that in Jesus Christ, they had stature. Across the chasm of all these years, I can still almost hear them singing "We are climbing Jacob's ladder, we are climbing Jacob's ladder, we are climbing Jacob's ladder." And they sang something we don't hear in that spiritual now: "Keep on climbing, we gonna make it."

Then they would sing another line: "Do you think I'll make a soldier?" They didn't say "soldier of the stars and stripes" or "of the stars and bars." They weren't soldiers of the United States flag or soldiers of the hammer and scythe. They sang "soldiers of the cross."

✑ 17 ✑

A New Title

First Pastoral Anniversary of Edward L. Taylor,
New Horizon Baptist Church, Princeton, New Jersey,
October 17, 1999

Thank you. Pastor Taylor and members of New Horizon Church, I'm delighted to be here this morning. Of course, when you have reached my age you're delighted to be anywhere, but I am particularly pleased to be here this morning. Your pastor has thrown me off because he has talked about food we are going to have after this service, and it makes me want to go to where it is. It's going to be difficult to get that out of my mind. I'm trying the best I can.

Seriously, it is marvelous to see a developing church. What we forget is that the New Testament churches were all in the beginning what you are now. They met together around their loyalty to Jesus Christ. They met from place to place, and bit by bit out of the warmth and richness of their fellowship they developed into the whole Christian enterprise. One sees great structures erected now, Christian structures. They are the children, the descendants of the early church where people met together in much smaller groups than you are now but with the power of Jesus Christ in their midst, and they went on from strength to strength.

I am pleased to see people here who are related to members of the Concord church. There are two sisters of one of your members who did all of the typing of my sermons, Otha and Ina Washington. They could actually understand my writing, so much so that they could understand my writing when I could not. But they are truly a blessing, and I'm glad they are here.

Now Pastor Taylor has shown a great courage in going forward. In 1926 — I know that sounds like before the flood to some of you — my father bought a Studebaker car down in the Louisiana country where we grew up, I grew up. And that car would sometimes lock; you would have to shake it, push it so you could get it to start again. Now, I never knew anything about automobiles, I still don't, but it was said that the problem with that car was that the engine was too strong for the transmission. And whether that was true or not, I don't know, but that was the explanation that the mechanics at the Studebaker dealership gave. Sometimes you run into people who are too strong for the situation in which they find themselves. This is a young man of great vision and great determination, great strength of character and spirit. And he has to be free to open to you the vision that the Lord has given to him. We have to thank God for people who are willing to catch the vision. So many of us don't want to do any better. When the farm agents began moving through the Louisiana countryside years ago, they would go from house to house telling people to come to the meetings. They went to one man's house, and he asked, "What's going to happen at the meetings?" They said, "Well, we're going to show you how to farm better. That's why we want you to come." He said, "Oh, I don't need to come to a meeting for that. I'm not doing all I know how to do now. No use my learning to do more."

Well, thank God for Pastor Taylor's vision, and now you've come to the first year that you've been together as pastor and people. God bless you and God strengthen you as you go forward. I preached this year at the Progressive National Baptist Convention in Washington. He was in attendance. I made a comment there that I'm going to make now. (Mrs. Taylor may or may not receive it kindly.) Here and yonder, people have asked the same question. They look at the book that he has just produced and with my name and his on it, Gardner and Edward, and they ask me, "Are you kin?" And I say, "Well, I don't know, and as far as I know, we're not kin." Of course, I did preach in and around the town where he was born, no question about that.

He is greatly blessed in having at his side this lovely lady who supports and strengthens and backs his ministry. I make a prophecy, not just a prediction today, I make a prophecy that you are going to go on to a future that you do not even begin to see today. God has in store for you great things, and as you know, the Lord has to sever old ties sometimes, break through to new ground, that his purposes, that his vision might be brought to pass. And this I predict, I prophesy, is going to happen here with this energetic and visionary young pastor and you together. He has shown me, I thought a little proudly, and I am proud, too, the watch which you gave him yesterday. It is very, very nice where a people and a pastor are joined together in harmony and in service to Jesus Christ. There is absolutely no telling what can happen, because God has no boundaries. There is no way to fix the limits to which God can lead people. Some of us who have come up out of very difficult situations are amazed at what God can do. I was born in the Louisiana swamp country eighty-odd years ago and I never dreamt, it just never crossed my mind, that the Lord would open before me so many opportunities and possibilities. Here as a church the Lord will open before you a future that you cannot begin to see now. And I prophesy again that you will look upon your beginning and you will say to yourself and you will say to others, "Look what God hath wrought!" I want to talk to you a little while today about "A New Title."

Somebody says, "What's in a name?" Shakespeare wrote in *Romeo and Juliet,* "A rose by any other name would smell as sweet." But I'm not so sure that names only describe. Sometimes they ascribe, sometimes they give meaning to things. They do not just describe what the thing means, but they make things mean something. I suppose that if you call a rose by some other name it might not smell as sweet as a rose smells. Take, for instance, that word, the *n* word, it wasn't just a description; it was also an ascription; it was forcing upon a people a certain attitude, a certain penalty. And there are words that are heard today in our country that are not just descriptions, but they are an attempt to give meaning, not to describe meaning but to give meaning to things. The word *quota*, that's one of those catchwords, a word that isn't designed to describe something, it's designed to indict, to charge. *Affirmative action*, that's not just a description, it carries with it another weight.

Jesus did not give people titles downward; he gave them titles upward. Listen to this word which he speaks here in the fifteenth chapter of the Gospel of John at the fifteenth verse.

"Henceforth," he says, "I call you not servants; for the servant knoweth not what his lord doeth: but I have called you friends; for all things that I have heard of my Father I have made known unto you." "No more do I call you servants," that's in the fifteenth verse of the fifteenth chapter of the Gospel according to John. Now if I were at any other church except New Horizon Church I would say that the Gospel of John comes after the Gospel of Luke. But I don't suppose I need to say that in New Horizon Church.

Marcus Dod called this verse the Christian's Emancipation Proclamation. "Henceforth I call you not servants." Now, the people who translated the Bible, out of some sense of sensitivity or out of some guilt, translated that word as "servants," but that word in the original sentence, *doulos*, stands for the word *slave*. Out of some sensitivity they would not put down that word *slave*, but that's what it stands for in the original language. "Henceforth I call you not slaves." What is a slave? In my youth, I know people who had passed through the pain of bondage. One of them, Mr. Ike Johnson, gave me the first six hundred dollars I ever had. He was not kin to me; most of what he gave was in old silver dollars. He told me as a child how the smaller children, as those who gathered around this altar this morning and were spoken to so becomingly by the pastor, would be left on the plantation in the care of some woman, or women, too old to go into the fields. And so these children would play, and at lunchtime or dinner, they would take mash or grits or what have you, a bucket of it, pour it into a trough and then pour milk in on top of it in the trough. And these little children with the dust and germs in their hands would dip into the trough, and you could see, he would say, the lines of the dirt in the milk. Thus our people ate like cattle, slaves.

I call you no longer slaves. I once had the privilege of riding with young Miss Candace Simpson, who was not ten years old. She used the word *slave* and I said to her, "My dear, what is a slave?" She said, "A slave is somebody who works and never gets paid." And then she said another thing: "A slave was not taught to read or write." That was close to what Jesus is saying, that "I call you not slaves" because slaves do not know what the master is doing. The slave works with no reasoning, no accounting, no explanation. Works, works. And they said that in slave days, the people sitting around the table with the house slaves serving them would spell so the slaves would not know what they were talking about because, as she said to me, slaves were not taught to read or write.

My own parents spelled around me. "Santa Claus" and all of that. I knew what they were talking about two years before I let them know. But a slave did not know what the master's plans were. And Jesus says, I do not call you any longer slaves. We must remember, we who are the heirs, the descendants of slaves, ought to remember that we have come from a breed of people who were dehumanized and would not lose their humanity, whose humanity was sought to be stolen from them and yet they would not give it up. They were crushed and would not bow down. You are their descendants and, my Father, with what honor you ought to carry yourselves. A people who made it anyhow in the face of all odds, against all disparities and disallowances, made it anyhow. You are their heirs. How sad it would be for those of you who have come now as their progeny, to fall down and fail, show yourselves miserably less than human.

I thank God for the protests that have gone on in New York City, but if minority people in my city's mayoralty elections had stood up when David Dinkins was defeated, we would have been spared the venom and poison and filth that come now out of the highest places of government in the city of New York. One hears talk about improvement. What improvement? When the great majority of young minority men are afraid to walk the streets? Improvement? It's a lie, and we ought to, as we get opportunity, meet this because there's a cancer in that city. See to it in the future that you do not face this kind of venom and poison and bitterness and vileness with which we are confronted day by day by day — vote!

No more, Jesus said, do I call you slaves. For a slave does not know what the plans are. But I have called you friends. Have you thought of yourself a friend of Christ, a friend of Jesus Christ? You boast about your friendships, I am a friend of the Savior of the world. Are you? Are you a friend of the Bright and Morning Star? A friend of the captain of the Lord's hosts? A friend of the Lord of life, friend of the Liberator of humanity? I am a friend of Jesus Christ, and above all earthly alliances, I take pride, I hope it's pardonable, in the awareness that I belong to Christ and he belongs to me. "He walks with me, and he talks with me, and he tells me I am his own. And the Voice I hear falling on my ear none other has ever known." Friend, I call you friend, he says.

A friend shares creative silence. If you have real friends, you do not have to talk all of the time. There's a communion between friends where language is unnecessary. There's an understanding between friends where one does not have to put into speech exactly what one is thinking. And now and again a true friend will say, "I was thinking" and the other says, "I was thinking the same thing," because there is the communion of a creative silence. And then there is the communion of shared secrets, and so we know the secrets of the kingdom. We do not have the blueprint, but we have the prospectus. You know, when our church was being built, before the blueprints were drawn, with the electrical lines and the plumbing and all of that, the artist drew a sketch. In the pastor's office you'll see it, the artist's sketch of what your building is to be like. Now we do not have all the details, but we have the artist's sketch of what it is to be like.

My late friend, Dr. Sandy Ray, traveling through Georgia, driving on a rainy evening, stopped for gasoline. He said to the attendant, "Where am I?" The attendant said, "What's the matter, you lost?" He said, "No, I'm not lost, I know where I'm going. I just don't know where I am right now." And, yes, sometimes we will not know where we are right now, but we know which way we're headed. We know where we are going, know what our goal is. We know who's waiting for us, and we know how it's going to turn out. We do not have all the details, all of the blueprint, all the plumbing and the electrical systems, but we know how it's going to turn out. God is going to win, make no mistake about it.

We've got a prospectus there in the Book of Revelation. Not a blueprint, but an artist's sketch. John said, "I saw a white horse and he that sat upon him was called Faithful and True. He led an army on white horses and they came out conquering and to conquer, and on his thigh was written the title King of kings, Lord of lords." I know how this battle is going to come out. It may be very difficult sometimes, but I know who is going to win. John has given us an artist's sketch, where the saints cry out, "Worthy is the Lamb." I know who is going to win. I know who owns the victory. I know who owns tomorrow. I know.

Somebody says, "Well, there are things I do not understand." There are things we all do not understand. Why are there empty places in our family circles? I do not understand it. Why do some of our own people languish in sickness, year after year? We do not understand it. Why is the way sometime so dark and lonely? Why do I feel discouraged and long for heaven and home? Why are our pillows sometimes dampened with our tears at night? Why is it sometimes we weep inwardly and we weep outwardly? We do not know. Somebody says, "Christ has not told me everything." Well, he says here in the next chapter, as a kind of postscript, a kind of afterthought, "I have many things to say to you, but the problem is you cannot bear them now." Not only dark things, but there are some bright things we cannot bear now.

The Bible does not tell us much about what heaven is like because we cannot stand that. We would be too anxious to get away from here if we knew. We have some outlines, some sketches. "I saw a new heaven and a new earth coming down from heaven as a bride adorned for her new husband, and I saw the new Jerusalem. And there shall be no more curse, no more death, no more sorrow, no more sickness, no more pain," but the details are not spelled out. It is a prospectus.

But I know this: that God lives. Dark may be the way some

of you travel now, steep may be the hill, but God lives, make no mistake about it. So Jesus said, "I have many things to say to you, but you cannot bear them now." But thanks be to God we have a promise, here or yonder, here or somewhere, when the mists have rolled away. Someday when the clouds have all parted, some day when we no longer see through a glass darkly, but then face to face, somewhere, somehow, when we know as we are already known, we'll understand it better, yes, we will. We'll understand it better when the morning comes. And while it is hard for us to say it now with all of the pains, when the difficulties are past, we shall thank God. We shall thank him for every tear and every fear. We shall thank him for every sorrow and every sigh. We shall thank him for every loneliness and every weakness, for every pain. We shall thank him for every enemy. We shall thank him and thank him.

Section Five

Eulogies

ᴄ⌒ɔ 18 ᴄ⌒ɔ

FAREWELL TO A FRIEND

For Marshall Shepard,
Philadelphia, Pennsylvania, February 25, 1967

Because I am for the moment the titular head of the Progressive National Baptist Convention in which Marshall Shepard was a moving and an inspiring figure, I have come to express his denomination's immense sense of loss and sympathy. Because I am a fellow pastor, I stand now in this pulpit; because I am a Christian, I come to witness his passing into the fullness of his inheritance; but because he was my friend, and I his, I come to weep and mourn over his fallen human form.

Marshall Shepard was my friend, the best friend I have ever known in the ministry or ever expect now to know. He was the jolliest of companions, the sturdiest of allies, the firmest of friends. He went about doing good. He and I traveled or met in the length and breadth of this nation and on beyond, London, Amsterdam, Copenhagen, on and on. Almost everywhere we went he knew someone who came forward to thank him for some favor he had shown somewhere along the way. He merited what was said in the early English saga of *Beowulf*: "The heart of man shall cherish and word of man shall praise the Master-Friend, when in the end his spirit goes its ways." Marshall Shepard was a master friend.

He loved this church and knew with it a growing romance for over forty years. This last September we met here, and I was privileged to preach his fortieth anniversary, his last.

He had an intrepid courage. Late last night a doctor friend who is a neighbor told me how he knew Marshall as Recorder of Deeds in Washington at the moment of the severest test of his public career. Marshall Shepard kept smiling and, knowing

135

he had done no wrong, went fishing at a spot he loved and which some of us here have shared for years, hard by Lake Cobbesconte at the Cambridge Gun and Rod Club.

Cille, dear wife, you were the fiber and muscle of his soul. He never would have made safe port and snug harbor without you, and he knew it. Lorenza, you will never know how much you helped your father as copastor here. He freely said to me that for years now as he sought to husband his failing energy that you have really been the senior pastor and he leaned upon you and never found you to fail him. Sammy, your father talked many nights of his love for you. Robert, brother, you two never lost your closeness. Beulah, Boston was for him a shining city because you lived there, and he knew you would have breakfast for him whenever we passed that way. Philadelphia, he loved you with a schoolboy's ardor and served your civic welfare as a priest at an altar. Mount Olivet Church, you were his and he was yours, and far on into the nights he would talk about your years together. Preacher, statesman, jovial prophet, lover of humanity, he lived life to the hilt. Above all, he was my friend, the closest thing to a brother I have ever had.

More than twenty-five years ago in Cincinnati, to which our denomination goes this year, Russell Barbour, of blessed memory, brought Shepard and me together well over twenty years ago in a restaurant and said, "I want you fellows to be friends." And friends we became. We traveled and roomed together in almost every state and city in this land. To know he was here in Philadelphia was to be aware of backing and strength and interest wherever I was.

I must not linger upon this. How often I called on the telephone and would say to Lucille, "Where is Shep?"

"O Gardner, Shep is not here," Lucille would answer. "He is in Washington, or down in Atlantic City at Aquila's, or Chicago, Detroit, Miami."

And then I would place the call again, and ask, "Marshall Shepard, please." "Speaking," he would invariably say.

Then I'd always quote that spiritual, "You can run, but you can't hide." And we'd laugh and talk. I'll not ever again have to ask, "Where is Shep?" I know where he is, and he secretly was ready and anxious.

In Mexico last winter he quoted to me in great weariness from Ecclesiastes: "The grasshopper shall be a burden...because man goeth to his long home" (Ecclesiastes 12:5). I know where Shep is. Somewhere where weariness does not come, where winter's chill never troubles and prejudice never poisons, where the flowers bloom forever, where the song never stills and the day never dies.

I know where to find Shep. "Old Partner, wait awhile. Watch for my arrival, and we'll sit at a welcome table and talk and talk and talk."

✑ 19 ✑

A PRESIDENT OF PREACHING

For Sandy F. Ray,
New York, April 21, 1979

Great and solemn considerations crowd in upon us all at this hour. Sublime and splendid recollections of our fallen friend and leader converge before us. We all have a sense of how much has been taken from us. The passing of his physical presence radically alters the landscape of our souls. Indeed, the spiritual climate of this borough and this city and this nation perceptibly cools with his departure. I have heard it said, in this connection, that this borough of Brooklyn in which he spent these glorious, shining thirty-five years has known the greatest array of pulpit gifts ever assembled in one place in America. Whatever truth there may be in this, we may be certain that the stilling of his golden voice greatly weakens that claim, maybe fatally weakens it. As saddened as we are, we cannot know yet how great has been our loss. Indeed, he was so intensely, infectiously alive that it is hard to realize that we do not have him among us as he was. As for me, I always felt better knowing he was in town. One may not feel the need to call him, but it was comforting, sustaining, rallying, steadying to know that he was there.

We stand too close to the shock of his passing to be able to see clearly through the film of grief or to draw accurate lines as to who he was and what he was. Some qualities he possessed and some circumstances his Lord gave him loom large.

His life was an epic, a grand tale woven by God himself. He spoke often of his family and the years long ago when his native Texas was a far different place from what it is today. He once branded onto the consciousness of many who heard him how as a child he saw his mother running alongside a sheriff's buggy, because his brother was under the threat of a lynch mob. His

138

unvarying support of every civil rights cause, his sterling record as a champion of the poor and oppressed, doubtless found a part of its inspiration in such a circumstance as I have mentioned.

His was a great adventure, a scenario written by God. Born as the twentieth century stood poised for entrance, he lived to within twenty-one years of the twenty-first century. What a weak comment! Centuries did not limit our friend; he moved as belonging to the ages, a man for all seasons, bound by no years, limited by no century. Now, Bill, his brother, alone of his once large family is left. God wrought a miracle producing a Sandy Ray from the arid political and economic and social circumstances of Texas in the early 1900s.

God does provide! How unmistakable is that comforting truth in the companionship his Lord gave him through his wife, who was with him when his summons home came. What a mercy that he was not alone in some distant city or somewhere where loving hands would not be immediately at hand. That she was there when he left us should not surprise anyone; for many of us watched the attention, the unobtrusive, quiet strength she gave to him wherever he went, without ever seeming to be supporting. He must have told this to you often, but since he told me, too, I thank you for him.

You who were his children know better than any of us how unfailing and unflagging was his love for you. You are left a noble heritage, and you carry within your veins the blood of one of God's noblest princes.

If some marriages are made in heaven, then the Lord himself must have united Cornerstone Church and Sandy Ray in holy wedlock. Does the history of the Christian church know any romance between pastor and people sweeter and more lasting than was this one? You honored him as pastor and freed him to be your preacher and my preacher and America's preacher. He made Cornerstone Church an affectionate and admired name wherever Christian people gather in this country. He said often that your appreciativeness and eagerness to hear the gospel made him yearn, and dig, to find fresh insights and to bring new treasure for your souls from God's Word. He strengthened you, and you strengthened him. At the end of thirty-five years in a great outpouring of love, you exhausted his power to thank you. This pulpit was his throne, and he made it to ring with good news and glad tidings. He sent thousands forth from here week after week with a fresh vision, a new walk, and a hope in their hearts in Jesus.

What was his rank beyond this place? He held offices in his denomination and convention, but he honored the offices more than they honored him. His true title? He was president of preaching, ambassador plenipotentiary from the imperial court of King Immanuel. He was a crown prince of the pulpit, a flaming herald of Calvary's news. He was a leader of the advance guard of the returning King of kings and Lord of lords. As such, he spoke of his Lord's right to rule heaven and earth. His gospel, like Jacob's ladder, was firmly rooted in the affairs of this earth. It disappeared into the heavenly places. We must never forget that after the awful carnage at Attica, it was he who opened the doors of the Cornerstone Church to the sad procession of caskets.

There was another side to him which only those closest came to understand. Many of us were critical, sometimes harshly so, of him for what we considered his distaste for the fire and fury of partisan conflict. It was only later that we came to know why. His was a heart so tender, a personality so delicately wrought that contention and misunderstanding and resultant bitterness chilled his soul. It was not that he could not stand contradiction or opposition, but antagonism was hostile to his nature. Only those who knew him best and to whom he talked most freely sensed that tenderness of spirit which brought about anguish and pain at the thought that he might have mistreated someone. He was nature's gentle man. He could bear opposition, but antagonism wounded his soul.

It would be a false picture to present him as someone who did not know great personal disappointments. He did, but he spoke seldom of them, and he was so gallant that he hid them behind that infectious and enviable humor which so characterized him.

There was something about his presence which guaranteed for him recognition and rank. He had only to enter a room for others to know how ordinary they were in comparison with him. You knew he was a prince, before you knew his tribe or location of his inheritance. He reduced us all to peasantry by his bearing, and yet it was something of which he was totally unaware. I carry locked in my heart a touching confession he once made to me about his feeling of insufficiency.

Supremely, Sandy Ray was a preacher. Our history has not produced his equal. Call the names of our loftiest pulpit figures among whom he moved as a younger man, and it is no disparagement to say that not one matched him in the sustained attractiveness of his pulpit work. Call their names: C. T. Walker and E. K. Love, Peter Bryant and Arlington Wilson, L. K. Williams and J. C. Austin, he outdistanced them all. His preaching at the last was as fresh as at the beginning. His imaginative power never dimmed. I heard him preach for thirty-five years, and I never heard one fake sound, one insincere pose, one artificial sentiment. He preached with a total sincerity and a touching humility. At the height of his pulpit oratory it was hard to tell whether one heard music half spoken or speech half sung. And when the glad thunders of that voice reached his climactic theme, the heavens seemed to open and we could see the Lord God on his throne. It is hard to believe that we shall not hear that clear, sweet voice again. How touching that he would be called at Easter. Are you struck with the strange sequence that Martin King Jr., to whose family he was so close so long, should be taken near Easter, that Adam Powell who admired him so much as a preacher should be translated so near to Easter?

How shall we look upon his departure? You will know your grief, as I will know mine. As for me, for nearly forty years I knew him, and for thirty years we labored here together. He supported and encouraged my coming here. Great winds buffeted our friendship, but it stood the test of time and stress. I have groped through grief for some word to speak to myself as well as to you. I looked again at the text at John 17:24, which Spurgeon

quoted on a Sunday late in March, following the death of his
dear friend, Charles Stanford, minister in Denmark Place Chapel,
Camberwell. The words are the words of Jesus. Who else has a
right to speak to us when death has invaded the fields of our affection? "Father, I will that they also, whom thou has given me,
be with me where I am; that they may behold my glory, which
thou hast given me: for thou lovedst me before the foundation of
the world."

"Father, I will that they be with me." There is almost a note
here of insistence, of determined demand. But not quite! For
what insistence is needed between a Father perfect in love and
an only Son perfect in obedience? To ask is to have; to suggest is
to receive. There is a note of authority, of the right to say it, a
royal prerogative, a regal option. "Father, I will." "Father, I want
Sandy now to be with me where I am." Our Lord seemed to favor that word "where I am" as if it makes all the difference. "I
go to prepare a place for you, that where I am there you may be
also." Now turning from us, Jesus turns to the Father, "Father, I
have told him that our house has many rooms and each room is
a mansion itself. I want him to see what I have prepared for him.
He has never seen the family dwelling. Paul told him that when
the little house he lived in could no longer protect him, he had
a house, another building, a house not made with hands, eternal. I want him to see what has been prepared for him. I want
him close now. He has talked about me so faithfully. Father, he
has called my name so sweetly, so long. I want him where I am.
Father, I will that he may be with me, that he might behold my
glory." Is it a strange request? You and I will know that success
has no sweetness and honor has no appeal unless we can share it.
We need others who will rejoice in what has come to us. "Father,
I will" — it is our bell to ring us home. "That Sandy may behold
my glory. I want him to see the 'seven times sealed book' open
in these nail-scarred hands. I want him to hear his Savior praised
by admiring, heavenly creatures who cry, 'Worthy is the Lamb to
receive riches and honor.' I will that he see the brow which once
wore thorns, now crowned with many crowns.

"I will that he see our city. He lived in the earthly metropolis of New York, but he has never seen a city four square, as long as it is wide and as wide as it is high, where there are no lights and no candles, but the Lord God giveth them light. He has never seen a city over whose streets no hearse has ever rolled, and within whose borders no 'goodbye' has ever been heard."

And so our friend crossed over! Quickly, quietly, he closed his Bible and crossed over! Left the pulpit the last time and crossed over! Took his last text and crossed over! Raised that magic hand the last time and crossed over! He did not have to wait for his transfer. He passed through Jordan standing up. He crossed too quickly for any watcher to see a break in his stride. That splendid figure never bent, those bright eyes never dimmed, and that unmarked countenance never wrinkled. He crossed over in full triumph. He crossed over Jordan standing up. His God hid his infirmity from all human eyes. A few years ago we were allowed but a glimpse of human vulnerability in him in his illness. But God and his wife, together with a faithful physician and members of this congregation, quickly removed that illness. We saw that his God would not let impious eyes look upon his weakness and the defacing of that great pulpit genius. He passed through Jordan standing up! His Lord kept him away from the fiery arrows. Death did not wrestle with him. There was no contest. He passed through Jordan unmarked and standing up!

Good night, old friend, your little day is over, ours nearly so! On some glad tomorrow, when the morning comes, and all the saints of God are gathered home, we'll meet and tell the story of how we've overcome.

ᏒᎧ 20 ᏒᎧ

A MIGHTY OAK IS FALLEN

For Samuel DeWitt Proctor,
Abyssinian Baptist Church, Harlem, New York, New York,
May 29, 1997

When I was summoned to this solemn responsibility, I realized that it was but a testimony to the long, enduring friendship that I knew with Samuel Proctor. And I knew then, as I know now, that I was not competent to do this.

To measure the meaning and work of Sam Proctor is as if one would take a thimble and try to empty an ocean. It would be as if one sought to measure the expanse of the heaven with the span of the human hand. Something vast and noble has passed from among us. It is like a mighty oak has fallen, leaving an empty and gaping and glaring space against the sky where he stood.

And to his wife, now widowed, sons, brothers, sisters, grandchildren, all, on behalf of Christendom and on behalf of a grateful republic, I want today to thank you for your willingness to make him available to all of us over so long a period of time and in so notable a fashion as he gave his service.

One thinks of a passage over in ancient literature — "Know ye not that a prince and a great man has fallen in Israel" (paraphrase of 1 Samuel 3:38). Few among us will hardly see his like again, for he was a meteor flashing across the sky. When Calvin Butts called me, I began canvassing Scripture for some appropriate word. But even in that rich treasure, I knew almost inevitably that I would have to summon a word from Jesus himself.

So I was inevitably and invariably drawn to that word which the resurrected Spirit said to the church at Smyrna. One beholds it today, modern-day Izmir, as it rises up from the Aegean Sea, crowned by the ruins of a magnificent castle. And as the ancients said, "with its feet resting in the sea." The Spirit spoke to me of what Jesus spoke to the church at Smyrna — one of only two churches to receive the full affirmation of the resurrected Spirit. It was as if the speaker and writer was looking in the direction of Samuel Proctor when these words were written. "Be thou faithful unto death, and I will give thee a crown of life" (Revelation 2:10). Amen.

Faithfulness belongs to all of us. It does not have to do with the length of our living or the extent of our capabilities. Faithfulness is within the grasp of the least of us as it is within the reach of the noblest of us. But one cannot help pondering that where more is given more is required. And Samuel Proctor was given abundantly.

He was born in the Tidewater; some of his contemporaries, brothers and sisters and others, still live there. He was born of parents to whom he referred with ever greater reverence as the years came and went. One gathered from his writings that his father and mother had been vaccinated against racism by the Spirit of Christ. That inoculation flowed through the bloodstream of Samuel Proctor. And it is passed on, I believe, to his children, to all future generations. With his equals he was a delightful companion, and to those who had not reached his level he was gracious and concerned. One would speak about his superiors, but there were none.

And so we gather around his mortal remains. What an odyssey — what a journey — what a pilgrimage of faith in Jesus Christ! Here was a man who by the very gifts of nature looked like a prince and talked like a poet. And many of us entering his presence felt like rough gingham in the presence of rich brocade. For here was one of nature's noblemen.

The word for him was "Be thou faithful." And he was faithful. How he traversed this land, believing that those who are challenged and down could rise up and that there are capacities and potentialities in the least of us to reach toward the stars and to scrape the very sky. He never gave up, in his confidence, on what young people could become, and so he traversed the land. We cannot know what he went through.

Oh, at some distance we may have some idea what he went through, but we cannot know all of what Sam Proctor experienced — packing bags — going in airports — getting on planes — leaving his family — getting off planes — going to hotel rooms — always with that burning in his heart. Somebody said he was driven; maybe so. If so, he was driven by his belief in the potentiality of the young, believing that they could measure up to some standard that they had not yet achieved. But Sam Proctor was not only driven, he was pulled by the magnificence of his Lord, who laid claim upon the fullness of his life.

We cannot know the deepest and innermost thoughts that he had. I saw him last sitting on the porch of the old Alex Haley Farm down in Tennessee, and that image I carry with me still in memory. That evening he seemed withdrawn, meditating; it was as if he heard some far-off cathedral bells ringing in his soul. I will carry to my dying day the memory of Sam Proctor that evening, as the sun left the sky down in Tennessee.

And so he worked and so he served. He went up and down the country, never stopping, never despairing, surely some times lonely, sometimes with great fears about his own health. But that was not his principal concern in his most recent years.

And then his crowning work here at Abyssinian Church — this legendary place, this historic edifice. Here he served and preached the gospel of Jesus Christ with clarity and power and insight, constantly touching the great mystery of faith. When he came toward the end, he had prepared this young giant to take up where he left off.

His was a grand story larger in dimension than many of us had ever seen or can ever hope to see again. We bid his spirit farewell today from this earthly round. But Sam Proctor never gave up. Be thou faithful — faithful at the lectern of the academy — faithful in the pulpit of Christendom — faithful as he walked among us — faithful in his encouragement. Faithful in his confidence about our black destiny in America and faithful about the nation's capacity to rise up to its fullest potential. Faithful! Faithful! Faithful! Unto. You will notice that the writer did not say until death, for that is a type of parallelism, a sort of "alongside," but unto death — that is, directed, aimed, purposeful, intentional. He was faithful not just until death; he was faithful unto death.

When I spoke with his wife and now widow, Bessie, she said how thankful she was that he did not have to suffer. And God be thanked! All of us might well wish that our end would be as his. For he went directly from the trials of this life to claim his reward. "For I will give you a crown of righteousness that fadeth not away." I will measure your service. I will take account of what you have been. I will remember how you went up and down the land. I will reward you.

And so with his sword unsheathed and his armor still in place he fell facing the foe. God be thanked for that. The medieval mystics had a notion that there was a resting place between here and yonder. They called it Sangreal. They conceived of it as a majestic castle with thirty-six towers and crystal crosses and hangings of green samite, guarded by its knights, surrounded by impenetrable forests and a glittering mountain of onyx. John Bunyan may have taken his idea for Beulah, which lies on this side of Jordan, just before heaven, from that picture of the medieval mystics. But Sam Proctor bypassed Beulah and did not stop at that castle at Sangreal near Onyx Mountain. He went directly to see the King. With the scent of the battle still on his garment, he went to see the King.

And so we bid him today farewell. I speak not now to this mortal castle of clay, though it was majestic in its time. But I speak rather to a liberated, redeemed, emancipated spirit. Sam, we bumped into each other in and out of airports, we laughed and talked together, but your flight was before mine. Mine is not yet, it seems, and so I speak now to his spirit as he leans over the balcony of heaven and looks down upon these ceremonies. Please come to the terminal. It ought to be that my flight time is already on the board. Do not stay in the terminal; come out to the arrival gate. I've never been to that land, but I understand that it's a land of pure delight, where saints immortal reign. I've never been to that land. I understand that the city is of perfect architecture, its length is as its breadth which is as broad as its height, but I've never been there. I hear the hills of Zion yield a thousand sacred sweets. We may taste of them all before we walk its golden streets.

So will you, old friend, will you, come out to the arrival gate. Meet me there. It cannot be long! We'll laugh as in days of old, and we'll go to see Jesus. God be with you, Sam. God be with you, till we meet! Till we meet, till we meet, till we meet on the other shore.

Section Six

Expository Sermons
on the Seven Churches
of Asia Minor

∼ 21 ∼

EPHESUS:
THE CHURCH THAT LEFT ITS FIRST LOVE

Revelation 2:1–7

January 17, 1988

The first chapter of the Book of Revelation sets the action for the rest of it. It qualifies the reporter, John. It declares and defines the central figure and the true author of the book, Jesus Christ. The second chapter, which we come to today, addresses or begins to address letters to the seven churches of Asia Minor. It identifies the church as the center of the interest of Jesus Christ. What a compliment! Think of the innumerable organizations. Ponder the countless institutions. Think of the myriad associations that exist in the world. And then reflect upon the fact that the interest of Jesus Christ centers upon the church.

So we come to deal in these Sundays coming with the churches and seeing if we can detect ourselves, reflected, for better or for worse, and, at last, we hope, for better. Two of the seven received no blame: Smyrna and Philadelphia. Two of them received no praise: Sardis and Laodicea. The other three received praise and blame: Thyatira, Pergamos, and, what I consider was the largest and best established of all, Ephesus, to which we come today. Ephesus: the church that left its first love.

And so it begins "unto the angel of the church." In my young days as a pastor and preacher in my native state, people sometimes in formal public address would refer to the pastor as "the angel of the church." Irony, as one of the church fathers thought it was so. Others have thought, including Professor Walter Wink at Auburn Seminary, that it refers to the particular spirit assigned to the care of the church. Well, if it does mean the address is to the pastor of the church at Ephesus, and if there are any pastors

151

who hear me this morning and feel somewhat proud about being referred to as an angel, I would direct your attention to the ninth verse of the twelfth chapter of the Book of Revelation, where it is said that Satan, the devil, was cast from heaven with all of his angels. As a matter of fact, we have associated a certain halo with the name, but originally the word *angel (angélos)* meant only "messenger." Of course, there's distinction in that, but not the kind of things we attached to the word *angel.* We have brought that word down out of the sky and put it in our romance, and surely that is not the meaning. So the next time you refer to an angel, you are talking about a "messenger" in the Bible.

Ephesus, what a city! Its citizens, maybe its chamber of commerce, called it the chief city of Ionia. Center of commerce and culture. Even when one sees the ruins of Ephesus, they are impressive. Its amphitheater, with its tiers of seats, is preserved almost intact, though in ruins. Its great elaborate brothel, with its drunkards' bath outside of it, where the people who got too drunk could douse themselves sober, are all there. You can go up and down the streets, overgrown now with grass and dust. Its centerpiece was the temple of Diana, one of the seven wonders of the ancient world. One of the ancient historians said that the temple was 221 years in construction. And when people came to look at the wonders of the world, the temple of Diana had to be considered one of them. But not only did the city itself have a great distinction, but also this church in Ephesus, had a great and distinguished beginning.

You read chapters 18 and 19 of Acts when you are home, and you will read something about this city of Ephesus and some of the great Christian figures who were a part of the early church there in that city. Apollos, the elegant Alexandrian orator, worked in Ephesus, spoke there. Timothy was there, and the brightest star of them all, Paul, spent time in Ephesus, and John, very likely the writer of the Book of Revelation. So the word is addressed to this church, and there are some words of praise for the church in Ephesus and for the church in Brooklyn. Concord, whatever church. The church in Ephesus, the church in Brooklyn.

The Lord who moves among the candlesticks has some words for the church. This reference to his moving among the candlesticks means that he has the church under close scrutiny, and when I speak of the church I hope that you do not think of something alien and separate from you. I've said that to you before, but it bears repeating ever so often. We talk about what "they" are doing at the church. The church is not "they," and it's not "them," and it's not that other contraction we have, "some of 'em." The church is you and I. So when the word is addressed to the church, it isn't addressed to somebody or something; it's addressed to you and to me. The Lord says to the church at Ephesus, "I know thy works." That's praise, and "thy labour," so that this was an active church at Ephesus. And God knows a church ought to be that. They may have had a clothing exchange in Ephesus, I don't know. They may have had an elementary school, they may have had a home for elderly people in Ephesus, I don't know, but the Lord praises them. "I know thy works, I know. I'm aware of your labor." It was a working church, and every church ought to be that.

There is something wrong with any people who have received from Jesus Christ the newness of life and of life eternal and who can sit down and do nothing. There is something wrong with a people who carry the name of him who turned the world upside down and then right side up and who are paralyzed. A do-nothing church is a no-Christ church. Work ought to go on in the church, it ought to, we ought to. Because Christ came for people's needs, the church ought to be dedicated to the needs of people, spiritual, physical, political, material, economic needs. God knows there are many needs around us. I said this week to one of our city officials that our city is in great need of healing. This is a bruised city. We are people of too many backgrounds for us to be at each other's throats. It won't work. I said to him, it is, God forbid, conceivable that a person who is black may not be able to go into a community that's not black, and by the same token, it is conceivable, and this is a dreadful thought, that a white person may not be able to pass through these black streets.

Abominable! We can't make it like that. Our social contract, if I may use Rousseau's term, has broken down. There are grievances and there will be, and as I tried to say to him, there ought not to be bandages or cosmetics over the grievances, but within the grievances we've got to contract some kind of livable arrangement here. And one of the things we need is to change the vocabulary of our public discussion.

We need a new language that does not incite and upset and anger and infuriate. We need to develop now a rhetoric of reconciliation. That's what we need. This church at Ephesus was a working church, and the Lord said, "I know thy works, and thy labour, and thy patience." What a wonderful tribute to a church if it had ended with "I know thy works." This is the Lord of the church talking who has scrutinized it and investigated it and examined it and who superintends it. "I know thy works." It was a working church. And God knows I pray and hope that this will always be a working church. By way of the death and resurrection of Jesus Christ to enter into a fellowship and then to do nothing about this society is to reflect unfavorably upon the Lord who has called us out of darkness into the marvelous light of his grace.

Then this was the church that did not tolerate false doctrine, evil, ungodly, and un-Christian principles. It speaks of the Nicolaitans in the sixth verse, "thou hatest the deeds of the Nicolaitans, which I also hate." It is believed that the author of that sect, of that heresy, of that unbelief, in the church of Ephesus was a man named Nicolaus, from which they got their name. And I hate to have to say it, but if you'll read the sixth chapter of the Book of Acts where the deacons are named, he's the last named deacon. Nicolaus started a mess in the church at Ephesus. We ought to be very careful and, I do thank God that I do not say this in reference to anybody in particular. We preachers sometimes preach fussing sermons at somebody. I am not preaching at anybody; I am preaching now at everybody, including myself. The higher we get in the church, the more careful we ought to be.

The Nicolaitans believed that once you came into Jesus Christ you had no obligation to live a godly life. Not only did you not have any obligation to live a godly life, but you didn't have to worry about not living a godly life. I have always said that most of us, and God knows I number myself in that number, will fall far short of what we ought to be as Christians. We ought not ever become content with being less than we ought to be as Christians. There ought to live in us a tension and an anguish that we ought to be more and more like Jesus. If that tension has gone out of your life, if you are comfortable in your failure, if you are satisfied in your moral collapses, then the Lord is not in you. There ought to at least be pain and anguish that we are not loyal to the Lord as we ought to be. There's hope as long as there is that "unsatisfaction" in us. The church at Ephesus the Lord praised, because they would not tolerate false doctrine.

We come to that fourth verse. I wish we didn't have that fourth verse there. But you put this down; the Lord tells it all. Now the King James Version, I must be honest with you, has done an injustice to the Scripture. It adds "somewhat," and no wonder the translators put it in italics, because it doesn't belong there. I'll tell you why it doesn't belong there. It doesn't belong there because "somewhat" means I've got a little thing! Nothing big, but I've got something, a little "somewhat." The New Revised Standard Version drops that "somewhat" and says starkly, "I have this against you." If you think that's a little "somewhat," you read on down where he says, "Remember and repent," if you think that "somewhat" doesn't mean much. Or else "I will come unto thee quickly, and will remove thy candlestick." I'll take your power away from you. I'll remove your scriptural authority, I'll deprive you of your apostolic commission, I'll reduce you from one of the elect. If you think that "somewhat" belongs there, you read that part, "Repent or I will come quickly. I'll take the candlestick away from you," and there's nothing so sad as a church which has lost its spiritual power. This going along, making motions, and acting like it is a spiritual entity when the fire has gone out in it and the Spirit has departed from it. It is doing nothing but going through ceremonies and form and fashion and outside show, as they used to say, to this unfriendly world. It's a sad thing to see a church when the power has gone out of it.

And what had they done? I want you to see the importance of it. You take that "somewhat" away; it doesn't belong there. Somebody tried to make it nice and put that "somewhat" there as if it were a minor thing. But verse 5 will rebuke and repudiate that notion. If you don't repent of what I have against you, I'll take your power from you. You'll be salt which has lost its savor. It'll be good for nothing but to be tracked under the feet of people, and that's what the world will do to you. A church which has lost its power, the world can do anything to it, but, my God, to a church which has the living presence of Jesus Christ, nothing can happen. No storms can ever blow it over, no fire can ever burn it down, no slander can ever smear it, no opposition can ever defeat it. When the power of the Lord is in the church, the church has power. Power, power, Holy Ghost power, power!

What was it the church had left? By first look at all of these other things, it is doing wonderfully, but it has left its first love. Now, what is, who is the first love of the church? I don't think I need even to tell you. The church doesn't have but one name to travel on. The church is the people in it, not something different from you and me. You, you have left the center around which a Christian life and a church have to be organized. Jesus Christ, that is the center, that is the core, that is the power, that is the generator! Left your first love. Oh, my God, what an indictment! I spoke earlier about this church's voter registration campaign being wonderful, but don't leave your first love. Mr. Franklin Thomas, now of the Ford Foundation, spoke about his time here as a child in the Boy Scouts. Wonderful, but do not leave your first love! Christ is the power of this church! Christ! Let the Lord be among us! Let Christ be all over us! Let Christ be all around us. Let Christ be all underneath us. Let Christ be all through this church! Let Christ's name be lifted up! Let Christ be all through here! Let Christ be praised here! Let Christ be our all and all!

When the Christfund, which we will not too long complete, was just getting underway, I was telling about it to a pastor in another city. And he said, "That's a wonderful thing, it ought to carry your name." I said, "Oh no, it might fail if it carries my name. If it's going to fail, it'll never fail bearing my name." But I knew what I was talking about. I said, "If it's going to fail, let it carry the Lord's name." I knew what I was talking about. I knew that if it has the Lord's name and the Lord's Spirit in it, it cannot fail. There's no way for it to fail. Put his name in it, and I know it is bound to succeed. The Lord's not going to let his name be dragged in the mud.

Well, I guess that's about what I've got to tell you today, except for one thing, and I'll let you go. If you want a formula for success, I'm going to give it to you this morning. If you've got some dreams in your life and they're worthwhile and you want to see them come to pass, I'm going to tell you how to get it done. You hitch yourself to Jesus. I'm going to put it another way this morning. Your car may not be able to move. The car of your dreams may not be able to move. And it may be a ragged car, but you hitch it to the Jesus train. Hitch your car to the Jesus train, oh yes, hitch your car to the Jesus train. I thank God I hitched my hopes to Jesus, I hitched my strength to Jesus, I hitched my dreams to Jesus, I hitched my future to Jesus, I hitched everything to Jesus' name. If you ask me this morning how is it going to be with me, I cannot tell you. But I can tell you I've hitched my car to the Jesus train. I do not know which way the road leads, but I've hitched my car to the Jesus train. If the road goes up or the road goes down I'm hitched to Jesus' name. My people, go on in Jesus' name! You hitch your car. It may be rundown and ragged, but you hitch your car to the Jesus train. You'll get to the place for which your heart sighs.

✧ 22 ✧

SMYRNA:
THE RICH POOR CHURCH, PART 1

Revelation 2:8–11

January 24, 1988

This subject I found confusing. I did not know whether to call this the poor rich church or the rich poor church. Which is which? And then I remembered a biography about Diana Barrymore, of whom it was said that she had too much too soon, and she was called the poor little rich girl. So it seems that the rich poor church is the apt word for the church at Smyrna.

Let me read again these words of the risen presence of Jesus, not a long address, but a meaningful one. You will remember before I read the Scripture that there were two of these seven churches of Asia Minor which received no praise: Sardis and the old, banking capital of Laodicea. Then three of these churches received mixed praise and blame: Ephesus, Thyatira, Pergamos; and two of these churches, one of which we come to today, received nothing but praise: Smyrna and Philadelphia.

The angel of the church in Smyrna writes,

These things saith the first and the last, which was dead and is alive;
I know thy works, and tribulation, and poverty, (but thou art rich) and I know the blasphemy of them which say they are Jews, and are not, but are the synagogue of Satan.
Fear none of those things which thou shalt suffer: behold, the devil shall cast some of you into prison, that ye may be tried; and ye shall have tribulation ten days: be thou faithful unto death, and I will give thee a crown of life.
He that hath an ear, let him hear what the Spirit saith unto the churches; he that overcometh shall not be hurt of the second death.

There is too much in that for me to exhaust today, or even another time, but certainly not today. Smyrna was said to be the most beautiful of the cities of Asia Minor. Ephesus was the chief city, though Smyrna never conceded that. It was said by the Asians that its feet were in the sea and its head was crowned by a great hill that rose over Smyrna. It had the most convenient and the safest harbor of all of the cities along the Aegean Sea. It sat at the head of the Hermes Valley, which was extraordinarily rich in grain. It claimed to be the birthplace of Homer, though later somebody wrote that when Homer was living he had not a roof to cover his head, but that is natural. It was a city of commerce and of culture; there was a public library, there was an *odeum*, music theater, and an amphitheater. It was greatly favored by the Romans, because at one difficult time in a Roman invasion not far from Smyrna, when the Roman legions were greatly in peril, the citizens of Smyrna gave their own clothing for the Roman soldiers. You can still see in the city of Smyrna the gray marble floor of what was once a temple to Tiberius. A temple to a man. Not just a monument but a temple.

We come again to that matter of emperor worship. They demanded, these emperors did, that a pinch of incense be taken and placed on an altar, and it be declared by everyone who wanted to enjoy citizenship that Tiberius, or whoever was the emperor, is God, is Lord.

This is what got Christians in trouble, as I have said over and over again, in this Book of Revelation. What is it? What is the lust in us that makes us want to be more than what humans were meant to be? What is it? I've raised that with you before. What instinctual lust is there in us that makes us want to pretend to be what we are not? Shakespeare said of our humanity, "how like a god," and there are grand and lordly and noble characteristics about our humanity, but we are still human. It is not an old thing. We hear of that kind of thing in what is called an imperial presidency, this temptation of our humanity to want to be more than what we are. We are already great creatures. Lordly spirits, noble, the very height of God's creation, but not gods. I'm not now talking about aspiration to be better men and women; I'm talking about the desire to be worshiped. We make poor gods anyhow. Two-legged, eyeglass-wearing gods? Bald-headed, pot-bellied gods? Teeth-decaying, hair-falling gods? It doesn't fit us. What we ought to try to be is the noblest of humanity that we can be. And we will have bitten off a large order right there. These emperors were already the most powerful people in the world, but they were not satisfied. They wanted people to worship them as gods. The Christians could not do it. And that word *atheist* was first applied to our spiritual forebears. Christians were called atheists because they would not worship Caesar. It got them into trouble. In this case it was the church at Smyrna. That word Smyrna means myrrh, the balm used for healing. There is still a Christian community in Smyrna. It was the church upon which a central persecution and suffering descended.

I would that I had time to tell you about Polycarp, who was pastor or bishop of the church at Smyrna. Perhaps on another Sunday I will have opportunity to do so, but a frightful persecution fell upon the church. The members of that church were not merely poor; they were deprived of their property. It was tantamount to being declared outside the law if one would not bow down and worship — such a person lost jobs, such a person had property confiscated. Such a person had no rights left. This is what Christian people faced.

And it is for that reason that we hear the words here of the Lord Jesus, "I know thy works, and tribulations, and poverty," and here is a parenthesis. My God, what a vast parenthesis. Did you look at it? "But thou art rich" — there are endless volumes of God's grace inside this parenthesis. The harmonies of heaven, said Joseph Parker, are inside this parenthesis, thou art poor but thou art rich. Poor, but rich. Let me talk a little while, if I may, about poverty. And let me throw aside a canard, a ridiculous false statement that used to be made, I don't hear it any longer, by so-called liberated blacks who spoke of church people as being foolish and singing "take all the world and give me Jesus." So said these poor, lame-brained, half-educated Johnny-come-latelies. Fools they were. Doctor William A. Jones has pointed out accurately that the people in our black community or communities throughout the country, by and large, who are going to work, and earning a living, and educating their children, and buying homes, and getting little bank accounts, are church people. Go into any city in America, any city anywhere, you will find that to be true.

The people who are getting ahead, by and large, are church people. I have been up and down this country from one end to the other. I do not know a single city or community in the nation in which that is not the truth. And the people who are supporting their community causes by and large are church people. That other crowd with their big parties and their all-night poker games and their smug sense of superiority support nothing but themselves. So I want to clear that ground.

Now let's talk awhile about poverty and wealth. Let me tell you this: in the eye of history, the worst thing that has happened is this era of greed, symbolized by the lives of the rich and famous, the popularity of *Dallas* on television, and *Dynasty*, which in their religious counterparts are the health-and-wealth TV evangelists. Listen to me this morning. I include their political counterparts in Washington, where greed and supposed success are the standards of life. The greatest condemnation of this is not that these people themselves are tainted with a false notion and smitten with an awful virus that cannot produce health. That is not the worst part.

The worst part is they have communicated to our children the notion that getting it is all that matters in life. A survey by the University of California of freshman students revealed that seventy-odd percent of the young people entering college said that their primary purpose is to make money. Fewer than thirty percent said that they felt that the primary important thing in their lives was to get a meaningful philosophy of life by which to live. That is the tragedy. Seventy-odd percent saying that the only thing that matters is money. Greed can destroy the nation, and we will discover that our greed has not only not saved us, but also, in the strange providence of God, in trying to get, we have lost.

This nation does not belong to the United States today. Have I said it to you before? We are $59 billion in debt to Japan. They're talking about buying the airport at Atlanta; they own the Exxon building in New York. They own every Westin hotel in America. Our greed has not got us anywhere. It cannot save us. I am not talking about not being industrious and not saving, but I am talking about worship at the altar of greed and gain. I do not say this in great condemnation, but one financier said the other year that there is nothing wrong with being greedy, everybody ought to be a little greedy, and you ought not, he said, feel guilty about it — as he got ready to go off to jail.

It will not work. And what is wealth, what are riches finally? Well, Mr. Edsel Ford, who was exactly my age, died a few months ago in the hospital which his money built. It is wonderful that he built a hospital, but all of his wealth could not save him at the last. How much of his wealth would this person of great financial holdings have been willing to give up in order to stand where I stand, or to sit where you sit today?

Health is wealth. To have the use of one's limbs is wealth. It is rich to be able to get up and come out here this morning, that's wealth. It is wealth to have family around us and friends who respect us. And, oh my God, to have Jesus Christ as our Savior, to whom we may look and upon whom we may depend and who has promised to guide us and to be with us and to take care of us in every shifting and changing circumstance of life, that is wealth. "Thou art rich," said Christ to the church in Smyrna.

What are riches? I ought to come back to that. It depends on who is talking. To someone who has nothing, a thousand dollars is great wealth. To a millionaire, a thousand dollars, twenty thousand dollars are not much. It is far beyond our grandest imagination when Christ says you are rich, for his holdings are all that God possesses.

These people suffered because they were Christians, and while we may not be called upon to suffer in such a grand and dramatic way, all of us are, in a way of speaking, penalized to some extent. There is some money we cannot take. No Christian dare make money out of crack or heroin. What kind of Christian is it who is willing to make money by scheming and depriving others of what is their rightful possession? Let me tell you, sometimes I daydream about winning ten million dollars in the lottery. And I think I would give the church five million dollars. But how would I ever explain to the church where I got the money? There is some money that does not belong to us, and we ought not to have it. It is no good!

Someone tells of a ragged, seedy man standing outside of a window of a convent. One of the young nuns could stand it no longer. She tossed out a note with a hundred-dollar bill attached to it, and said on it, "Keep your courage. Sister Marie." The next day the man came back. The Mother Superior answered the door. "Sister Marie here?" "Yes." "I have a thousand dollars for her." "A thousand dollars?" Mother Superior was surprised. "Yes," he said, "a thousand dollars." "Where would Sister Marie, the nun, be getting a thousand dollars?" And the man said, "Keep Your Courage paid twenty to one at Aqueduct Race Track."

I know that some of you do not quite hold with this, but there is money that does not belong to Christian people, so these people had lost greatly. And the Lord Jesus was saying to them, "Stand up, I know your work." The Lord sees your tribulations, your hardship, your anguish. He was saying to them to stand in his name. What we do may not matter much, if we are representing only ourselves. What we do takes on infinite significance, however, if we are wearing the colors and uniform of Christ on the playing field of life. That matters!

It does not make much difference what you do, what I do, but Christ's name is at stake. The Lord's name is tied up with your name and with my name. That's what makes it important how we bear ourselves in life. Oh, I hope you'll remember that this thing has haunted me through these years, knowing my own faults and failures. Have I ever said to you that I have desperately wanted, under God, not to disgrace his people, not to disgrace the Lord who has called me out of darkness into the marvelous light of his grace? And Jesus is saying, "I know your tribulation, I know it is hard. Many have given up, some are bowing down, but stand up, don't give up. You are wearing my colors!"

There was one of the church fathers, Erasmus, who confessed openly that he was not made of the stuff of which martyrs are created, that he did not have it in him, and many of us sympathize with that. But if we will put our hands in the Lord's keeping, he will give us strength. For whatever it is that we have to face, he will give us strength. And he says to you and to me and all of us that we have our struggles. Life is not an easy business; it is a struggle from the cradle to the grave, the infant struggles for balance and equilibrium. The little children going on to kindergarten or first grade struggle to find a place in a new environment. Young people struggle for their identity and against the awful temptations that are all around us. Those in their middle years struggle against all kinds of doubts trying to make something decent of life, and those of you who come to old age struggle against the fear of what might happen, and when we leave here, we are likely to struggle for our breath.

Life is a struggle from the cradle to the grave. And the Lord Jesus says, "I know your works. I appreciate you." I'm so glad he said that he knows what you are going through. "You are not off in the corner somewhere passing through your hardships by yourself, unknown and uncared about; I know. Trust me," he says, "lean on me. Depend on me. I will give you strength. When the hour comes I will be there. Whatever it is, I will raise up friends for you." How well do I know that this is true! "I will open doors for you. I will put bread on your table and I'll put a roof over your head. I'll be what you need. Trust me, trust me."

That's what he says to us: trust me. And I cannot help asking, Will it work? And I come back to that hinge, yes, that hinge upon which the whole New Testament turns, that linchpin which holds the axle wheel in place, the very axle of the New Testament. The pivot. You follow me — the turning point, the core, the heart, the sine qua non of the New Testament — how can I trust him? Can he see about me?

You have not got to the heart of Christianity until you've come to that faith: "I am he who is dead and I'm alive." That's what the whole New Testament is about, my people. It looks at your troubles and hears when you ask, Can God do anything about my plight? Then the New Testament replies, "God raised Christ from the dead." That's the heart of the whole matter. Can he make me mount up with wings, to run and not be weary, to walk and not faint? Can God do it? He raised Christ from the dead. If God could do that, nothing, nothing is too hard for him.

Whatever your trials, whatever your circumstance, however difficult the road you travel, God raised Christ from the dead and, praise his name, he can see about you and me. Is God able? He raised Christ from the dead. Can God take care of me in all my shifting circumstances and changing conditions? He raised Christ from the dead. When I am sick and it does not look like I can get well, can the Lord put me on my feet again? He raised Christ from the dead. When my friends turn their back on me and I have nowhere, it seems, to turn, can I believe it will be all right? He raised Christ from the dead. Yes, God can see about me. No matter how far I drift, through whatever circumstances to which I come, God can bring me through. And so, because of that, it pays to serve Jesus. Never forget that. I do not know what your condition is, but it cannot be any worse than what God faced when Christ was in the tomb — and the tomb became empty. What God has done for others, particularly Christ, God can do for you.

✌ 23 ✌

Smyrna:
The Rich Poor Church, Part 2

Revelation 2:8–11

February 7, 1988

From whence names come we do not know, but these were people in Smyrna who knew a name. And that is why we're talking about them. It is amazing! Some people whose names we do not know knew a name, *Jesus*. And here we are, talking about Smyrna and some people there, nineteen hundred years later. What a power there is in the name of Jesus!

If I could summon today no other evidence for his being the Son of God, the fact is that we are here this morning toward the end of the twentieth century talking about an obscure town, more or less. When we went there, we had to travel down the whole European continent, down to Istanbul, down to where the continent of Europe almost touches Asia, and then fly over an hour from Istanbul to Smyrna. But they knew a name there. And they were not people who built up the name in a chamber-of-commerce hype. Things can be built up by hype. Public relations, if you've got enough. Promoters built up last Sunday's Super Bowl game just by hype. Now the fate of the world was not decided in San Diego last Sunday. I got up early the next morning in a hotel room in El Paso, and the sun still came up. They hyped the Super Bowl, they attached the Roman numerals to it, XX, to give it cosmic significance. The only other place I see Roman numerals today is in the Bible. These people in Smyrna did not have any of that, but they did know a name. And we know something about them.

We know that they were a church under siege; the heaviest

artillery of the empire was pointed at their heads, so to speak. We know some of what the trouble was; we talked about it last week. They were accused of treason, disloyalty to the government because they would not acknowledge — and I will be saying that again and again — they would not acknowledge Caesar as Lord, and they were therefore called traitors. These Christians. Some of you may have seen a program on public television this week in which my late colleague and friend Dr. Adam Powell was saying that there is a law, the law of God, which is above the law of human beings. It is bad when any people, or any segment of people, try to act as if the law of God is equal to the laws of people. That's one of the things Martin King was all about. There is a higher law. And while we can be Americans and be proud of it, there is a law higher than the laws of America. Older and higher.

I was on an army post this week, and I can understand how that goes on, but I caught the determination to make our country and God the same thing. It can be done, but not by bringing God down. It can be done by our reaching up to where he is. I rather get the feeling that the attempt is not so much to get us up to him but to get him down to our level, and that will not work. So the Christians in Smyrna were accused. They were accused of treason, disloyalty. They would not take an oath that they believed compromised their faith in Jesus Christ. And then they were subjected to the charge of blasphemy, of atheism.

Now to put it in its real meaning, they were slandered, they were blasphemed, they were slandered partly as being immoral. These early Christians had night meetings, and did you know that in the early church an unbeliever could not look upon, I'm not talking about participating, could not look upon the Lord's Supper. It was closed, and that's where the idea which I heard about when I first came to this church still existed, the idea of "closed Communion." It is now changed, but an unbeliever could not look upon it. It was too holy. Those who watched these early Christians enter the place of worship for these nocturnal hours of worship said that something terrible and immoral must be going on, because we're always tempted to look on the worst side of everything, including each other.

How little do we look upon what is good about the other. How quick we are to pounce upon what we fancy to be real that is negative in somebody else's life. Those were two charges. Disloyalty, blasphemy, and they were slandered. They were, therefore, in tribulation. You would have thought, though, that the Lord would have said to them, "That is enough. You've gone through enough." He did not do so. There was, and I hate to have to bring it up, but there was antagonism between early Christians and Jews, and sadly enough it has gone on down through the centuries. I have promised God that I would never in this pulpit, as far as he will let me, speak a divisive word between people, but there was a difference between them. The world divides too much into "we" and "they," and "us" and "them." The singleness of our humanity needs to be lifted up. Those who persecuted them were, these early Christians said, of the synagogue of Satan. It would seem that the Lord would have said to them, "Enough. You've suffered slander, you have suffered the charge of treason, your property has been confiscated, you've lost your jobs, you have been declared noncitizens, your whole movement is an illicit society, branded by the government as subversive, outside of the law. Enough. Enough." He does not. He says to these people, "I know your tribulation," and then he goes on in the next verse to say "Other things will come upon you. The devil shall cast some of you into prison that ye may be tried," and it did come upon them.

There's an account in the early church of a young lad, because sometimes whole families were fed to lions in the arena. The young lad, with his father's arm around him, looked up at his father saying, "Father," as the lion came out of the chute, "will it hurt?" And the father said, "But for a little while, but he that overcometh shall not be hurt of the second death." We have a record of Polycarp, who was bishop of Smyrna, murdered on February 23, A.D. 155. They tried to get him to say that Caesar is lord. The Asiarch, who was the high priest of the civil religion, said to him, "You're old; it won't hurt you to renounce Christ and say that Caesar is lord." Polycarp said, "For eighty and six years I have served him, he has never done me wrong, how can I now denounce my Lord, my King, who has saved me?" So they burned him in the amphitheater. Indeed he was enveloped in a cloud of flames. The church at Smyrna in their minutes set the date of Polycarp's martyrdom with the words, "Statius Quadratus being Proconsul, but Jesus Christ King forever."

I wish I knew why suffering comes upon good people, well, if not good people, then upon people who try to serve the Lord. I do not know. I have no answer. I know some clues why we suffer. We suffer partly because the nerve which can tingle with joy and pleasure can also throb with pain. I know that the body which must sink and die is the same body that is born and grows, and these things are somehow mixed one with the other. I know that. But I could not tell you today why suffering comes upon you or upon those whom you love. I have no answer to that.

I do know this, and I believe it with all my heart, that the Lord God who is the Father of Jesus Christ will not for nothing let us be hurt. That he will not allow us to suffer without purpose, I do believe with all my heart. And I believe also, as our forebears said before us, that God knows the limits of our ability. He knows the outer frontier beyond which we cannot bear. He knows that. And I do believe it with all my heart. I know for some of you it is very difficult, and I know, fellow pilgrim, that sometimes you wonder how you're going to make it through another day. I realize that there are times when you feel like literally screaming, because the load gets heavy and the hill is so high and you seem to be all in it by yourself. Oh, but I know this too, that there is no road so long that it does not have a turning. And I know this, that whatever you are passing through, this too will pass away. And I know this, that somewhere and somehow the load lifts, and the burden rolls away. I know that. I know something else. I know that God knows just how much you can bear. Though the load gets heavy, keep on toiling. Though the teardrops fall, your heavenly Father knows your capacity. He knows.

I read here a word that makes me shiver. "He that overcometh shall not be hurt of the second death." What is this? All of us have staring us in the face what we call the grim reaper. But this word here speaks of something grimmer still, the second death. I will speak to your souls very earnestly this morning. When we leave here the first time, we leave here amidst the actual physical presence of those who love us. But, my God, the second death, that speaks of an awful separation from God. Out in a place of endless loneliness, of a misery unending, "the second death." I pray God that nobody here may ever know what it is to be banished, as far as we know, forever from the presence of his God, to feel that abandonment like an endless nightmare, the second death. Grimmer, more terrible than the first one. God grant that every soul here will turn to Jesus Christ whom to know is to live, indeed, that you might not go out into some dark and lonely eternity without him, separated forever, forever, forever from the presence of God Almighty. The second death!

God deliver us from that. God deliver every one of you from that. It speaks of something so dreadful that it may be better not for me to deal with it. Let its unspeakable and indescribable implication stand by itself, "the second death." Men, women, boys, girls, do not call me morbid, but death day belongs to us, and beyond that, something else. Something else! God deliver us! Christ deliver us! Holy Spirit deliver us! "The second death."

I must not detain you much longer. "Be thou faithful unto death, and I will give thee a crown of life." I must keep repeating in this series that the importance of what is said depends upon who said it. And have I not said to you before that there are things that can be the wildest, the largest things said by people, and you know that what they say isn't worth a penny? And do not our business houses take great pride and do they not communicate their strength to us in terms of how old they are? And do you not see in the advertisements "since 1855"; "in business since 1930"? They refer to that with great pride, as bringing confidence in what they advertise, that they have been in business a long time. When we contract for things, we want to feel that the people with whom we are doing business will be in business. That the warranties and guarantees that they have issued will be backed up by their presence, that they are not fly-by-night business houses. When we call them, when we need to question the guarantee, we do not want to be told that the line has been disconnected, they have left town, they are not in business any longer. No. We want to do business with old, established firms. And we want to do business with firms that seem to have a stability that will indicate that they will go on, so that the warranties and guarantees they have given us will be honored.

Well, here it is, said the First and the Last, "Be thou faithful unto death, and I will give thee a crown of life." Christ said, "I am the First" (Revelation 1:17). How shall we discover what that means? What backward flight must we take to discover what the Lord means when he says "I am the First?" Back behind innumerable years, we must travel to get back to where he says "I am the First." Back behind the years into which countless centuries have sunk and disappeared. Before the morning stars sang together or ever the sons of God shouted for joy, "I am the First." Before the first star was placed in that mysterious dome above, "I am the First." Before the oldest planet flashed its light upon the face of the universe, "I am the First." We must travel back before Isaac, and before Abraham, and before Adam. "I am the First. I make the promise. I will give thee, if thou art faithful, a crown of life. I am the First." How far back must we go? Before the earliest song the elder seraphim sang around the lily-white throne, "I am the First." Till our spirits are chilled and we stand shivering in the pavilion of eternity where only God's heart reigned and God operated and God's words spoke. Before he said "Let there be." "I am the First. I promise it."

And what confidence can we have about the future? "I am the Last." How far must we travel out in front of us? Through what slow-passing centuries must we move? Beyond what eras and eons must we pass to find out what he means, "I am the Last." Until time collapses and its funeral sermon is delivered with the words "There should be time no longer" (Revelation 10:6), "I am the Last." Until the final sun's rays have risen and the final sunset has gone down, "I am the Last." Until the ultimate cry of rebellion or repentance from the ranks of humankind has been lifted before the presence of God, "I am the Last." Until all that is shall be no more, "I am the Last." Until "the elements shall melt with fervent heat" (2 Peter 3:10), "I am the Last." Until the trumpet shall sound and the dead in God shall be raised incorruptible, "I am the Last. I am the Last." Be thou faithful, not smart, but faithful. Not brilliant, but faithful.

Hold on, when the world turns against you, hold on. When it looks like every star has disappeared and the sun is about to run down in a crimson stream, hold on. When you've got no friend anywhere and it is like you're all by yourself and your strength has given out, hold on. Hold on. Stand the storm. It won't be long. We'll anchor by and by. Hold on. "I will give thee a crown of life."

This is his command. These are our marching orders.

∽ 24 ∾

PERGAMOS:
THE CHURCH NEAR SATAN'S THRONE,
PART 1

Revelation 2:12–17

February 14, 1988

I talked on the telephone last night with my friend Dr. Nelson Smith, and he had heard one of the tapes of our music here which touches the heart as well as the feet. Our choir is singing this month some of our great hymns. For a while, we seemed to grow a little cool about our own music. I preached recently in the First Presbyterian Church of Dallas, Texas, one of the most influential and wealthiest churches of that city, and they were singing that Sunday morning, "I don't want to run this race in vain." Let us continue to cherish the music which has been our drumbeat.

Pergamos or Pergamus, pronounce it either way you will, was the church where Satan's throne was. We come this morning to the northernmost of the seven churches, some fifty-five miles from Ephesus, twelve or fourteen miles inland. The people of Rome called it the last outpost of civilization. That was not exactly true, but it was the way they characterized the city of Pergamos. It was, outside of Athens itself, the most Greek-influenced city of that region of the world. There were two hundred thousand copies of parchment, which were the predecessors of our books, in the library at Pergamos. It was second only to the great library at Alexandria. Two hundred thousand, and the word *parchment*, many believe, comes from the name "Pergamos."

We who live in this time take sometimes the attitude that ancient people were all primitive, not quite civilized. We were

173

brainwashed with that about Africa for a long time, until we learned of the great kingdoms that existed in Africa. And what drew Africa away from the main role of rulership, if I may call it that, was the accident of where gunpowder was developed as a weapon. Judged by certain standards, we in the West may be the primitives, the savages. Certainly our language is founded upon the languages of the ancients, and many of our words in the English language come directly out of the Greek and Latin, so who are the primitives? If the judgment is made that respect for human life or lack of respect for human life marks the primitive, the savages, as over against respect for human life marking the civilized person, we in the West may be the primitives. For in our last two great wars, more human life was destroyed than was destroyed in all of the wars in the history of the world.

Who are the primitives? It is a disease of the young to feel that all who went before their generation were stupid and backward. This is an age which we all pass through I guess. We were sure our parents did not know anything of what it was all about. And we carried that idea over to the people who lived in an earlier time. Who are the primitives? No generation has courted death by inhaling, as for instance marijuana, on the scale that we do. Or smoking crack, or shooting heroin, or sniffing cocaine, no generation has courted death on so broad a scale. Who are the primitives? Who are the backward people? And no age has had a plague more deadly than AIDS. Who are the primitives? . . .

I've said all of that to get to something else this morning, because this is going to be in a way a peculiar sermon, and I'm going to come back next time we are together to the "white stone" which is mentioned here. There's something else I want to get at today, if you will grant me time and lend me your ears.

Pergamos was a center of ancient culture and learning. Was that what was meant by Satan's throne being located there? Galen, the ancient physician, did his work in Pergamos; he was second only to Hippocrates, whose oath the physicians take. Asclepius, the god of healing, was one of the chief gods of Pergamos.

He had as his insignia the serpent wound around a stick, which is still the medical fraternity's insignia. A hospital was located there. I went to that hospital once. It has in it the ruins of a little amphitheater where, two thousand years ago, they had what we would call now therapeutic drama. And the hospital had a healing room, in which small amounts of morphine were introduced in order to give the patients a feeling of well-being. It was said that nobody died in the hospital in Pergamos — because if you looked like you were going to die, they put you out! So the ancients said. But this was their worship, really, a mixture of medical science and pagan superstition, in the cult of Asclepius. *Asclepius Soter*, they called him, Asclepius savior. The seat of Satan was to be found in the fact that eight hundred feet above the city — that would be four times the length of this church — there was a pagan temple on the brow of the mountain and then above it an altar to Zeus, the father of the gods. What was the secret? Why does the spirit of Christ call this the seat of Satan's throne? What is the seat? Let me read this to you again.

> And to the angel of the church in Pergamos write; These things saith he which hath the sharp sword with two edges;
> I know thy works, and where thou dwellest, even where Satan's seat is: and thou holdest fast my name, and hast not denied my faith, even in those days wherein Antipas was my faithful martyr, who was slain among you, where Satan dwelleth.
> But I have a few things against thee, because thou hast there them that hold the doctrine of Balaam, who taught Balak to cast a stumblingblock before the children of Israel, to eat things sacrificed unto idols, and to commit fornication.
> So hast thou also them that hold the doctrines of the Nicolaitans, which thing I hate.
> Repent; or else I will come unto thee quickly, and will fight against them with the sword of my mouth.
> He that hath an ear, let him hear what the Spirit saith unto the churches; To him that overcometh will I give to eat of the hidden manna [I want to come back to that in a moment — the hidden manna], and will give him a white stone, and in the stone a new name written, which no man knoweth saving he that receiveth it.

What was the seat of Satan? What was the throne of Satan? Was it this proud medical knowledge, these two hundred thousand parchments in the library, or was it the pagan superstition that existed there? This was a capital city of the imperial cult, of the worship of Caesar in that region. What was it? Many of the beliefs were a combination of these things, great advancement in knowledge mixed with a foolish, childish superstition. I want to suggest this morning that the worst thing that can happen to us is to get a mixture of great accomplishment tied up with a lot of foolishness. That is what I believe was meant by "Satan's throne."

My friend Dr. Smith, whom I mentioned a moment ago, says that it is a terrible combination when someone is dumb and mean. I am not sure that this *is* the worst thing that can happen to us. I think it is far worse when we are smart and mean. The "dumb mean" can find only so many ways to exercise the meanness. But the "smart mean" is resourceful in finding ways in which to manifest the meanness. A dumb crook was never as dangerous as a smart crook. A dumb crook might steal chickens. A smart crook will steal cities and countries. And the problem about our greed today is not just that we are as greedy, or greedier than any other generation within the last ten years or fifteen years. It is that our greed is able to exercise itself in world markets. Not just hoarding a few dollars under a mattress, but affecting the population of the world with our greed. I believe such was what was wrong in Pergamos. What made it the throne of Satan was that it had a great deal of the highest knowledge, all inexplicably mixed up with some of the lowest superstition and paganism. That is what made the earlier Duvalier in Haiti so deadly. He was a medical doctor and a believer in voodoo. The greatest knowledge tied up with the sleaziest kind of superstition. That is awful.

My young people, let me say something to you this morning, there is something terribly destructive about getting a head fixed up when the heart is out of fix. It won't work. The old Scripture is right, "the fear of the Lord is the beginning of wisdom" (Psalm 111:10). And to get your head straight, with your heart out of fix, makes you a terribly destructive and futile personality. It is this mixture, if you see what I mean, that is definitely destructive. If it were one or the other it could be dealt with more easily, but when this ugly composite comes together, we've got something destructive. What makes some of these television bigots masquerading as religious people so dangerous is that they smile and speak the ugliest racism in support of South African apartheid and in honeyed phrases dripping with the name of Jesus Christ, but mixed with hatred. If they were just plain mean, that would be one thing, but when you get meanness, a mean purpose, or a mean thought tied up with a charming smile, you have a dangerous condition.

I was speaking with Dr. Michael Graves of Nashville this week, and we were talking about people who are very proper in their religious beliefs. He spoke about one state — I will not name it because some of my friends are there, but it is considered to be the purest state in America as far as we Baptists and our doctrines are concerned. The doctrines are purer, but that orthodoxy, that doctrinal purity, that biblical faithfulness, never mentions the dangers of bourbon whiskey which is produced by their distilleries. Oh, have I given the state away? I am sorry. The problem, my people, with so many doctrinally pure people is that they use the purity of their biblical beliefs to avoid dealing with the problem of race. And if I may bring it home this morning, why is it that the people who come among us sometimes, the people who call the Lord's name loudest, are the people meanest to the Lord's people? This is Satan's throne.

I pulled up beside a car some months ago near Utica and Church Avenue. A lady looked over and recognized me. She leaned out and she said to me, "I'm so and so." I said, "Yes"; she said, "I used to belong to — " and she named one of our sister churches. And then she said, "Until I saw the light." But the meanness, the belligerency, the hate, when she said "I saw the light" made me not want that kind of light. How can the saints of God be the meanest people around? And isn't there something wrong when the closer we claim we get to the Lord, the more distant we get from other people? Satan's seat. Satan's throne. And then the spirit of the Lord says, talking to that little church in Pergamos, "thou dwellest... where Satan's throne is."

Well, that's where the church of Jesus Christ belongs. I am glad that this church is located right in the heart of Bedford-Stuyvesant; that's where a church ought to be. This idea of our taking flight from need does not belong to Jesus Christ. He took his place among the disinherited and the disallowed and those who were farthest away from authority and power. "The Son of Man is come to seek and to save that which is lost" (Luke 19:10). They that are well, he said, do not need a physician; but they that are sick. That is where we belong, doing our work in the midst of need, where life is harsh and difficult.

I would not claim at all this morning that this is an easy thing to do. It is not easy for one to dwell in an environment where everything is against what one believes in. But Jesus does say — and I take great notice of this word — "where thou dwellest." Not where more often than not the Christian community is comfortable and in control. Our job is to take our stand right where need is. I know this is difficult. I know sometimes this is very discouraging if you are in a family where it is difficult or awkward for you to profess your Christian faith. But that is where you dwell; that is where you belong to make your witness. You women and men who have worked with your marriage partners to bring them to Christ and they have not come, your job is really there. In fact our job is to witness. You cannot save anybody; the Lord can save them. And the Lord will save them. All you've got to do is to keep on. I've seen it happen over and over again. A long time they may reject Christ, but after awhile that steady influence, that bright and sunny disposition, that faithfulness, that light of faith in your eye, that calmness in the midst of criticism, that peacefulness will have its effect.

"Where thou dwellest." I know that it is hard sometimes, but stay there. The Lord has put you there; stay there. Because, he says, I will give you of the hidden manna. You've got to go back to the sixteenth chapter of the Book of Exodus to get hold of this meaning. It happened when Israel started out from Egypt toward Canaan. They came to the place in the wilderness where whatever little food they had flung across their shoulders for the journey ran out. And there was no vegetation they could eat along the way, as they put it themselves, in that "waste howling wilderness." They cried out against God. They said to Moses, "Would that we were back to take what rude comfort we could find in being slaves. Would that we were back at the fleshpots of Egypt and eating the bread of Egypt rather than to die in this wilderness."

God said to Moses, "I will give them food. I will test them by my goodness" (Exodus 16:4). If you read the sixteenth chapter of Exodus, you get that sense. "I will test them by my goodness." For the Lord does not only test us by hard things that happen to us. The Lord tests us by our prosperity and tests us by our blessings, and some of us can stand blessings less than we can disappointment. I suppose that more people have been ruined by success — at least that is my observation — than have ever been ruined by failure, for some of us cannot stand success and some of us cannot stand blessings, some of us cannot stand prosperity. It intoxicates us; it makes us lose our balance. Some of us cannot stand high places. We get dizzy. The Lord said, I will bless them, I will bless them. And so the next morning, when the dew had dried, they saw the little round circles left on the ground, the cakes, their food. They called it manna. The bread of heaven, manna.

It was thought by the old rabbis that a pot of that manna was preserved and put in the ark of the covenant, the sign of God's deliverance. The rabbis said further that Jeremiah took the pot of manna and hid it in a cave. It was the belief, according to the legend of the rabbis, that when that pot of manna would be rediscovered, it would be like the first manna: sufficient for all the congregation, and they would all eat upon it.

Here the Lord says, "I will give to [them] to eat of the hidden manna," of the bread of heaven, and God will do that for us. He will give us to eat of the bread of heaven, the bread of joy in our time of sorrow, the bread of provision like Abraham found on Mount Moriah, when we have need of it; the bread of calmness in a troubled time; the bread of deliverance when it looks like we've got no way out. "As thy days so shall thy strength be," says the Lord God of hosts. "I will give you to eat of the hidden manna." The secret food of God comes, and none can know it except those who take it. We are promised the food of God in the quiet, still hours of troubled nights, when the Lord feeds us with manna from on high. And so the hymn, "Bread of heaven, bread of heaven, feed me till I want no more." "I will give to eat of the hidden manna." The world cannot know or understand when you are being fed or how. They may think you are exhausted when the Lord is renewing you right at that moment. And so being fed and renewed, we are made equal to the issues of our lives.

✂ 25 ✂

PERGAMOS:
THE CHURCH NEAR SATAN'S THRONE,
PART 2

Revelation 2:12–17

February 21, 1988

I spoke to you last week about Pergamos as a cultural center. I do not know if I mentioned to you that it was the largest city of Asia Minor. It could not claim the commercial importance of Ephesus or of Smyrna, for they were located on the sea. I sat next to a man on a plane one evening. It later turned out he was an oilman from Texas. He said, talking about the cities of Texas, that one could account for the other cities of Texas being there, but not for Dallas. It turned out he was from Houston, but he said that Dallas is not located on any waterway to speak of. They have a small river there, the Trinity River, but Dallas has not a particularly choice geographical location in the state. Yet somehow Dallas has become a great city.

That conversation led me to reflect upon the fact that almost all of our great cities have been built on the water or else they were geographically located so that they could be hubs out from which spokes of commercial and other kinds of influence might spread. Pergamos was fifteen miles inland and so could never match Ephesus and Smyrna. It was fifty-odd miles from Ephesus, but it was the capital city of Asia Minor, and it was that which gave it its political and commercial significance.

Capital cities have a quality of their own. London, Paris, Edinburgh, Washington. They have an atmosphere of their own. They have about them the aura of the pomp and circumstance of state occasions, the buzz of political gossip and rumors, and the dazzle,

181

the momentary dazzle of political personalities. Who here can re-member who was Secretary of Transportation during the last two years of the Carter administration? Don't ask me. Momentary dazzle quickly passes.

We do not know the name of a single one of those regional officials who governed in the name of the Roman Empire in that whole province of Asia Minor from the city of Pergamos. We do have the name of a doctor there, Galen, but that is an obscure name, and one has to search far to get to it. But there was the name in Pergamos of one who was spoken of by Jesus Christ — "Antipas...my faithful martyr." And while the name of Antipas may not be a household word, it is posted in history, most as-suredly in salvation history. That name, whether it is dwelt upon or not, cannot help being read and reread wherever Christian people come together and read this second chapter from the Book of Revelation.

"Wherein Antipas was my faithful martyr." That word *martyr* means "witness." These people who were martyrs witnessed unto death. The Lord Christ singles him out as "Antipas, my faithful martyr." He gives to this obscure Christian whose name, as I've said, is now posted in salvation history, the same title which the Lord Jesus himself has in the fifth verse of the first chapter, where the Lord is referred to as "the faithful witness." And here Antipas is spoken of as the faithful martyr.

Mark my words, there is a reputation, if I might put it that way, and there is a certain notice which belongs to people who are faithful to Jesus Christ. I have said many times that I have seen people in this borough who were supposed to count for a very great deal. I have seen them pass away. I remember a notable example, one Sunday afternoon. It was not our funeral, but they asked that this sanctuary be used for the funeral because they were expecting that no other place would accommodate the people who wished to attend. The deceased was supposed to have been one of the outstanding people of Brooklyn. I came in to see the vast horde of people. There were three rows of family sitting in the pews and not another soul, except for maybe two or three other people.

I have, on the other hand, seen here people that hardly anybody, outside of this fellowship, counted for anything. They have died. And I have seen, in snow, cold, far greater numbers who came to pay their tribute. I am not saying that a funeral service's size is the mark of a person, but it is one clue. Beyond that, there belongs to those who serve the Lord a network of influence that goes on long after they are dead. I was saying to a visitor this week that there are people I remember out of my childhood, simple people, brickyard workers, oil refinery people, domestic workers. They live on in memory. I was preaching the other week in Nassau in the Bahamas, and those people from my past came before my mind's eye, sixty years later. Why? Because they counted for Jesus Christ, and their influence lives on, at least in my life. Sometimes in the still watches of the night their faces pass before me. I remembered how they prayed and how they sang and what radiance, what glow would come upon their faces when they talked about Jesus.

There is a reputation, if that's what you want, that belongs to those who are faithful to Jesus Christ, that will last long after temporary, worldly popularity has passed away. Because it is true that the world wants us for what we can give, and that is not all wrong. But when they have squeezed the juice out of the orange, they are through, and they go on to a fresh orange to squeeze.

"Antipas...my faithful witness." Here we are, on the other side of the world, not just a few miles from Pergamos, but across the Aegean Sea, across the Adriatic. Go up the tip of the boot of Italy, up to Rome; go up through middle Europe; go up through northern Europe. Cross the Atlantic; come here to New York, and here we are, calling the name "Antipas...my faithful martyr." Thank God for people who served their day and generation faithfully in the name of Jesus Christ, not looking particularly for any great notoriety or reputation, but they fastened themselves upon our hearts. I dare say that there are many of you here listening to me now who can look back over the years and remember people who inspired your life by their own example and to whose memory you turn now when things get hard and remember how they stood up to life. Thank God! Antipas! May each of one you be an Antipas.

You may not pay the supreme sacrifice of sudden martyrdom, but you can pay the price of service to Jesus Christ so that there will live on in this church and in your families and in this neighborhood or wherever you go the memory of what you were and what you tried to do and how you sought to serve the Lord Jesus. He will not forget. The world may, but he will not forget. And only what you do for Jesus will last.

Still, everything was not all right. And so the spirit of the risen Lord said, "I have a few things against thee because thou hast there them that hold the doctrine of Balaam." The name *Balaam* occurs as one who committed error. You will get reference to this name in the fifteenth verse of the second chapter of Second Peter. It speaks of Balaam "who loved the wages of unrighteousness." And you will get reference to this name in the eleventh verse of the only chapter there is in the Book of Jude. He said, "Because thou hast there them that hold the doctrine of Balaam." Now I have not the time this morning to go into all that Balaam did. Suffice it to say that Balaam, a prophet, entered into an easy and questionable working relationship with Balak, who was the king of Moab (see Numbers 21–25). A heathen king consorting with the prophet of God!

It was not a totally harmonious relationship, but Balak, king of the Moabites, and Balaam, prophet of God, had some kind of understanding between them. They had an arrangement whereby they were dealing with each other with promises of preferment. Balak, the heathen king of Moab, and Balaam, supposedly the prophet of the Lord, got together. Balaam and Balak formed an alliance. It was this shadowy partnership which was not pleasing to God. There ought to be some tension between those who are God's people and those who are not. We may, therefore, say that there must be some line of demarcation between the people of Christ and those who are not the people of Christ.

Now, I do not for one moment say, and God knows I do not believe, that we ought to claim any superiority, but there is a difference between the life which has acknowledged Jesus Christ and the life which has not acknowledged Jesus Christ, and that line can not be erased. The church of Jesus Christ ought never to be merely an echo of the culture or the political system in which it exists. It may from time to time cooperate because, as Paul Tillich used to say, there are "history-bearing groups" who momentarily represent the purposes of God even though they do not call God's name. But there must never be an alliance between the people of Christ and those who are not founded upon their mutuality and agreement. There's a line. No church ought merely be a spokesperson or a spokes agency for government.

I made many mistakes in these years, but I thank God for one thing: I have never spent one day on the payroll of any government. Every dime I've gotten has been from the people of God, and therefore I am under obligation to no secular person. Never! Prophets ought not to eat from the king's table. No church ought to be bought by anyone. It is not ours to buy or sell. It is the Lord's. No church ought merely be a church for white people. No church ought merely be a black church. I honor my background, I thank God for it, but the church of Jesus Christ is larger than any race, larger than any class, larger than any nation. This is the church of Jesus!

If I may comment this morning, a lot of money is to be made by mixing Christianity and racism. I preached in a Southern city, and a man carried me out to see this vast empire of buildings. They said, I later learned, that the empire is worth $140 million. I said to that man that evening, "There isn't a thing to this." I was echoing my Lord Jesus. His disciples came to him, and they saw the magnificent glory of Herod's temple, its burnished roof, its gold roof glistening in the sunlight. They "marvelled" at Herod's temple. Jesus, knowing that Herod's temple was founded upon political chicanery and expediency, said to them, "There isn't a thing to this." Those are not his exact words, but that's what he said. He said, "There shall not be left here one stone upon another" (Matthew 24:1–2). And a lot of the things we slavishly admire do not amount to a hill of beans, as my forebears would put it.

A lot of money is to be made in this country today mixing a little Christianity and a little racism together. That's right. Call the name of Jesus, stand over against people's progress, you can make money. There are a lot of very rich people who are ready to give it; there are a lot of poor, poor fools ready to contribute, also. When a church gets to the place where it is in captivity to whatever is around, that church is in trouble because the Lord's hand is removed from that place. I tell you this now, no church of Jesus Christ can go on if the Lord's hand is taken away from it. You hear me this morning. With all that is here, let the Lord's hand be lifted from this place, and it will wither and wilt and become an abomination and a shame before God and a laughingstock before this community.

There were some other people there in Pergamos, the Nicolaitans. Now, I've said this to you before: they said that the Lord had set them free and therefore they could again mingle with the rest of the people in Pergamos. They could go to their feasts and eat their meat which had been offered to idols, do anything else they chose. And this matter of fornication really is a reference almost always to idolatry, which is what the pursuit of sex represents. And the Lord's Spirit said, I am against it. The one word to us when we are moving contrary to what the Lord says, no matter who we are, is not a comfortable word. It is not a suggestion, it is not a quiet, polite entreaty. Oh, to be sure, the Lord does plead with us, but the Lord's voice can get mighty strong and mighty sharp and mighty cutting and mighty devastating. And I'll tell you again, the Lord's Word can bring one down. You can get so high, if you want, that you figure you're on your own and you don't need anybody, anything, and you don't need him, but he will bring you down.

And so the word is not a nice, courteous, polite, conventional suggestion. Old Ben Perkins in Cleveland used to say that if a person's house is burning down, if you've got any care about the person, you do not walk very politely up the pathway and knock on the door and say to him, "You know, I've seen smoke coming up through the roof and that suggests to me that there might be fire and you might want, whenever it's convenient, to call your children and your wife and, at your convenience, go out, because I saw smoke and I think there might be fire coming through the roof." No, you holler, "Fire!" because there's no time for politeness. That's a time for movement and urgency.

And so the word is *repent*. Not "if you please" or "when you get ready." Something foul may be growing in your life today. I do not stand here as preacher in this pulpit and therefore having at least some responsibility for your souls, to speak to you quietly and calmly in subdued tones with a suggestion that maybe in your judgment and your wisdom you might want to change it. Repent! Something is growing foul in your life. It is blocking your communion with God. Repent! Turn around, about face.

Now, I really wanted to get to this white stone. "I will...give unto him a white stone." Long before color got all tied up with race, the white stone was the mark of acquittal in a court, the old Phrygian and Scythian courts. And it has been carried forward in the black ball fraternities and sororities designed to keep people out. A white stone — acquittal. If the decision was acquittal, not guilty, those rendering judgment cast the white stone. The Lord here is saying, "I will give you, if you're faithful, if you will try to do your best, I will give you acquittal. Not guilty!" That's where I stand today. I don't know where you stand. Not guilty. Not because I have been found innocent, but I am not guilty. Not because I have measured up to what I should have been, but I am not guilty.

Why, you ask me, am I not guilty? I'm not guilty because the Judge of all the earth has acquitted me. He has said to me, "It is all over, you're forgiven. I sign it in my blood. You're free. You're not held, you're not in bondage, you're at liberty, you're in the glorious liberty of the sons of God. You're free, free!" My soul is free! Thank God Almighty, I'm free! I have been acquitted. The Lord Jesus has given me the white stone. I have been acquitted. And I thank God that I have today his name to call upon. I ask you this morning, is it well with your soul? Are you acquitted? Has the Lord exonerated you? Have you been turned loose, are you free, free, in Jesus? Free!

Then the white stone, the *tessera* it was called in Latin, was given to gladiators when they had fought many a battle and were retired. They were given the white stone. It was their lifetime pass into the games in the amphitheaters and in the great Coliseum in Rome. It was their lifetime pass, and they had a special section reserved for them. No gatekeeper could keep them out when they presented the white stone. It was the mark that they had contended and had overcome. And they had a right in any public function, any public festivity, any public games. To merely present the white stone was a ticket of admission.

Thanks be to God if you've got the white stone, nobody can keep you out. Wherever Jesus is, you've got a right there! Angels cannot keep us out. We can pray there when we want and sing there when we want, and nobody can turn us out, as my elders put it. In that white stone, is "a new name written which no man knoweth save he that receiveth it" (Revelation 2:17). Now, I do not know what your name is in Jesus, and you cannot know what my name is because our name is the sum total of what we are to the Lord Jesus. "I will give him a white stone, and in the stone a new name written."

No wonder in the bayou country redeemed people sang so lustily. I can hear them still:

> There's a new name written down in glory,
> And it's mine, oh yes, it's mine.
> And the white-robed angels tell the story,
> "A sinner has come home."
> For there's a new name written down in glory,
> And it's mine, with my sins forgiven.
> I'm bound for heaven, never more to roam.

～ 26 ～

THYATIRA, PART I:
THE CHURCH THAT HARBORED
A FALSE PROPHETESS

Revelation 2:18–29

March 6, 1988

We move now Sunday by Sunday into this Lenten season, as we face reflection upon our Lord's death and upon his resurrection. And we follow the path as we come today to the fourth of the seven churches of Asia Minor, the church at Thyatira.

If you were to travel the route, we would have reached the northernmost point; we now turn back toward the hill country, and the town of Thyatira lies between Pergamos and Sardis. Thyatira was the smallest of the towns of Asia Minor. It may be true that the church in that town of Thyatira was the smallest of the churches, though we do know that Thyatira was the smallest of the cities, maybe not the least important, but certainly the smallest.

That may be why we have the longest letter written to the smallest city. Someone has said that if God made the country and man made the city, then the devil himself must have made the little town. I do not know that that holds true in the case of Thyatira, but this letter lacks some of the features of the others. It is similar to all of the others in the sense that in each one of these letters, you will find a pattern. There is the superscription, or to whom the letter is addressed, and there is the inscription, or who is addressing it, together with a description of the message of the letter. In the case of Thyatira the sender is described as the one with eyes flaming like fire and feet like fine brass, which we read first in the opening chapter.

189

A diagnosis of the condition of the church follows. Next are the demands which the Lord made upon the church for correction of the church's faults. And then, fifth, the church is to be cured and the promise is given to those who overcome. Then the whole matter in each church branches out to a universal dictum. Not alone let them that have ears hear what the Spirit saith to this particular church, but what it says to all of the churches, because all of them share to some extent what was wrong in either one of them. And so the specific address broadens out into the universal.

Thyatira was not a city in which emperor worship was as pronounced as it was in others. I would not for a moment say that it was not present in every settlement in the empire. That whole contagion, the infection, disease, of emperor worship had spread. I talked about that over and over again during this series, but emperor worship seemed not to be the most pronounced problem in Thyatira, nor was external antagonism.

The paramount problem in Thyatira seems to have been internal. It ought to be said in this connection that the church of Christ has specific promise of protection from external enemies, as in "the gates of hell shall not prevail." The church does *not* have such a warranty against internal opposition. I will not read now this entire passage, but let me just pick up the thread of it.

> And unto the angel of the church in Thyatira write; these things, saith the Son of God. [This is the first time that we come upon the Lord referring to himself in this book as the Son of God.]
>
> Who hath his eyes like unto a flame of fire, and his feet are like fine brass; I know thy works, and charity, and service, and faith, and thy patience, and thy works...and the last to be more than the first.
>
> Notwithstanding I have a few things against thee, because thou sufferest that woman Jezebel, which calleth herself a prophetess, to teach and to seduce my servants to commit fornication, and to eat things sacrificed unto idols.
>
> And I gave her space to repent of her fornication, and she repented not.
>
> Behold, I will cast her into a bed, and them that commit adultery with her into great tribulation, except they repent of their deeds.

And I will kill her children with death. . . .
But unto you I say, and unto the rest in Thyatira, as many as
have not this doctrine, and which have not known the depths of
Satan, . . . I will put upon you none other burden.
But that which ye have already hold fast till I come.

You can see a new emphasis here. The outstanding feature of
Thyatira was its guilds. It was what we call now a labor town.
It was a town in which the various occupations had — I won't
call them unions — guilds, organizations, associations. The tan-
ners had a guild, the bronze workers had a guild, the dye people
who worked in dyes had guilds, the cotton weavers had guilds.
It was a labor town. It was a town of labor unions, of sundry
workers' organizations.

The guilds enjoyed great influence in Thyatira. They were organizations of prestige. If you did not belong to your particular
guild, you suffered economically. You were not on the inside. To
use but one example, you would not know where the trading was
going on unless you were there to pick up the rumors and gossip
and the information. That was a part of it. There was something
else about these guilds, these labor unions. They were not merely
professional organizations. They were also social organizations.

It is almost impossible to eliminate this social aspect of life.
An organization may come together solely to promote trade, but
sooner or later it takes on certain social characteristics, and there
were celebrations in these guilds. They had periodic feasts, meals
together, and that is a part of business. One of the problems that
minority people have had in dealing in business affairs in this
country has been that they have not been where the business talk
was being done in social settings in country clubs and whatnot,
where people come together and carry on business while eating
and drinking.

So the guilds in Thyatira had become unavoidably social organizations. They had great feasts; they would have them in one
temple or another, and the whole guild — I keep wanting to say
labor union — the whole guild would come together. And as these
things go, they had lavish feasts.

Often in these temples, these feasts were dedicated to this god or that. The food they ate often was food that had been offered to idols, to the gods. I'm not saying that the guilds themselves were heathen institutions, but it was the kind of thing that was done. Naturally, these feasts took on another character. People had a good time, and they drank and drank heavily, like Christmas parties in the offices in America. And the wildest sexual parties took place also. All of these things came one after the other.

Here is where Christian people had a problem. There were Christian people in Thyatira who could not help feeling that these guilds were the fashionable places, that they were the in thing. If you weren't in the guild, then you didn't get an invitation to the guild affair. You were an outsider. These were the fashionable, prestigious organizations of Thyatira. Many Christians came to feel that their little house church, perhaps on a back street, was a little something off to the side, but what really was happening in Thyatira were the affairs of the guilds. They were the important entities. Here was a danger.

We've just celebrated Black History Week or Black History Month. I went into a church and looked around at the pictures of black people on the walls. There was this deputy so and so — not the head person usually, because black people have not usually been the head people — but deputy, the first deputy, or second vice president, of this or that. And there were some other people whose careers depended upon philanthropy to carry them on, and there were some other pictures of people who were now and then in earlier years in the news. I saw in this church not a single picture of Richard Allen, who started the African Methodist Episcopal church. Not a single picture of George Liele, who began the first black Baptist church. Yet the church of black America has been the salvation, socially, economically, politically, psychologically of black America.

You talk about black history. Well, let me tell you about it. George Liele started the first black Baptist church in the late 1700s at Silver Bluff in South Carolina on the Savannah River. I must say that the people of Jamaica have had better sense.

They named their education building in the East Queens Street, in Kingston where I have preached, the George Liele Building, because George Liele went from South Carolina to Jamaica. Not a single picture of George Liele, not a picture of Adam Powell Sr., who led churches into a new self-development sense in Harlem, did I see. But all these deputy so-and-so's. It is because you do not regard the on institution that you own. You do not. Now you can look at me and bow as much as you want, but you do not. Young people, sad it is that your heroes must always be made by other people. You do not make your own heroes.

I have a friend, William Hudgins, who was president of a black bank, a black person, and the state banking commissioner complained because the bank's loan mortgage portfolio was overcrowded with churches, that they were out of proportion, that there weren't enough businesses. But what that state banking commissioner did not realize was that, for better or for worse, the black church is our General Motors. Did you get that? I'm going to give it to you straight this morning. This is our United States Steel, it is our statehouse, it is all we have. Anything else you've got can be given to you and taken away from you, and will. I'm not interested in whether you like this sermon, frankly, it doesn't make one particle of difference, but you will never be a great people until you make your own heroes and your own heroines.

One of the problems in Thyatira was that there were Christian people who thought that other organizations were all that mattered. And if you were going to announce that you belonged to something, you wanted to announce that you belonged to such and such a guild. And when you prepared your little biographical sketch and your little curriculum vitae, you put down proudly that you were part of the dye guild of Thyatira, or whatever. But you didn't worry about putting down that you belonged to the church, because it was not the important thing in Thyatira. That was one of the problems.

There was in Thyatira a movement which sought to integrate the church and the people of the church with the guilds of Thyatira, and the only time that a woman is mentioned in these seven letters, she is mentioned here. I do not believe that this woman was named Jezebel. Dr. Moffatt translates this to read "that Jezebel of a woman." The name *Jezebel* goes back to the sixteenth chapter of the First Book of Kings, and then at the ninth and tenth verses, the ninth chapter of the Second Book of Kings, where we read about the rise of Jezebel and her fall. Jezebel was the daughter of a Phoenician king. She married Ahab, the king of Israel, and introduced all forms of idolatry to the nation. Almost always when the Bible speaks of fornication, it is speaking about a certain spiritual whoredom where the people of God turn to false gods.

It was Jezebel who led her husband, Ahab, into the worship of Baal, and finally Elijah the prophet withstood Jezebel. They went to Carmel, where fire was rained down from heaven and that word came, "Let him be God who speaks by fire." That was the biblical reference to Jezebel. I do not believe that this passage in Revelation refers to any woman in Thyatira actually named Jezebel, and I'll give you a reason. There has been some theory that the woman referred to may have been Lydia, who was a businesswoman from Thyatira, whom Paul met and converted, in the sixteenth chapter of the Book of Acts. Some people believe she had picked up false doctrine and some strange ideas and had brought them back to her home, because the sixteenth chapter of the Book of Acts says that Lydia was from Thyatira. There is no evidence for that, however, and it may be purely libelous and blasphemy against this woman to suggest it.

There is also an old manuscript which speaks of "your wife Jezebel," which may have suggested, though it is not to be trusted, that it was the wife of a business owner who was head of the church of Thyatira. We have no evidence for that, and for obvious reasons I'll leave that very quickly. But I do not believe that there was any woman named Jezebel, for a simple reason: no mother and father in Israel would name their child Jezebel, just as I dare say not one of you has known anybody or very few of you have known anybody named Judas. And likewise, no mother and father in Israel would have named their child Jezebel. So I take it to have been what Dr. Moffatt said, a Jezebel-like woman. She had seduced the church, and I'm not competent today to deal in the differences in the sexes. I know there is a difference, and I know beyond that, that women enjoy a sensitivity that very few men have. And I know also that women have — I don't want to use the word *shrewdness* — a cleverness that most men lack. I know that. And I know also that women have an attractiveness that all men lack — and like.

What I'm trying to get at this morning is how carefully must we use gifts that have been given to us. There is a level that belongs to womanhood which must be treated as a sacred trust, and I say this to you, my young people with whom I have spent time Friday night, there is a difference. I do not know how you look upon it, but a woman drunk and slobbering down the street, under the influence of crack looks worse to me than a man. I don't know how it looks to you, and you have a right to your opinion. I claim to support feminism, but a woman wallowing, pulling hair, and fighting in the street is a more disgusting sight, to at least one person in this room, than a man wallowing in the dust and wrestling and throwing punches. And I hope, young black women, that you will forever remember that and that there is a singular dignity which belongs to you. There is a sensitivity in women that is superior. I present but one evidence for it this morning: Pilate. Had he followed his wife's advice, he would have been spared writing his name forever in infamy when she sent word to him to have nothing to do with the mockery of a trial which was going on in connection with Jesus. Have nothing to do with it, she told her husband. And many a man has been saved from disaster by the sensitivity and thoughtfulness of a good woman.

Well, there was a Jezebel-like woman, clever, persuasive, attractive, tender, and sympathetic, but who had got hold of some false doctrine. It was she who said to the people in Thyatira, the Christian people, If other people can eat this meat offered to idols, you can eat it too. It is no difference. Christ has died for you. You don't have to put forth any effort. Do anything you want. Christ has died for you. That was the false doctrine, and if I read correctly this reference to many who "have not the doctrine" or the "depths of Satan," something else was mixed with this heresy. It was perhaps sorcery and astrology and all of the weird magic of that part of the country.

I pray God that everybody here is delivered from that, but I was born ninety miles from the capital of all of this kind of pagan practices. Voodoo, they call it in Haiti. I knew a man who was wonderful to me in my childhood. He died really from high blood pressure, but he died believing somebody had done something to him by magic. You could not convince him otherwise. And somebody listening to me here this morning in this church is entangled in that same kind of weird, primitive belief.

I pastored in New Orleans many years ago — did I ever tell you? I went to early morning prayer meeting one Sunday, and a man named Jenkins called me outside, pointing out some powder underneath the steps. He said to me, "Some people are trying to get you out of this church." I don't know whether I said it to him; I know I said to myself, "I hope all they ever do is sprinkle that powder underneath these steps." This may have been the kind of belief in Thyatira that threatened the church.

The sad part here is that in almost every other church except Pergamos, the Lord's Spirit says to the church, "Repent," straighten up. But the Spirit does not say that to the church at Thyatira. What an awful thing that this church had gone so far that the spirit of the Lord does not call it to repentance. There is no conditionality. Mark my words this morning, a church can get so far from God that he takes away its candlesticks, removes its power. I've said it to you before; I must go on saying it to you again and again. You can meet here in great numbers, you can give what you will and be what you want, but you can get so far from the Spirit of God that he has nothing to do with this church.

There is no word spoken here as to what the church ought to do. It is as if some have not bowed down to this new doctrine, as if some people are the church in the church, the invisible church in the midst of the visible church. This came out in the Reformation's distinction between the *ecclesia visibilis* and the *ecclesia invisibilis*. It may well be that, as it was in Thyatira, so it will be with Concord Church. All are not to be saved, only as many who are willing to serve the Lord.

And so the spirit of the Lord says not to the church but to as many as are faithful, "Hold fast." Whatever the trouble, hold fast. Whatever others do, hold fast. Whatever fate you might find all around you, hold fast. Whatever insults are heaped upon you by wicked people inside the church, hold fast. Whatever slights may come your way, hold fast. Hold on. For the first time in this book, we come upon the words "till I come." Stand the storms. It won't be long. We'll anchor by and by; wait till I come.

The Lord is coming. I do not know what your trouble is this morning, but hold fast till he comes. The Lord is coming to make up his jewels. The Lord is coming to set wrong things right. The Lord is coming to bring down what is high and lift up what is low. The Lord is coming to straighten out what is crooked. The Lord is coming to bring every mountain down and to lift up every valley. The Lord is coming. There is "a bright side somewhere; oh, don't you rest until you find it." The Lord is coming. Whatever your lot, the Lord is coming. He said "Till I come." The Lord is coming... *Maranatha!* The Lord cometh!

ᓚ 27 ᗡ

THYATIRA, PART II:
THE GREAT POSSIBILITY

Revelation 2:24–29

Palm Sunday, March 27, 1988

Thank you. That remarkable preacher, Paul Scherer, used to say that he dreaded special days because they demanded a shift in whatever direction his mind was being led. Well, this poor mind of mine pondered much as to how this announced series would fit with Palm Sunday. We are at the church in Thyatira. Thyatira is hundreds of miles from Jerusalem, and the events are separated by a generation. Then it came to me that the Bible is a unity, and wherever one picks it up, what is there matches with whatever else is there. So let me read, then, and we'll talk this morning about Palm Sunday and Thyatira, the great possibility.

> And he that overcometh, and keepeth my works unto the end, to him will I give power over the nations: And he shall rule them with a rod of iron; as the vessels of a potter shall they be broken to shivers: even as I received of my Father. And I will give him the morning star.

I say, then, that the Bible is a unity, and it has two themes. One, and this is the initial one, is the God theme. The Bible is about that long campaign of God to win back his children in whom he has taken the awesome risk of making them free. For in doing so, he gave us the privilege of saying yes and no even to God. Yes or no to each other, yes or no to ourselves, yes or no even to God. That is one side of it. The Bible is the account through the centuries of how he goes about that, culminating in Jesus of Nazareth, to get back what was his, whose possession is now in some doubt because he has made his children free to say yes or no. That is one side of it.

The other side of it is the human side, and you put these two together and you've got the biblical account from one end to the other. The human side of it is the great "if," a great possibility. Your life and mine are made up of a huge *if*. If we decide to live, we can live. If we decide to die, we can take our lives. I'm not now talking about the consequence, I'm talking about the *if* which is open to us. If we decide to try to be good, we can be good. If we decide not to be good, we can be bad. That *if* is the hinge of our freedom. It is the confidence God has expressed in us in giving us the capacity, let me say it that way, the *if*.

And so wherever one comes into the Bible and looks at our side of it, in one way or another he or she will see that *if*. That's what your life is all about. It's a big *if*. That's Christian humanism. A lot of these new Christians with their television distortions are always talking about secular humanism. I do not think they know what they are talking about, really, because they're mostly shallow people. There is in us a Christian humanism, the great *if* in our lives. You must not denigrate or downgrade that capacity. What I'm talking about now is what makes you somebody or something.

You say, well, a dog can make choices. Yes, but not at the level you can. The dog is almost completely driven by instinct and appetite. You are not. To some extent instincts influence, but they do not control you. You may fast yourself to death. A dog will hardly, around food, fast himself to death, because he does not have that big *if*. It's a dangerous thing, too. It has in it life, and it has in it death, and wherever one comes across the Scriptures and looks at our side of it, he is or she is looking almost invariably at that *if*. Moses, far back before Israel has got to the land of promise, at the time when he realizes that he will not make it over, this venerable leader of God's hosts, now in the evening of his years, gathers the congregation before him. You read the fourth chapter of Deuteronomy. It pictures Moses talking to his people, and he is saying to them that when you come into this land of riches and promise and when you have been there a while, you are likely, when things have gone well with you, to turn from your God. If you do so, Moses is saying then, the consequence of what you do will have to happen. God can forgive us, but he cannot forgive us consequence. "If you turn from God...."

Years ago Dr. Benjamin Mays stood in this pulpit and spoke about a lad driving a nail into a board, and the nail should not have been there. His father removed the nail, but he could not remove the imprint that the nail had made. God cannot do anything about and will not do anything about consequence. And so Moses is saying, when you're over there a while, you're likely to turn from God. Then comes that great *if*. "If," God says, "you will seek the Lord your God with all your heart, you will find him...."

Centuries go by, ages pass. In the Second Book of Chronicles at the sixth chapter, Solomon is dedicating the temple, standing in awe of its pristine glory, its dome shining in the sunlight. He is saying to his people that, again, they are likely to turn from God. If they do so, pestilence will be in the land, locusts will eat their crops, the skies will dry up and become brassy. But even then, if the people who were called by God's name will humble themselves, if they will pray, if they will seek God's face, if they will turn from their wicked ways, he will hear from heaven, and will forgive their sins, and will heal their land (2 Chronicles 6:38–39). *If!*

And Palm Sunday is a great *if*. It is really our Lord's final *if*. His time among us was one long appeal to our capacity to say yes or no. He said to a young man agonizing over what way his life would go, if you want the fullness of life, sell what you've got, it's eating you up. Bless the poor with it, and come and follow me. *If*. And again he said by his words and by his healing and by his Spirit, "If any man will come after me, let him deny himself, and take up his cross daily, and follow me." And this is what is said to you Sunday after Sunday when whoever it is stands before you in this church, or whatever church, and gives you the invitation to membership. It is to put in your hands the response to that great *if*. You can say yes and you can say no, and some of you have been saying no to God all of your lives. All of us have been saying no to God some of our lives. *If*.

That is what Palm Sunday was all about. I shudder when I read the account of that day. For the Lord acts in a most uncharacteristic manner. He never flaunted himself before people, never paraded himself, never made a show of things. It was not his way. And yet on that Palm Sunday, in one last desperate overture, he presents himself. Look at the scene.

It is a bright, sunlit Sunday. Great throngs are making their way to Jerusalem for Passover. In the city itself, teeming throngs of people crowd the narrow streets of Jerusalem, jostling, shoving one another. It is a great crowd. The sun shines upon the glory of Herod's temple. Its golden dome reflected the brightness of the sun. Great crowds were moving on the highways, singing some of their pilgrim songs, some of which have been preserved for us. And suddenly, in their midst, riding on a jackass, comes the meek and lowly Savior, offering himself. Offering hope, offering peace, offering life, offering light, offering the Bread of heaven, offering water from the everlasting Fountain. He said it himself. "If thou hadst known, even thou, at least in this day, the things which belong unto they peace! but now they are hid from thine eyes" (Luke 19:42).

The crowd made its noise, shouted its hosannas, cried, "Blessed is he that cometh in the name of the Lord." But they did not turn. They exercised their option. They turned from the great possibility. They gave themselves over to darkness. Here is the great hazard of our freedom. Look! Man, woman, your relation to God is in your hand.

So my text says, "To him that overcometh." It does not declare that anybody is disqualified. It does not say that anybody is ineligible. It does not say that anybody has inability. It does not say that anybody is disabled from doing this. "To him that overcometh." I take it that if it had not been possible for all of us to overcome and to keep his Word, the Lord Christ would never have put it upon us to do so. No, the power is in your hands. Your relationship to God is in your hands. There's a great power that belongs to us. Do not neglect, do not look casually upon what I am saying to you today. You men and women, you boys and girls, have a great power in your hands. That *if*, that tremendous possibility.

I say particularly to these young people today — you can. Your future is in your hands. Oh, I know the difficulties, the odds, the problems that you face, but your future is in your hands. Many people have gone through the same things you go through. Many of them sit in this pew, and they have overcome, and if they have done so, you can do it.

Be done with the notion "I can't." You can! God has given you the power. He says in the morning of creation, "Thou shalt have dominion over everything that crawls and that swims and flies. Thou shalt subdue the earth. It's in your hands." You can rise to whatever level you want to. You put God in your life, and if you will offer yourself, even in half a commitment, the Lord will bless your life. If you will open your spirit to him, he will guide your footsteps, yes he will. If you will ask him to lead you, he will direct you. If you will ask him to give you strength, he will give you strength. If you ask him to keep you from temptation, he will preserve you in the midst of temptation.

In a few weeks now I will go back to Oberlin College for their commencement address. Fifty-one years ago I went to that school with all of its distinction and honor. They did not know that I was coming out of a high school where there was absolutely no library. The only books we had were textbooks. I am going back to that school, which has a library of four or five floors. There was no library in the school to which I went. We did have dedicated teachers, but we had to scrounge the best we could to pick up whatever extra knowledge we could pick up. The folk at the Oberlin Graduate School of Theology did not know when I went there that I was coming out of a little poor black Baptist college whose library was one room, not any larger than one of the education rooms there. They did not know it. But by the grace of God, fifty-one years later, I am going back there to receive Oberlin's highest honor — because God is able. If you will put yourself in his hands, if you will ask him to direct your footsteps, if you will let him lead you, if you will try to be faithful to him, he will raise you up, yes he will!

So the word is *if*. "To him that overcometh," *if*. "I will give him authority over the nations." Oh, you say, what kind of poetry is this, what wild fancy is this? Authority over nations, we poor Christians, give us power over nations? You do not know what God can do. Twenty years ago and less than that, who would have believed that yesterday in the state of Michigan a black man would receive the largest number of votes for the presidency of the United States? Would you have believed twenty years ago that in the state of Mississippi for the presidency of the United States a black man would receive a great number of votes? Do not tell me what God can and cannot do. God can do anything but fail, yes he can. "I will give you authority over the nations."

And then let me conclude. "I will give him the morning star." What does it all mean? I know that in the twenty-second chapter of the Book of Revelation, the Lord Jesus says, "I am the bright and morning star." Of course we shall have Jesus, but I take it that there is another meaning here. I will give him the morning when promise is on the way. I will give him the signs of dawn, of the coming of daybreak, morning when strength is at its most powerful and when hope is brightest. I will give him the morning, when the bird is on the wing and the dew is on the grass. I will give him the morning, when weariness no longer hampers the weary soul. I will give him the morning, filled with promise and hope. I will give him the morning. The promise to us is that we shall know of the morning power, when strength is at its greatest, and I take it to mean that you and I will overcome. We at last will come to that place where our human nature will know the great strength of an eternal morning — when this human nature of ours, cross and clumsy, will at last be delivered into the most exquisite and into the most consummate heights of its power; when all that hobbles us and halts us will he cast from us, and we shall rise up, in the mighty power of the Spirit of God, erasing every difference that lies between us and holy creatures. No, more than that.

There shall be no line between us and God. The line that separates our humanity from his divinity will be erased, and God and Christ and the Holy Spirit and angels and we shall be the identical twins of Jesus Christ. "I will give him the morning star." It belongs to us, a brighter day, a better day, a day when we are delivered from all that cripples us and all that shackles us and all that imprisons us. And we are set free, free in the Spirit of the Loving God! Free! If! I will give him the morning star.

SARDIS:
WORDS ABOUT DEATH AND LIFE

Revelation 3:1–6

Easter Sunday, April 3, 1988

Easter leaves us speechless or so touched that we cannot express what we feel. Our minds turn irresistibly, as Cardinal Newman put it, to those whom "we have loved long since and lost awhile." A hope in us, which is almost always so fragile that it seems about to flicker out, flames up with warmth and brightness at Easter. We know some of the wistful hope in agnostic Robert Ingersoll when, standing at the grave of his brother, he said, "Life is a narrow vale between the cold and barren peaks of two eternities. We strive in vain to look beyond the heights; we cry aloud and the only answer is the echo of our wailing cry. From the voiceless lips of the unreplying dead comes no word; but in the night of death, hope sees a star, and listening love can hear the rustling of a wing." Vague, indirect, but he speaks of that longing, most times so insubstantial, so almost unreal in us, but which at Easter becomes vivid. We ponder, and we sense that we were there when they crucified our Lord. And that we were there in his resurrection.

We turn today to look at Sardis in this series, the Book of Revelation, the fifth of the seven churches. Let me read again the words that we've read as our Scripture.

> I know thy works, that thou hast a name that thou livest, and art dead. Be watchful, and strengthen the things which remain, that are ready to die.... Thou hast a few names even in Sardis which have not defiled their garments; and they shall walk with me in white: for they are worthy.

I remember our coming upon Sardis, travel-stained and weary, after night had fallen, with a full moon beaming on the ruins of the old city. It was a strange and eerie feeling. Sardis was a city that had seen better days. It was the capital of Lydia and one of the most fabled people of wealth. King Croesus had reigned there. It was once the capital of the wool-dying business. And it was the first city in which gold and silver were minted. But it had seen better days. Its glory belonged to the past.

Ephesus and Smyrna, located on the sea, had superseded Sardis in importance. It was a city built high on a bluff, and it was believed that it was impregnable, unassailable, and invulnerable on three sides from attack. The fourth side was carefully guarded and fortified. It was supposed to be the one side from which an enemy could successfully launch an attack. But when Cyrus and his Persian army came against Croesus and his people in the city of Sardis, either by treachery or through accident they found a ledge or a passageway unguarded. While Croesus and his people slept, the armies of Cyrus entered the city, and they who went to sleep feeling secure awoke to find themselves overrun and captive. That itself is a parable of life. For we believe that at some point, at one particular stage of our lives, that we have it all worked out, that we have shored up ourselves, fortified ourselves as much as we need, that we are protected, that we are equal to anything that can happen, that we are sufficient for any circumstance. And then, suddenly, we discover that from an unguarded source something has leaped out to bring us into great danger and under awful peril. That is a parable of life.

Well, there was a church in Sardis, and because Cyrus attacked it once by night, the people in Sardis would have understood well the words of the risen Lord when he said, "I will come on thee as a thief, and thou shalt not know what hour I will come upon thee." Sardis had experienced such an attack. There was a church in Sardis, but we do not know much about it, except that we know that the spirit of the risen Lord said about that church "thou hast a name that thou livest, and art dead." You read it, and it makes you shiver. A name that "thou livest, and art dead," and I would say to you this resurrection Sunday morning that there are many forms of death.

It is hard for me to say this and perhaps hard for you to believe it, but the least anguished, the least threatening kind of death may be that death which we fear most, physical death. I find it hard to say, but it may well be. There is the death of purpose and ambition, when the soul no longer rises to meet any challenge. Drifts, wanders, a derelict with no goal, no direction. One sees many of our young people with their nervous systems under trauma and shock with drugs. Their eyes staring vacantly. Reeling, up and down the streets of this neighborhood. Dead. No purpose. The breathing dead, and I say, not merely because I have reached the years I have, I believe I would rather be physically dead than dead to interest, dead to purpose, dead to goals. Then there are those, and some perhaps who hear me this morning, who are dead to gospel pleadings.

You have heard from this preacher, or some preacher, so many claims of Jesus Christ presented to you and you have become momentarily alert, but then it passed. And now the name of Jesus does not touch you. You hear it, as some of you hear it now, but it does not assault your consciousness, does not penetrate beyond your hearing, does not get at you in the deepest places of your spirit. Some are dead to the divine mercy. Some of us take things out of God's hand every day but never a glance at the direction from which they have come. Neither sorrow nor joy moves us. The glories of the sky and how the Lord has given us this world as a fit theater for the drama of our humanity leave us totally unmoved.

Anatole France has a sketch about this man. It is a lovely legend of Pilate, old and arthritic. (Many of our people insist on giving another name to that condition and call it Arthur Right-is.) Pilate has long finished his tenure in Judea, and he has gone to the watering spa at Baiae, favored by Romans. He is sitting sunning himself, old, broken in health. Someone comes up to him and asks him, "Do you remember a case when you were governor of Judea? The name of the person was Jesus." "What?" said Pilate. "What did you say was the name of the accused?" "Jesus." Pilate's brow furrowed. There's puzzlement in his eyes; he tries to recall, and then finally he says, "Jesus? The name I faintly remember, but the case I have forgotten."

Here was a man who in one night twice stood in the presence of the Savior of the world, but his awareness was dead, dead to God, dead to grace, dead to mercy, dead. There are some of us so self-centered that we are dead to any interest around us. And some of us are so confused that we are dead to love. Dead. And there are people in our country who are dead to the winds of God. They are so deadened, let me put it that way, by tradition and their blighted history that they cannot recognize the winds of God's purpose blowing fresh and clean upon them.

I am told, oh forgive me this, that there is a reporter here from one of our national publications who wants to talk with me about the present presidential campaign. Let me have — and I do not say this in any flippancy — a part of the interview now. This question is whether the nation is alive to the winds of God. Of course, if the nation wants, insists upon, and is determined to have a Caucasian president, then of course Jesse Jackson is not the candidate, he's not the person. But if the nation wants a new vision, strong in compassion, which is the only greatness there is before God, and someone with enough self-confidence that he is not psychotic about any other nation, and the calling of another nation's name does not send shivers of terror and anger through the candidate and the body politic, then that is a different matter. The question is, are we dead to a new and exciting society?

The sad part about the church at Sardis was that it had a name that it was living, which I had almost said was worse than dead, for it had a name that it lived. It and the world looked upon it and thought it living. And the people inside of it thought it was living. The world admired the grandeur of its worship, the eloquence of its preaching, the apparent vigor of its life, but it was dead. It had Christianity in name but not in reality. Nominal Christianity — that's what that word means, in name, but there was no vital spark there. Whatever energy that group of people, supposedly Christian, produced came out of their own animal energy. It was self-generated. That church was not fed from immemorial springs. Whatever moisture it got and whatever fluid, whatever liquid, if I may use that figure, it received for its life it produced itself. And, therefore, it was stagnant.

The world marveled at how wonderful it looked, but the spirit of the living Lord looked upon it and said that it was dead. On resurrection Sunday, may I remind you that a nominal Christianity is no good. In-name-only Christianity will not stand you in good stead in the swelling of Jordan. In-name-alone Christianity will not give you an anchor to hold within every stormy gale. In-name-only Christianity will not bear you up in this cruel world, and it will not protect you in temptation's fury.

"I know thy works; thou hast the name that thou livest but art dead." I asked myself this morning, as I ask each of you on this resurrection day to ask yourself, do you live in Christ? Or is there in your lives a counterfeit Christianity? It has no reality in it, and therefore in the great stress of life it cannot hope to stand firm.

What an apparent contradiction we have here. "Thou art dead" and "be watchful." They do not go together. Not with human reasoning. Either dead or watch, but not dead *and* watch. That's God's talk. No scientist can talk to us like that. Thou art dead; be watchful. There is no human resource that can deal with us at that level: thou art dead; be watchful. That is what someone told me is an oxymoron, a combination that is impossible to be brought together. Dead! Watchful! That has to come from somebody beyond the sphere of our rational procedures. This is illogical; this does not make sense. No, it is not illogical; it is supralogical, it's above logic, it is a logic that does not rise up from underneath and does not move horizontally. This is a logic that comes down from above. It has to be spoken only by that One who says, "I am the resurrection and the life." I do not merely bring you any reports about it. "I am the resurrection and the life." I do not give you any clues to it. "I am the resurrection and the life." I am not merely reporting something to you I heard. He says. "I am the resurrection and the life." You cannot talk like that, and I cannot talk like that.

This is one who can say "I am he that liveth, and was dead" (Revelation 1:18). That's a language that comes out of another dictionary. That belongs to the lexicon of faith. It belongs to the power of God in Jesus Christ: dead yet alive; finished yet beginning; down yet up. Only Christ can talk like that. You will listen in vain, a lifetime or two or twenty, for anybody else who can talk with any authority like that. "Dead." "Be watchful." Because it is the power of God we have seen in Jesus Christ which can raise the dead. That is the hinge which God has given us for our faith about our dear dead. And when we carry our people to graves as deep as love and as long as life, the only hinge we've got to hang our faith upon is not some pronouncement of some poet or some preacher or some scientist or some philosopher. The hinge is that God has raised Christ from the dead. If that did not happen, forget it. Let us all go to our graves likes dogs and cats. It is all over. Finished. Our longing will make no difference. Our lives are at the mercy of death, and the things we hold dearest can be attacked and slain by the things we hate most.

If God did not raise him from the dead, your being here this morning is mere vanity. If God did not raise him from the dead, your being here is merely a social event, and my standing here to preach to you is merely an exercise in human speech. If God did not raise him from the dead, your going to cemeteries is in vain. If God did not raise him from the dead, your loves, whatever they are, will soon be cut off forever. If God did not raise him from the dead, you are of men most miserable because there lives in you a hope which is vain, a myth, a foolish fancy, a childish dream. But God *did* raise Christ from the dead. For two thousand years this has stood the test. God did raise him from the dead. It did not look like he could. Everything seemed against

Jesus, all odds were against him. He was ending his life at a time when most of us are beginning our careers. He had no chance to, as we put it, get set. He never moved on the great stage of history as we look upon it. He lived his life in an obscure corner of a third-rate province, off the beaten highways of the world. He was not a member of a majority people; he was a member of a downtrodden minority race. He grew up in a city which had the reputation of being completely worthless, a city from which anybody of any merit whatsoever could never come. All of the odds were against him.

He had nothing on his side. His very birth was under suspicious circumstances, so the Gospel writers tell us. He grew up in the dusty village of Nazareth and worked in an obscure carpenter shop. All odds were against him. What did he have on his side? Nothing! Nobody but God. Wicked men plotted against his life while he was still in the morning of his years. He had nobody with him but God. Ones whom he had befriended turned on him and betrayed him. He had nobody with him but God. Another who had walked close with him denied him. He had nobody but God. Friends forsook the best friend the world has ever had. He had nobody but God. They arrested him by night. He had nobody but God. They hauled him from judgment hall to judgment hall. He had nobody with him but God. There was nobody to speak a word in his defense except a woman who sent a message to her husband, "Have nothing to do with this just man." That was the only vote he had that night. Everything was against him except God. The men who killed him spat in his face. Everything was against him except God. Then they hung him on that tree on that darkest of Fridays. Everything was against him except God.

Alas! It looked like God himself had left Christ, but he had not. The sun refused to look at him and fled from its appointed place and hid itself in the folds of darkness. Everything was against him except God. They put him in a tomb. Everything was against him except God. Until the appointed day came, and when that Sunday came, and the first streaks of dawn began to disturb the darkness, God brought him forth. God raised him from the dead, and he took the sting away from death, and in that victory he stood in resurrection power and declared, "All power in heaven and earth is in my hands." Yes, "up from the grave he arose, with a mighty triumph over his foes." He lives, and we shall walk with him in white, in the garments of victory. For that's what white garments meant in the ancient world. Let that word sound in every heart and thrill every soul Christ lives.

ᵔ 29 ᵔ

PHILADELPHIA:
THE OPEN DOOR

Revelation 3:7–13

April 17, 1988

And to the angel of the church in Philadelphia, write; These things saith he that is holy, he that is true, he that hath the key of David, he that openeth and no man shutteth; and shutteth, and no man openeth;

I know thy works: behold, I have set before thee an open door, and no man can shut it: for thou hast a little strength, and hast kept my word, and has not denied my name.

So we come now to the next to the last of the seven churches, the sixth, Philadelphia. And I know that when I speak the word *Philadelphia*, many of you think of a city in Pennsylvania. But I am thinking of a city in Asia Minor. And when I speak of Philadelphia you are thinking of a city ninety miles south of New York; I'm thinking of a city twenty-five miles south of Sardis. The word literally means "love of a brother," and you will hear in the first part of it an English word, *filial*, that is, love of a child for a parent. Philadelphia, modern Alashehir.

I remember arriving in that old city and someone allowing us to go up on the second floor of a home built along the old wall and to look down and to get just a bit of mortar from the ancient city wall of Philadelphia. Philadelphia's importance was due to the fact that it was on the imperial postal route that ran from Rome to Troas and on out to the east. It may surprise some of you to realize that ancient Rome did have a postal system. I hope it was better than some others about which we know. The letters that we have here in the New Testament very likely were either delivered by private courier or by the old Roman postal system.

213

The significance of Philadelphia was that it was on the route from Sardis to Pergamum. It has been rescued, how shall I put it, from the dump heap of history because it came indirectly in touch with Jesus Christ. I am quite certain that if it had not been for the Lord Jesus, though he did not touch this city directly, that we would hardly be speaking about it at all in this sanctuary today. Oh, somebody digging around in ancient history, some research scholar would be talking about Philadelphia, but it would be of no importance to us. Its significance is grounded in the fact that at least indirectly it was touched by Jesus Christ. And it was touched indirectly by him because there was a church which bore his name which met in the city of Philadelphia.

I have said often from this pulpit, and it bears repeating now and again, that almost all of us have been rescued from oblivion by Jesus Christ. Had it not been for him, very, very few people would know anything about most of us. Our immediate families, but there would be no great notice paid to us. Almost all Christians who are a part of a community of faith can say truthfully that Christ has rescued us from obscurity. We would have lived, most of us, and passed our days and died and would have been, for the moment, mourned perhaps by a few people, but very little notice would have been paid to us. I might add that had it not been for him there would have been very little about us worth noticing. You will say, or someone will say, there isn't much about us worth noticing now, and that may very well be true. But think how much less likely would we be to receive any notice at all.

You know people talk about Christians not being as good as they ought, but think how much worse we would be if it were not for Jesus Christ. People talk about how the world is so bad and the spirit of Christ has been abroad in the world for all of these years, but how much worse would it be had the spirit of Christ not entered the world? Think about that sometimes when you are ruminating in your critical moments of looking somewhat sourly at things. We are so much better, maybe not what we ought to be, but far better than we would have been had the Lord Christ not come into our lives. He performs miracles in our lives. Miracles day by day. And we do not recognize them often. John Hutton, a Scottish preacher of an earlier generation, was preaching in a Yorkshire town when a miner leapt to his feet and sang the doxology. Again and again the man cried out, "Praise the Lord, praise the Lord!" After the service Dr. Hutton sought out the miner and talked with him and said, "You seemed to be enthusiastic about the Lord Jesus. What do you do?" "I work in the mines," the man said. "Well, that's a pretty rough bunch of fellows down in the mines, isn't it?" "Yes." "How do they react, how do they take to your enthusiasm about Jesus?" "Oh," said the man, "they say this and that. One said to me the other day, 'You do not really believe that story about Jesus turning water to wine, do you?'" "What did you say to him?" said Dr. Hutton. "Oh, I said, 'I do not know whether he turned water to wine, but I know that in my house he turned beer into furniture.'" Miracles are going on in people's lives, in your life and mine day by day, sometimes unnoticed, passed over, but still there.

Let us look at this church in Philadelphia, ancient Philadelphia, modern Alashehir. It is one of only two of these seven churches that were not criticized. Two of them were not: Smyrna and Philadelphia. But read the account of Smyrna when you are home, and read the account of Philadelphia, and not even Smyrna received the accolades which the church at Philadelphia received. It stands alone in the lack of criticism and in the amount of praise which it received from the Lord. We read the words, "I know thy works: behold, I have set before thee an open door," so that there is vital connection between the open door and the works. "I know thy works... I have set before thee an open door."

There are many of us who want things of the Lord, and we ask. And we say that if the Lord will do so and so, I will do so and so. If the Lord will help me to educate my children, I will obey him. If the Lord will help me to get my health back, I will acknowledge him. If the Lord will help me to get a good husband or a good wife, I will serve him. Ah, my friends, we are putting the thing backwards, the cart before the horse. I read where it says, Ask and receive. I read nowhere where it says, Find and then seek. It says very clearly, "Seek, and ye shall find" (Matthew 7:7). I read nowhere where it says, It shall be open unto you, then knock. It says, Knock, and it shall be opened unto you. We put it backwards. If I can ever understand the gospel, I will believe. Read the seventh chapter of the Gospel of John where it says clearly, "If any man will do his will, he shall know of the doctrine" (John 7:17). Our effort must come first. That is faith.

When the Lord says, "I know thy works," it is not to mean at all that the works at Philadelphia were perfect. The Lord really is pleased, not so much at what we accomplish, and do not misunderstand this, but at what we are willing to attempt to accomplish. You and I will never do enough. We will never do enough to be proud, where the Lord is concerned. Never, because of one simple thing which I have again and again said here: you can never get the Lord in your debt. You may try, but I have come across these seventy years nearly to tell you that the Lord never gets in our debt. The more you try to do for him, the more he pours out his blessings, so that we will never do enough to feel proud about what we do for Christ.

But the Lord takes the yearnings of our heart, our sincere desire to be well pleasing in his sight and accepts that. He accepts that as if it were an accomplished deed. In David's day, David failed to build the temple, but the word came from the Lord, "Thou didst well that it was in thine heart" to build it (2 Chronicles 6:8). To some extent, the Lord is as we are with our children. What parent, when a little child comes bringing a smudgy, clumsily wrapped package with some little shabby gift inside of it, would say to the child, "This isn't worth anything; I can go to any shop and buy something better than that"? No, that dirty little clumsily wrapped package is as precious as if it held the riches of the world, because out of the child's heart and out of the child's effort and sacrifice, he or she brought the gift. It is precious not in terms of its intrinsic worth but in terms of the heart's spirit. And so the Lord accepts what we do and what we want to do. "I know thy works." Wherever anybody seeks honestly and sincerely to please the Lord and to do his will, thanks be to God for his mercy, he accepts that as if the effort and the work were a great and marvelous success.

Hear what he says. In the twenty-fifth chapter of the Gospel of Matthew, "Thou hast been faithful," not over a great thing but "over a few things" (paraphrase of Matthew 25:23). Well done! I am always greatly touched when I read that passage where the disciples come back from a preaching mission, you remember, and they report to the Lord that they had had a great success. Jesus immediately moved from that small, that parochial, that tiny, that puny effort of theirs to say, "Behold, I saw Satan as lightning fall from heaven" (Luke 10:18). He takes our little and accepts it as if was a great deal. So our first effort is to make the attempt, try to be faithful, seek to be well pleasing in his sight. Try to obey what he has said. He accepts that. And he says, "I have set before thee an open door."

"I have set before thee," he says, "an open door," and I believe with all my heart that this coming Tuesday an open door is set before us in the pending election. We will be able to declare that we want a piece of the pie. That's what it is all about. A door open before us. Some young person, some young man or woman, boy or girl, sitting here before me this morning is of the opinion that the door is shut in the matter of your getting an education. Don't you believe it. Trust God and try. My whole life is a witness. I could testify to that by day and by night.

I think I will share this word. My father died before I was thirteen. My mother was left with me to see about me, and it didn't look like there was any way I would be able to make it. I stand before you to testify that the Lord can and will open doors for you. There is, for instance in this Concord Times, a scholarship, a memorial scholarship for fifteen hundred dollars waiting for somebody to take it, and that can be multiplied many times. There is a way. Trust God! Try him! Obey him! Ask him! He will open the way! There is nothing too big for him to do. "I have set before thee an open door." It is open, open before you. If you've got the faith, you can walk in, and, I ought to add this morning, when the Lord, as he says here, opens the door, it is open indeed.

If there is something that the Lord wants you to have, nobody on earth can prevent you from getting it. And if the Lord wants to raise you up, twenty devils or twenty thousand cannot keep you down. And if the Lord wants to make something out of you and you're willing to have something made out of you, it is done.

"I have set before thee an open door." Some of us long for more spirituality. It is available. The door opens wide for you and for our church. We shall yet discover that we have not begun to praise God as we ought. We have not begun to worship God as we ought. We have not begun to serve the Lord Jesus Christ as we ought and as we can. There are steps of holiness and powers of consecration without limit. When the Lord opens the door, it is open and nobody can shut it. Never mind what anybody says about you or thinks about you. Never mind what criticism may be leveled at you. Never mind who says you can't. If the Lord says you can, you can!

I tell you something else that God will do. He will make people who said you cannot watch you while you can. Yes, sir, he will make them watch you. That's what is said in the Twenty-third Psalm. The Lord sets a table before me while my enemies are standing around the wall watching... "in the presence of mine enemies." "My cup runneth over." And the same enemies who had to watch that full table have to watch that full cup. Don't you ever believe that anybody can stop you. And if they seem to stop you in one place, you go scooting through another door made ajar by the goodness and mercy of the Lord. "I have set before thee an open door."

You must know that this is no neophyte speaking here. I think perhaps I ought to conclude this morning by saying who it is who says "I have set before thee an open door." It would seem by the time that we got to this sixth church that the Lord's titles would have run out. In Ephesus, he is the one who holdeth the seven stars in his right hand and walks amidst the seven candlesticks. In Pergamos, he is the One who has the two-edged sword. In Smyrna, he is the One who was dead and now is alive forevermore, the First and the Last. It would seem that his titles would run out. In Thyatira, he is the One who has eyes that are like flames of fire and feet like burnished brass. And in Sardis, he is the One who has all of the spirits of God, the seven spirits, the perfect number.

Here, at the sixth church, I read more about him. It says here that he is the Holy One, the *hagios*, the Wholly Other, the Different One. For that's what that word *holy* means. It does not mean what we think it means, that we won't drink or won't smoke. Well enough, don't do those things, but that is not what *holy* means. In the Bible, it means "separated," it means "different from." Christ is the Holy One. And it says here that he has the key of David, the power to "open, and none shall shut; and he shall shut, and none shall open" (Isaiah 22:22). So the Lord is able to unlock any door. He says in resurrection power that he has the keys of hell and death in his hand (Revelation 1:18). That is as tight a lock, as closed a door as you will ever see, "hell and death." He can unlock any door; he can open any pathway. He can straighten out any confusion. He can lift up any bowed-down head. He can fix anything that is wrong. He can help the helpless. He can give strength to the weak. "I have the keys," says the Lord Christ.

↬ 30 ↫

PHILADELPHIA:
THE KEEPERS ARE KEPT, PART 1

Revelation 3:7–13

April 24, 1988

It has become clear to me that I shall need perhaps one more Sunday, maybe two, but one more certainly after this, in connection with this church at Philadelphia. Today I want to talk about "The Keepers Are Kept." I do not know how it is with you, but I would like to have been able to worship in one of these ancient churches.

Some years ago I was in Cleveland and I drove out one evening to Elyria in which is located the first church which was willing to have me as pastor. I noticed that there were lights in Bethany Baptist Church, so I went in. Nobody knew me there. They were having a session of some kind, a public meeting. I looked around in the church, and I saw different faces from those I had known so many years ago. In my memory I saw Ben Carter, Jim Brown, Sherman and Leslie Benberry, the first person I baptized. I saw in memory Mother Rich and Mother Hammond, all gone now. At the end of the meeting, the pastor, a pleasant-looking and earnest-appearing young man, asked who I was, and I told him. Then, by my name, he knew. It was a joy to go into that church that evening after forty years. I wish I could have visited one of the seven churches of Asia Minor.

What kind of folk were they? I can imagine them, not in a formal place as we are, but in someone's house. How did they greet each other when they arrived at church? What was the spirit of their worship? Were there any conflicts in the church? How was it? Well, some of us may need to look back through the haze of twenty centuries and see a perfect people with a purity

220

of faith and a passion for witnessing and an extraordinarily high level of conduct. You may well need that kind of picture of these churches, and if it serves you well, then who am I to say nay to this, to hinder it? If you have to believe that about those churches, that they were indeed a faultless congregation of great vigor and virtue and purity, hold on to it. But you must not read the New Testament, because if you do, you will quickly have your minds disabused of that notion. I say this not to reflect upon our spiritual ancestors, for that is what these people were, but rather to indicate what the Lord has had to deal with all along down until now.

If you read the fifth chapter of the first letter which Paul wrote to the church at Corinth, you will discover something disturbing, and I am almost embarrassed to say it, but there it stands in the Scripture. The great apostle is saying to those Christian people at Corinth that they were having sexual practices that were unmentionable even among unbelievers. There was a problem in that church about the Lord's Supper. People were coming to the Lord's Supper and bringing their own refreshments, and they were gathering themselves into little circles and cliques and shutting other people out. Paul said to them, You ought to eat at home. I'm merely trying to get at what the Lord has had to deal with from then down until now.

In the first church there was a contention, a murmuring, the Scriptures say, that broke out between the widows who were of Greek background, very likely all Jews really but people of the *diaspora*, the dispersion, and the Jerusalem widows in connection with the benevolent gifts that were being given. And, my brethren, we ought not to forget, and I think it is a wonderful tribute, that deacons were begun in order to stop that kind of confusion. And I say this easily to you because of your great spirit: Deacons were created to stop confusion; not to start it but to stop it. And here in the seven churches we have seen that Ephesus has left its first love. Pergamos has, in the interest of some kind of superficial harmony, tolerated false doctrine. Thyatira has accepted and apparently not only accepted but also adopted the strange doctrines of a woman who is referred to as a prophetess in the church at Thyatira. Sardis is a church that is pretending that it has life in it but is dead. So that already out of seven churches we've got four of them with problems.

This is really to show how patient the Lord has been and how he deals with so many of us who are so far less than we ought to be. There was a scene in Mark Connelly's *Green Pastures* in which that stellar actor of an earlier generation, Richard B. Harrison, starred. Remember that Noah now was the only link that God had between the past and future. If you read the account in Genesis, everyone else had been taken away. Noah, drunk, looks up at God, at the Lord, as the play runs, and says, "I ain't much, but I'se all you got." How patiently the Lord has dealt with us, and what weak people we are. We come to the church at Philadelphia, to these words in the eighth verse: "I know thy works: behold, I have set before thee an open door, and no man can shut it." But particularly what I want you to look at is this, "Thou hast a little strength."

Now, a biblical expositor is free to look at that "thou hast a little strength" in two ways. There are New Testament scholars who take either side of what I am about to say. The meaning may well be thou hast but a little strength. Thou hast just a little strength, that may be the meaning. Or, the meaning may be you do have some strength. Get the difference. You have but a little strength; you do have some strength. Look at it either way you want. It is true of all of us, and how often we need to be before God because we have, and let me use the first part, but a little strength. Not much, not much. And that strength needs to be renewed every day. You and I are not equal to the issues of our lives by ourselves, and if we are equal, if we are sufficient unto them today, we are very likely not sufficient unto them tomorrow. Thou hast but a little strength. It is true of all of us. But we do have some strength, and what we need to do is stop excusing ourselves and holding others to such high standards.

I want to give you this morning a formula for making this a far better world. Are you ready for it? Here it is: be hard on yourself and easy on others. Require of yourself what you have been requiring of others, and require of others what you have been requiring of yourself. Hold yourself to high standards. Forgive the weaknesses of others. This would be almost a perfect world if we ask of others what we ask of ourselves and if we ask of ourselves what we ask of others. Turn it around. We have but a little strength, but we do have some strength.

We have drugs sweeping through this country. I talked on Thursday with one of the chief officials of the borough of Brooklyn. He said to me that we are barely holding our own in the matter of this drug trade — this from one of the leading police officials of this borough and of this city, for that matter. We are only holding our own. In other words, what he was saying is that we are not gaining any ground on bringing drugs under control in our communities and in our American society. That is the most we can say, that we are not losing ground, but he was not even sure of that. For the drug business has, we read, a $65 billion income every year. Now, sadly enough, the highest officials in our country went on television and made a great to-do about our waging an all-out war on drugs. They acknowledged in that address that the drug industry is now $65 billion, and then said in a strong voice of fierce determination, "We are going to commit $3 billion to solving the problem." And American people went "ga-ga." In the same speech. Sixty-five billion dollars the enemy has, and with a note of victory, the declaration was made that we are going to commit $3 billion to fight a $65 billion industry. Ah, we have but a little strength, but we have some strength.

We can try to educate our children about the deathly destructiveness of this whole drug culture. We can do more than that. You can slip to some pay telephone, if you're afraid to do it at home, when you see drugs being sold in your community and you can call the police department. You don't have to give them your name, and if nothing happens you call me and I will get in touch with that police official. We have but a little strength, but we have some strength. We will never get rid of this plague until we are all committed to using what little strength we do have. Thou hast but a little, but thou hast a little strength. We're not helpless. Oh, to be sure, we do not have all the power we would like to have, but we aren't powerless!

This past two weeks a lot of poison has been spread through the body politic of this city. A lot of inflammatory rhetoric has been uttered. We do not have a great deal of power to stop it, but we have some power. I hope you're going to get the difference here I'm trying to draw this morning. Not a great deal, but some. We are not helpless. We can watch, and, yes, we can remember. We can do that. We can remember from wherever this poison has come as we face the next election. We can do that. We have not much strength, but we do have a little strength. What I'm arguing for this morning is that we do not confuse a little strength with no strength. And we can watch people who rush out to make statements that will ultimately harm us.

I spoke out at Brooklyn College this week to the Jewish community, celebrating the fortieth year of Israel's life, and I am sure all of them have great questionings now about things that are occurring. I have no prescription for what that community ought to do in their situation. I admitted that before them, but I do have one suggestion. They are the children of the prophets. Consult the prophets. Ask what Amos says about what they ought to do. And Habakkuk and Hosea and Micah and the rest of the prophets. Beyond that we can all start a process of healing in this city. This city is broken and bruised and divided, and that is why I went out to that salute to Israel.

All of us are terribly distressed because the Jewish community gave to the candidate who happened to be black only 12 or 13 percent of its vote. But we never stop to think that the black community gave hardly 5 percent, that's right, of its vote to the candidate who was not black. Why don't we ask of others what we have been asking of ourselves? I know the extenuating reasons; you do not have to tell them to me, and we have never had a black President of the United States. Well, the Jews have never had one either. Why then are we so upset with them because they would not give a black candidate more than 13 percent when we would not give a white more than 3 or 4 percent? I plead guilty also. If we're going to deal with this thing, let us be honest about it. And if we're going to carry on a charade, let us acknowledge what we're doing.

You, of course, do not have a great deal of strength to win thousands of people to Jesus Christ, I grant that. You do not have that. You are not privileged to speak to great masses of people, and if you were, very likely as many of us do find out, it still would not be decisive. But you do have some strength. You have kin, people who need to be spoken to about the Lord Jesus. You have brothers and sisters and nieces and nephews and aunts and uncles and cousins, first, second, and third, and friends among whom you work. While you may not be able to preach like Paul, as the spiritual has it, you may not be able to tell the whole world, but you can tell somebody that Jesus died for all. You have but a little strength, but you *do* have a little strength. Use it, that's our job. Not to complain about what we do not have, but to thank God for what we do have and to put it to service.

Then the Lord Jesus says to this church in Philadelphia that "thou hast kept the word of my patience." That word *patience* has always bothered me. Those of us who came along in advance of our civil rights movement remember how we were told when the slightest murmurings of protest representations were made, be patient. So! That word *patience* has always troubled me. I was so troubled by it that I went back to get its etymology. I wanted to find out from where it came. Now, there are forms of patience that I do not take to be referred to here. There is the patience of the slave who prostrates himself or herself before the master. But that isn't the word that is stated here. That is not Christian patience. When the New Testament says to you and me to be patient, it is not talking about dumb submission, surrender, and resignation. It is not. That word *patience* has been misused. Christian people are not called on quietly and calmly and meekly to submit to everything. I plan to establish that in a few minutes.

Dr. Sandy Ray used to say, and he was right, that we are here to be used, but we are not here to be abused and misused. And I pray God that that will be forever the case in this church. We do not humiliate each other in this church. We do not subjugate each other in this church. We do not castigate each other in this church. If anyone persists in that, then the architect has built seven doors. One, two, three, four, five, six, seven, and they open out, out, out.

We talk about the Lord Jesus being meek, but that word in the New Testament does not mean cringing around in corners, afraid to speak or to be spoken to. Read the account of his life. I see nothing skittish and retiring about Jesus, and he is my example. I cannot measure up to him, but I have accepted him as my Lord, and he is my standard, and I have no other standard equal to him. There is no other doctrine of any other person that I equate with the example of my Lord and Savior. He is my standard. Nobody ever faced the odds which he faced, but he did not back away from them. His way was to march straight forward.

In the thirteenth chapter of the Gospel of Luke, some friendly Pharisees came to Jesus and said he ought to leave that city because Herod the king was out to do him in. Do you know what my Lord did? He said, "Tell that fox Behold, I cast out devils and I do cures today and tomorrow... Nevertheless, I must walk today, and tomorrow, and the day following: for it cannot be that a prophet perish out of Jerusalem" (Luke 13:32–33). That is not the meaning of *patience* as we use the word! And so Jesus says, "I must walk today and tomorrow and the day after." He never backed up. Great obstacles loomed before his pathway. He kept going forward. Mighty enemies sought to block his ministry and light. He faced them one by one and said, "I must go on today, and tomorrow. There's trouble ahead, but I must go on. There is a judgment hall waiting for me, but I must go on. There is a bitter cup from which I must drink, but I must go on. There is a trial and there are lying witnesses, but I must go on. There's a cross, a hard bed upon which to lie, but I must go on." And so the New Testament says that he steadfastly set his face to go to Jerusalem (Luke 9:51). Unbowed, his shoulders back, he marched on into the storm and through the storm into the morning of endless life. That is the patience of the New Testament.

And so I say to you this morning, talking about "the word of his patience," let us continue, let us keep on, let us not give up. The clouds may be dark and heavy in your life, but somewhere the sun is shining. The road may be steep and hard, but somewhere it levels off. Thanks be to God, the Lord will open a way. He opened a highway through the desert and through the sea itself. Nothing can stop God's people. Let us go on to see what the end will be. "Walk together, children, don't you get weary. There's a great camp meeting in the Promised Land." Hold on, keep on trying, keep on praying, keep on serving, keep on hoping, keep on believing. There is a bright side somewhere. Somewhere the sun is shining, somewhere the burden rolls away, somewhere enemies give up trying to hurt us, somewhere confusion is no more. Because "thou has kept the word of my patience."

⇜ 31 ⇝

PHILADELPHIA:
THE KEEPERS ARE KEPT, PART 2

Revelation 3:7–13

May 1, 1988

We have been blessed with rich and worshipful music today, and for that God be thanked.

I come now today to a second sermon on the church at Philadelphia. It is entitled, as was last Sunday's sermon, "The Keepers Are Kept." The keeping of the keepers. Let me read this passage at the tenth verse of the third chapter of the Book of Revelation.

> Because thou hast kept the word of my patience, I also will keep these from the hour of temptation, which shall come upon all the world to try them that dwell upon the earth.
>
> Behold, I come quickly: hold that fast which thou hast, that no man take thy crown.
>
> Him that overcometh will I make a pillar in the temple of my God, and he shall go no more out: and I will write upon him the name of my God, and the name of the city of my God, which is new Jerusalem, which cometh down out of heaven from my God: and I will write upon him my new name.

This text takes on, I believe, added significance because it is one of the last covenants, one of the last agreements mentioned in the entire Bible. That word *covenant* means "contract," but something more than contract. It has to do usually with matters that are of greater significance than houses and lands or silver and gold, those commodities about which we usually enter contracts. A covenant is a contract with something more holy about it than a mere contract. I'd say that this text takes on added significance because it is a covenant and because the Bible is a book

228

of covenants, and we serve a God who is a covenant God. We are a covenant people.

One of the first covenants of the Bible is found in the fifteenth chapter of the Book of Genesis, to be taken up by Paul thousands of years later in the fourth chapter of the Epistle to the Romans. There Abraham is being dealt with, and in that early covenant in the fifteenth chapter of Genesis, Abraham believes God. In the face of many questions and uncertainties he believes God. If I had the time, I would stop to inquire of you this morning, whom do you believe? Abraham, the fifteenth chapter of Genesis says, believed God. Is it not to argue that there are not many other places in which one may invest, if I may use that term, one's belief. I believe that what we have here is stronger, much stronger than an opinion. An opinion does not have any blood in it. It may be scarcely anything more than a notion, an arms-length idea. A belief has an investment of blood and risk in it. Abraham (I wish I could stay here a while) believed God. And God said to him, I will bless thee. There is a covenant. He believed God.

Then in the fifteenth chapter of the Book of Exodus, there is another covenant where God is saying to the children of Israel, "If you will diligently hearken unto my word, I will spare you what has happened to the Egyptians" (v. 26). That is a covenant. There are others in the Bible, but I think these are some of the great covenants of the Old Testament.

You and I who have entered into a relationship with Jesus Christ are a covenant people. Read Matthew 26:12–13 and Luke 22:28–29, and in each one Jesus is establishing covenant relationships. In each of those chapters as they stand now, the Lord Jesus is offering his pledge in exchange for an action by his followers. The ordinance of the Lord's Supper (Matthew 26:26–29) is a covenant of remembrance and promise. What an awful thing that the Prince of Glory would come here and die for us, and we would forget it. But there are many people, some of them so-called Christian people, who do not carry in their hearts and minds the memory. So we are called to witness this, he said, "in remembrance of me." That makes you and me a witnessing people. For a witness is another investment of one's self. I stand upon this. I witness it. We have here in Revelation one of the last agreements of the Bible: "because thou hast kept the word of my patience." Why does not God move first in this covenant business and then let us react as consequence in this covenant business?

It ought to be pointed out that God, even before the covenant, has already done something. He's given to you and me the power to make a covenant. And he's given to us the freedom of choice; that was the term in educational circles some years ago in New York City. Why does God not make us enter into a covenant? That would be to disrespect our freedom. If we do not want to be blessed, is it right for God to thrust upon us blessings anyhow? If somebody insists on going to hell — on being irresponsible, immoral, while having capacity to choose otherwise — is it fair for God to force another action on that person? If you commit yourself to hell by your actions and by your beliefs and by your outlook, is it not presumptuous of God to violate your freedom and not let you have your way and go to hell?

"Because thou hast kept the word of my patience." In other words, what the risen Christ is saying to these people in Philadelphia is that they had taken God seriously. I am not sure how perfectly they had kept his word, but they had taken God seriously. Our problem so often is that we do not take God seriously. I am not now talking about those knee-jerk prayers we blurt out in desperation. I am talking about allowing the spirit of the Lord to permeate, to saturate, to fill us not in what we say from time to time, but in our waking thoughts and in our actions.

Many of us will not take God seriously. Something is set down clearly in Scripture and we say, "God did not mean that." That is to make God what we are. We do not take God seriously because we do not take ourselves seriously. We say something to somebody, and if it is wrong, that does not make much difference to us because we do not take ourselves seriously. When we walk away from a mistake we have made in talking to somebody or in dealing with somebody, and feel no shame or need for apology or correction, that means we do not take ourselves seriously. There ought to be a hurt in you if you have made a mistake; you ought to be agitated. If we do not look seriously at what *we* say, we ought to take seriously what God has said. He enters into covenant with us by declaring "Because thou hast kept the word of my patience, I" — that's the other side of the covenant — "I also will keep thee from the hour of temptation."

"I will keep thee." I take great comfort in that. It does not say that maybe God will keep thee. I see no *perhaps*. There is no hint of *perhaps* here. "I will keep thee." I see no reference to extent, limitation, exceptions, qualifications. "I will keep thee." That means if ten thousand times, ten thousand enemies arise, "I will keep thee." If the floodwaters rise and threaten to cover your soul, "I will keep thee." Where the fires of trouble and persecution burn hottest, "I will keep thee." When people speak unkindly about you, "I will keep thee." And when everybody's hand turns against you and the world muddies your name, "I will keep thee." In youth, in the morning light, when the years stretch before you, young people, "I will keep thee." In the middle years, when the burdens press heaviest and the load is hardest to bear, and the sun beats mercilessly upon our weary heads, "I will keep thee." And yes, when the sun goes down, evening comes, and the chill of darkness is upon your life, and you are growing old and feeble and everything becomes a burden, the promise stands: "I will keep thee from the hour of temptation."

Those of us who study the New Testament are sometimes divided. What does Christ mean? "From the hour of temptation"? Does it mean to preserve us in, or to lift us out of? I do not know. Let me talk about the hour of temptation for a while because for the first time in the Book of Revelation, we have come upon one of the mysterious doctrines of the New Testament. Again and again we see reference in one form or another to the hour of temptation. This phrase does not refer to those minor irritations through which we pass, those small testings of our daily lives. This speaks of some great seismic testing which confronts the soul.

The Bible talks of "the great tribulation," of some type of major judgment when everything will be called into question. This is not talking about any little bruises we get, little cuts of the hand that we might endure. This hour of temptation is the hour of which Jesus speaks with almost a gasp. He says that there shall be wars, rumors of wars. He's talking about an "age on ages telling," a dread hour of sifting.

He is talking about a great assize, a great court hearing when the Lord divides the sheep from the goats. He is talking about some final decision making, the great hour of trial. Jesus says that "nation shall rise against nation, and kingdom against kingdom; there shall be famines, and pestilences, and earthquakes..." (Matthew 24:7). He said that there will be a time like there never has been before. I have never said this to you before. It goes against all my training in Western civilization with its idea of inevitable progress, but I say it to you with all my heart, I am driven to the belief we are right at the hour of "the great tribulation."

Look around. War is here and yonder. Children kill their parents. Parents kill their children. The plague of AIDS has descended upon the world, taking away some of its finest talent. Drugs have taken charge of our country. I do not see how this country is going to get back. When this awful drug was confined to some certain neighborhoods, nobody took it very seriously. It was a matter of casual comment, but now it is everywhere, from the highest to the lowest. It touches all colors and classes as it has seized the country. I believe that the time of great tribulation is upon us. And this is the dreadful time the Book of Revelation comments upon, this awful issue of final judgment.

Suppose the Lord Jesus comes right now. Are you ready for him? I say to you with all my heart, I am ready for him. Come Lord Jesus! A great and terrible time is upon the world. Do you think we can get out of the grip of what we are in now without the Lord's deliverance? Not on your life. One of our officials was saying just the other day that we ought to federalize our war on drugs. The problem is that our use of drugs is already federalized. When governors or senators or representatives or preachers or whoever are called together, how many of them are drug addicts?

"I will keep thee." Does it mean in the midst of? But if so, a psalm comes to mind: "as the mountains are round about Jerusalem, so is the Lord will be round about his people" (Psalm 125:2). And if we are to be preserved in the midst of the great tribulation as the three Hebrew children were insulated in the fiery furnace, so in the fires of the bad trial we will be protected. Or as the Lord stood between Daniel and the lions, so "I will keep thee." It means in the midst of. But it may well mean "from," or that the people of God are to be lifted out. That's what the Second Epistle to the Thessalonians says, that the Lord shall appear with a shout and the dead in Christ shall arise. Then we who are alive shall be caught up, to meet him in the sky (2 Thessalonians 4:16–17). That's what conservative theology has called the "rapture," to be caught up to meet him in the sky, caught up where sin and sorrow will last no more. Caught up where trouble cannot come. Caught up where sickness and sorrow, pain and death are felt and feared no more. Caught up. Caught up out of sorrow and trouble. Caught up, to meet him in the sky.

Give me but a moment. And to "him that overcometh will I make a pillar." Now it's remarkable about this room that there are no pillars supporting this vast stretch. It is an architectural marvel that this great sanctuary's ceiling has no vertical support. But in almost every temple a pillar supports. It is permanent, and it is prominent. "I will make thee a pillar in the house of my God," and I will label you. The Lord says that he labels his people. He puts on them the name of the city of God. Have you ever addressed an envelope and sent it somewhere? You put a name on it, and then you put an address on it. I do not know about you, but this first Sunday morning in May, I am labeled. I hope you are labeled. I am addressed. I am not wandering. I am on my way somewhere. I am bound for the Promised Land.

I will write "upon him my new name." I do not know what the Lord's new name is. I know he has many names. He is Malachi's messenger of the covenant. He is, from the Song of Solomon, the Rose of Sharon and the Lily of the Valley. He is the Bright and Morning Star as the canon comes to an end in Revelation (22:16). He is the shadow of a great rock in a weary land. He is the Lamb of God. I do not know what is his new name, but he has many from which to choose. Whatever, it is enough!

✑ 32 ✑

Laodicea, Part I:
The Great Amen Speaks
Revelation 3:14–18

May 8, 1988

We have come now to Mother's Day, and in our worship journey to the last of these seven churches, the church at Laodicea. What relationship do these early Christians have to Mother's Day? Let us turn that around. These early Christians, these people of whom we speak in this little church in Laodicea, were people who were clustered around the name of Jesus Christ. It was his name. It was his death and resurrection which brought them together. So let us turn the matter around. It is not a question of what relationship these early Christians have to mothers. It is rather a question of what relationship mothers have to the faith which brought these people together. What the Lord has done stands. He has opened the highway. He has given us a right of way. He has torn down the wall of partition. He has removed the enmity, the differences that stood between us and God. He has rent the veil, so that the holiest things of religion are no longer the preserve and prerogatives of the few but belong to all who will have them.

It is not a question of what relationship these people in Laodicea have to mothers. It is a question of what relationship mothers have to the faith which brought these people together. There has never been a time when the rearing of children, when real motherhood was not greatly augmented and strengthened by the love of the Lord. There has never been a time. And if some of you will say to me, as some of you well might, that you were reared in a good fashion by those who were not Christians, I say to you that you would have been reared in a far better way if they had been Christians. And if there had been no other reason for that better way than you would have had, as we say to these parents who bring children to this altar, an example of people who love the Lord who went before you. And whenever you thought of them, or think of them, their relationship to the Lord would have come also to your mind. There never was a time when the rearing of children was not greatly strengthened by the love of the Lord.

But also there never was a time, I believe, when the love of the Lord was so much needed in the rearing of children as right now. Perhaps I have no right to make that kind of comparison, but I do so. I do so because I believe that never in the history of the world has the rearing of children had the complexity and the difficulty and the obstacles that it has now.

Oh, always there were problems, but look around at the crack houses up and down every block almost and in every neighborhood. Look at the pornography which is publicly displayed at a time when children's minds are not able to discern and to discriminate. Look at the things that are thrust upon them. There never was a time when the Lord was needed in the rearing of children as much as right now. "If you never needed the Lord before, you sure do need him now."

So we come to Laodicea, fifty-odd miles from the ancient city of Philadelphia. We have now almost completed a circle. Ephesus and Smyrna, up to the northernmost portion to Pergamos, down to Thyatira, around to Philadelphia and Sardis, and now to Laodicea, the last of these seven churches. The great Amen is speaking. Let me read now, if I may, the text.

"And unto the angel of the church of the Laodiceans write; these things saith the Amen" — that is the Lord Jesus talking about himself — "the faithful and true witness, the beginning of the creation of God." He was establishing in this introductory comment his authority, and he is presenting to the ages his credentials. "The Amen," the so be it. When Christ says amen, ours has a tinge of our hope in it. We say let it be. Whatever the extent of our faith and our Christian confidence, our amen has in it a hope and almost always some little shadow of doubt. It has not yet happened. So may it be. The Lord says "Amen" and means "So be it." So be it. We say amen because we believe it. The Lord says amen because he knows it. And he is talking now.

I find it interesting about this city of Laodicea, the old banking capital. Somewhere in Syria, a Roman orator comments upon having cashed (we thought our banking system was modern) some letters of credit which he had brought from Rome to the city of Laodicea. I will speak at a later time upon this city as a center of the clothing industry and the rare wool that was grown in Laodicea. I will also speak of it at a later time as one of the outstanding medical centers of that part of the world and how the fact that it was a clothing center relates to what the Lord says and how it being a medical center relates to what the Lord says.

But I find it of great interest and alarming, too, that this is the one church about which nothing good is said. What an awful thing! Well, of course Smyrna and Philadelphia are the two churches that received only praise. Ephesus, Sardis, Pergamos, and Thyatira received mingled praise and blame. But when the Lord comes to Laodicea, there is not a single word of praise about this church. What an awful thing! What an awful thing about anybody when not one single thing can be said in his or her favor. You would think that, no matter what one's character or conduct or representation might be, you ought to be able to find something good if you pry deep enough and dig deep enough, but not one such word here. And this is the scrutiny of what one old preacher called the "superintending gaze" of God upon the church, and he finds nothing favorable.

Have I ever told you that I used to hear my father tell of a minister who had the reputation of saying something nice about everybody? He never criticized anyone, never said anything about anybody that was negative. I will never qualify for that, nor do I want to. This minister always said something nice, and then the worst man in the town died. This man was a drunkard, a wife beater, everything that was wrong, and the people crowded into the little church to see what the minister would say about this ne'er-do-well. The minister said, "I will say this for John, he was not as bad sometimes as he was other times."

But here, there is not a single redeeming, positive, favorable word spoken about the church at Laodicea, not even by the Lord, who makes so much of so little we do. I hope that never happens to this church, but not even the Lord could find anything good to say about the church at Laodicea. I must point out to you that it may have been because the church had bad leadership. The Scriptures do say clearly that where there is no vision, the people perish (Proverbs 29:15). There is another saying: "like priest like people." The church at Laodicea may have suffered from bad leadership.

There is a third-century letter that still can be read in which Archippus is mentioned as the first bishop, who was then the pastor. There were no denominations, but the bishop was the pastor. There is the letter that Paul wrote to the church at Colossae. Colossae was ten or fifteen miles away from Laodicea. There were three cities close at hand: Colossae, Laodicea, and Hierapolis. I remember having refreshments in Hierapolis, six miles from Laodicea, because it is a great resort center with mineral waters. And in the close of the letter to the Colossians, Paul says, have this letter which I'm sending to you Colossians read in Laodicea, and have the letter to Laodicea read in your church. Exchange the letters.

Then he says, tell Archippus to take heed to the ministry to which the Lord has given him, that he might be faithful in it (Colossians 4:17). So I feel I am fairly safe in saying that Archippus was pastor at Laodicea and there was something in the leadership of Archippus which led Paul to tell the Colossians to tell Archippus to take heed. And you and I, whatever position of leadership we might be in, in the family, mothers in the community, on your jobs, as officers, as ushers, we need to take heed. Those of us who preach ought to take heed that we rightly divide the word of truth, that we do not mislead people with false doctrines and fancy notions that have no roots in the divine Word of God. And those of you who usher ought to take heed, for somebody you greet at those doors might have a heart that's breaking and may not be able to stand one more bruise and one more hurt. Take heed.

We parents ought to take heed what we say around our children, because our children don't know what to repeat and what not to repeat. And they will say things they heard you say, at exactly the time you do not want them to say it. It is no use getting angry with them. They don't know when to say it and when not to say it. They heard you say it. And if you've got to say something questionable you ought to wait until they are at the place, wherever it is, where they can tell when to repeat it and when not to repeat it. But first you ought to learn what to say and what not to say. Take heed. I know this may sound foolish, but let me tell you. You parents ought to be very careful about talking about other grown people around your children. I thank God that when I came along old people, grown people, did not talk about other grown people in the presence of children. There were some terrible things back then and some things that needed correcting, but God knows that was not one of them. You do not need to be talking adversely about other grown people around your children. Your children will find out soon enough that there isn't much to adults, when they become adults. You don't have to give them that kind of advance knowledge. Take heed.

It may have been bad leadership in Laodicea. I want to get directly to this. The great Amen is talking. He said, "I know thy works, that thou art neither cold nor hot: I would thou wert cold or hot. So because thou art lukewarm, and neither cold nor hot, I will spew thee out of my mouth."

What is the Lord saying here? Is he saying that it is better to be completely outside than half in and half out? Better to be hostile, better to be cold, than to be indifferent? Exactly. Too many of us are take-it-or-leave-it people, neither hot nor cold. He's talking about you once-a-month worshipers who are not regularly in divine worship, that you might get instruction and guidance. He's talking about those of us who are never at the Lord's table that we might receive and be reminded that we are to keep the Lord's name before ourselves and before others. "I would thou wert cold or hot," but thou art lukewarm. Half in, half out. An African Methodist Episcopal bishop said to me that they have a name for many AMEs. He said that another meaning of AME is "After Mother's Day, Easter." If that be so, then many Baptists are AMEs too — lukewarm, neither hot nor cold. Half in, half out. Take it or leave it, Jesus died for me, that's all right, but it's not that important. He has established the church I that might be nurtured; that is all right but it's not important. As for my money, I do with it what I want and I'll throw at him a portion of that I would not dare present at a theater ticket window. Lukewarm, in, out, in and out. Half and half. Cold.

The Lord can do something with us if we are committed one way or the other. Paul went to Damascus breathing out threats. Hostile, but not lukewarm. And the Lord met him, turned him around, knocked him down, picked him up, closed his eyes and then opened them, put a new song in his heart with new words on his lips. "Thou art lukewarm. I will spew you out of my mouth." If I had used the word that the Lord uses here, you respectable people would raise your eyebrows this morning, and when you go home you would sit around your dinner table and talk about how tasteless I was in the pulpit and how I have gotten to the place in my old age where I don't know what to say and what not to say. But I'm going to tell you what the Lord says here. The word he says is *spew*. The King James Version has made it nice, but it stands for the Greek word *emeo*. The word here is not *spew*; the word is *vomit*. I will vomit you out. That talks about sourness and sickness and bad odor and something that won't stay on your stomach. I will vomit you. That *spew* (*emeo*) is so polite. That's just spitting. You're going to talk about me anyhow. That word *spitting* by comparison is so nice, it's so polite, but *spew* really means vomit. The stomach won't hold it, and what is half digested comes up all sour and impure, and smelling, and odorous. I will spew you. I will vomit you out of my mouth. I would that thou wert hot or cold.

Let me talk about hot just a little while. I would that you were hot or cold, that this church were on fire for the Lord. I wish to God that all preachers were on fire, afire with the gospel, that there was a fire set up and when we tried to be calm, we couldn't be calm because the fire burned inside. R. E. W. Harris, the Methodist preacher I knew in my youth, used to say — and I say this to any preacher who may hear me this morning — that if the preacher will catch on fire, people will come to watch him burn, even if they don't have any fire themselves. It is a wonderful thing when a Christian is on fire. Never mind what the world says; in a home where somebody is on fire, that one person can warm the whole household.

Now you can call this fire anything you want. Call it enthusiasm, call it the joy of your salvation. Our holiness friends call it "the latter rain." Call it what you want. Call it fanaticism, as I heard somebody refer to one of our members once, but if you're on fire for the Lord, it has its effect. Fire. Fire that burns, fire that cleanses, fire.

I think I once told you of what happened to me on the day after they buried my father. I was twelve years old. I asked my mother on that Sunday morning through that closed door with my father dead, "Mother, what will we do now?" I think I told you what she said to me. But I don't think I ever told you what it did for my little aching heart. Out of the fire that burned inside of her and her love for the Lord, she spoke to me. It wasn't just putting me off; I would have understood that. This was 1931, fifty-odd years have come and gone, but I can still hear that morning when I asked through the door, "Mother, what will we do now?" I can still remember the ring that was in her voice, I can still remember the force of conviction with which she answered me. She said, "The Lord will provide." It was not a half-hearted, tentative comment. It was not a passing enthusiasm. It was something I could tell even through the door, something which welled up in her heart and made her believe that the Lord would provide. That fire ran through that door and warmed a little boy's heart.

That was 1931. Then 1941 came, and I found out that what she said to me through the door still held true. The Lord will provide. Came 1941, 1951, 1961, 1971, 1981 — and I found what she said that Sunday morning of 1931 was still true: The Lord will provide.

I'll tell you, that fire can get you through. That fire can save your family. That fire can bring your children back from ruins. That fire can keep them out of prison. That fire can make something out of them.

LAODICEA, PART II:
LUKEWARMNESS REJECTED

Revelation 3:14–22

May 29, 1988

So then because thou art lukewarm, and neither cold nor hot, I will spew thee out of my mouth.

Because thou sayest, I am rich, and increased with goods, and have need of nothing; and knowest not that thou art wretched, and miserable, and poor, and blind, and naked:

I counsel thee to buy of me gold tried in the fire, that thou mayest be rich; and white raiment, that thou may be clothed, and that the shame of thy nakedness do not appear; and anoint thine eyes with eye-salve, that thou mayest see.

Herein the Lord rejects lukewarmness. We are all for enthusiasm, everywhere except in Christian discipleship and in divine worship. The football stadium echoes and reverberates with thunderous roars whipped up by attractive somersaulting cheerleaders; well and good, as long as enthusiasm does not enter the house of God and our acts of Christian discipleship.

At Churchill Downs and Pimlico and shortly at Belmont race tracks, thousands and thousands of people will scream and shout, hug one another, pat each other on the back; well and good, as long as there is no enthusiasm in the house of God. At political rallies, family reunions, school gatherings, everywhere, as long as it is not in the house of God. And I am not talking merely now about vocal outbursts, though I do not eliminate that. There is also an enthusiasm so deep that one is left mute, speechless.

A music critic a few days ago was commenting on a rendition of one of the major symphonies under the direction of Zubin Mehta, the director of the New York Philharmonic. He said that when the final movement of that symphony had come to its close, those who were privileged to hear Zubin Mehta at his best conducting and that orchestra at its best sat for a few minutes as if it found them speechless. That is emotion also. And over against that is lukewarmness, indifference, coolness. I don't know of anything that's worth dealing with which is lukewarm. Coffee, cold or hot, for many of us preferably hot, but, my goodness, not lukewarm. Tea, hot or cold; it may have ice in it and be very good, but, for heaven's sake, not lukewarm. Food itself, if it is a cold plate at certain times, fair enough, hot, yes, but my goodness, lukewarm food? The Lord does not like it.

I will not go into that almost obscene description I gave you the other day about what he will do with lukewarmness. I saw some of you arching your eyebrows and turning up your noses at what I said. I'll not go back into that, but it does stand there. Everywhere else, enthusiasm, but not in God's house, and the enthusiasm we do have we have about things that really are not worth a cent when they're over. We get all worked up about a lot of different things. It's all right to enjoy them, but we ought not believe that they represent the beginning or end of the world.

There was a time when we got great enthusiasm in supporting something that was regional, something or some team that came from a section that we figured was not as friendly to us as the other. But the nation is homogenized now. There is no difference between North and South today.

And then there was a time when our enthusiasm was related to race. My friend Jack Robinson played baseball for the Brooklyn Dodgers, and at that time our enthusiasm was built around the fact that here was a black fellow in what had been a white sport, actually performing. But now, race ball is gone. Because that's about all you see, in almost every sport. But show no enthusiasm in the house of God, and the Lord says he does not like it.

That is what had happened in the church of Laodicea. It had become cold. The people in that church had confined the Lord to the margins of their lives. They turned from him. They were indifferent. There was an English preacher, a poet, who wrote about

Jesus coming to Charing Cross. That's at the center of London, and the people passing by see him standing there, with arms outstretched at the very center of London. People are rushing hither and yon, to and fro, great crowds of them. The Lord stands there. They do not turn away from him, and they do not turn toward him. They are too occupied with their affairs, and so they pass him by. Now and then someone casually looks in his direction for a moment, but it does not last any time, and they rush on. At the end of the poem, the lonely Christ is pictured weeping and crying for Calvary. That would be preferable to cold indifference.

Such had happened at the church at Laodicea, and it can happen and sometimes does happen in our lives. Rarely enthusiastic, cool, we become less interested, not, mind you, disinterested, but less interested. As I said the other day, it is with us a take-it-or-leave-it business. It's all right either way. You want to go to church, it's all right; but on the other hand, if you don't, that's okay too. And you will have to decide within your own mind and heart whether that affliction has come or is coming upon you. A scholar friend tells me of a shiftless brother of his, who when asked about this or that will say, "Whichever way the wind blows." That describes many of us spiritually.

The Lord is calling for people who are ready to be with him. Not half with him, but with him, because the Lord's business is serious business. You may not know it or you may have forgotten it or it may not make much difference to you, but there is a great fight going on. The Lord is out to win back what belonged to him originally and what at last must acknowledge itself to be his. I'm not arguing whether or not the Lord owns you and me and whether he owns the world. I'm arguing that he is out to bring to pass the day when it will be acknowledged. That's what terms of surrender are all about. When Robert Lee was beaten at Appomattox Courthouse, they sat down in a farmhouse owned by a man named McLean. The fight was over, the battle had been won, but they sat down to acknowledge that such was the case. There is a brutal war going on, and you can see it if you look around you in the streets of this borough. Where do *you* stand?

I was in Houston speaking earlier in this week. People used to talk about getting out of New York to get where it's safe. There is not a hamlet or a village in this country today that's safe. This whole drug thing has got hold of us and gotten out of hand. It's a brutal war, a great struggle is going on. It's a question of whether the whole drug culture and all that it suggests is going to take charge of things. When it started, many people in positions of authority either winked at it or smiled at it and pushed it off as nothing but a quaint quirk that rises in some communities that are different from theirs. As long as it's there, there's no use worrying about it. That was the attitude in the country.

It reminds me of what happened where I grew up. There were in my childhood open ditches, there were no curbstones, and down in that tropical climate, mosquitoes got to be a hazard during hot weather. The authorities would spray the ditches in their section, and in the section in which most of us lived, they ran out of whatever the spray was. The idea was that the mosquitoes would know what neighborhood to stay in, but the mosquitoes did not know anything about the segregation laws. So they thought that the mosquitoes would not fly from the neighborhoods where they had sprayed, and would not fly into the neighborhoods where they had not sprayed. At last, with the great Anglo-Saxon wisdom for which our nation is famous, they decided that maybe in order to protect their neighborhoods they had better spray everywhere. It was all right, but the mosquitoes did not know where to stay. Mosquitoes do not know where to stay, and drugs do not know where to stay.

I get on a plane and I try to peer up into the cockpit. I wish I could see the pilot's eyes. It might not tell me anything, but I'd feel better if his eyes were clear. You get on a train, and you don't know what you're riding with. I'm not sure you know when you go in these courts what you're looking up at. I'm not sure in our city halls and statehouses and our national capital whether anybody can tell who is wearing what uniforms. There is a great battle going on. And it's not clear who is on what side. I'm not sure sometimes in these pulpits. The Lord needs people to come on out and take a stand. As Luther said, "here stand I." The whole world can stand whichever way it wants, but I stand here. There are some things that are forever right, and there are some things forever wrong. The Lord wants people who will take sides. This fence straddling and working both sides of the street will not work in the Lord's business. He needs people who will stand up to and for something. It does not make any difference where you are, what age you are, what school you go to, where you live. Some things are right and some things are wrong. The stars do not change. There are transcendent values. There are eternal truths that no one can make out to be a lie, and there are lies that nobody can make to be the truth.

Years ago I tried to preach a sermon here about that house where there was a demon and they swept the house out, cleaned it out, got all the cobwebs out, got all the litter up, got everything out, drove the demon out. Then they left the house empty, neutral, and so the demon returned and brought along seven others. And, Jesus said that the last state of that house was worse than it had been before. In this life, there's no place for neutrality! There's a great fight going on, make no mistake about it, and the struggle is hard and tough, and one of the problems of our country today is the problem of indifference. Nobody cares. Everybody looks the other way. Nobody wants to get involved. If it doesn't touch me directly, it is not important.

That's what has happened to our country. The commission on minority participation has made its report this week. Two former presidents, one Republican and one Democrat, served as the co-chairs of the commission. It says that we have fallen back, that 31 percent of minority people in this country live below the poverty level. The president of the United States said in Helsinki the other day, and rightly, that thirteen years after the signing of the Helsinki pact, it is difficult to understand why the matter of divided families and people unable to immigrate should still be on the East-West agenda. But he and we ought to be reminded that not thirteen years after the Helsinki agreement but 212 years after the nation signed the Declaration of Independence, 123 years after the nation signed its intention to become a democracy with the best blood of the land shed in the Civil War, thirty-four years after the Supreme Court said we will not be a society separated by race, twenty-three years after the 1965 civil rights legislation, 31 percent of minorities live below the poverty level. It is difficult to understand, to quote the president, how 212 years later, not thirteen years later, as in the case of the Helsinki pact, but 200 years later, there's a great fight about whether America is to be a democracy. The problem is indifference.

When our civil rights struggle brought this whole matter to the considerations of the nation, we sought to change what was a disgraceful condition in this country. Let me digress a moment. If it had not been for black and white people who got out and suffered and died, and some of us saw the inside of jails, what would anybody representing this country have looked like talking to anybody about human rights now anywhere? Who would have had the nerve? Even for an actor, who deals in make-believe, to talk about human rights if our civil rights struggle had not at least to some extent cleansed the nation of its shame and its guilt would have been laughable comedy — no, sheer tragedy. But the irony of it is that the people who talk the loudest about human rights are the same people who have opposed every single move about civil rights during their long lifetime, which is nearly a century.

There is a great fight, and the problem is indifference. I'm not saying, and God knows I wouldn't say it because it is not true, that people in America are evil people. There are wonderfully kind impulses in the whole American populace, but there is this tendency not to get involved. And as somebody said, the only need that evil people have in order to carry out their purposes is for good people to keep quiet. You say, what does this have to do with me? I'm just one person. Did you know this is going to be a presidential year? I don't know how many people will vote, but did you know that every election ever held, in the history of the world, has been decided by one vote? Let two million people vote; let a million vote on each side; let one, one vote on one side or the other and that side wins. You say that what you do does not matter. My God, it has forever been that one person standing up has started others. You and I can do some things. You can make telephone calls, you can complain, you can write, you can protest, and you can keep an interior decency within yourself so that you do not feel comfortable in the presence of what's wrong.

Our trouble is being at ease in Zion, where it doesn't make any difference. Shame on us! Christ did not just die for the world, he died for "whosoever," that's one, you, me. You say to me, preacher, what does this have to do with religion? I'm trying to get to heaven. If you read the twenty-fifth chapter of Matthew, you'll find out what Jesus said, and he's the Judge. He said that we are going to be, you and I are going to be divided, not by any creed, not by any church we attended. Our purpose at church should be to be alert and to be sensitized to what we ought to be and what we ought to do. But he said he will divide the sheep from the goats. How? By deeds. "I was hungry." Lord, when saw we thee hungry? "Inasmuch as you have done it unto one of the least of these my brethren, ye have done it unto me. I was hungry, and you gave me meat" (Matthew 25:31–45, paraphrased). Stand over here!

Oh, but Lord, I recited the Apostles' Creed backwards. So what! I was naked, and you clothed me. Did you know that your eternal destiny is to be decided by your attitude and your care and your deeds toward God's children? You are going to heaven or you are going to hell forever, and I, on the basis of how we have looked upon need around us. That's the religion which is in what I'm talking about.

Let me move on. I said the other day that the church in Laodicea may have had bad leadership, and that was a terrible thing. Prosperity was a problem also. This was a banking center, and people tended to be self-sufficient. It was a clothing center. It was a center of the garment district. They had some of the finest wool grown in all the world, and it might have been said that the prosperity of Laodicea moved upon the backs of sheep. That's what they used to say in Australia. And then it was a highly prestigious medical center, particularly in ophthalmology, whatever science they had and whatever the skill they had in the matter of treating eye conditions.

It may be that this proud city, rich as a banking center, the center of manufacturers of wool, prosperous, a medical center, led the people in the church there to become cold toward the Lord. For prosperity is a more dangerous thing than adversity.

It's not hard to be humble when you're down. In fact, there's hardly anything else for you to be except humble when you're down. It is not hard to pray when every need is upon you, and you know you need. That's not hard. But there is a great danger, when things go well with us, to forget. There is a great danger that we will assign the credit to ourselves. There is a great danger that we will not remember the rock from whence we were hewn and the hole or pit from which we were digged (Isaiah 51:1). It's easy to forget. Well, you say, how can I avoid this lukewarmness? How can I not be lukewarm? How can I get my enthusiasm? How can I?

The Lord says, do business with me. "Buy of me gold tried in the fire" (Revelation 3:18). Some things gold will not buy, and this world's gold can do much, but a lot of things it cannot buy. I know it cannot buy me my youth back. You saw on television the other week about the death of Aristotle Onassis. Even though he was one of the world's richest people, his wealth couldn't buy life nor enable him to stay here.

Do business with the Lord if you want enthusiasm. Be in divine worship. Never mind if the music is dull, if the preacher is boring; be there in season and out. God can talk to you not only through the music and through the preacher, but he can talk to you in spite of the music and in spite of the preacher. Be there. Be constantly in the Lord's presence. Ask him to help you, to strengthen, comfort, and keep you. He is able. Pray often, meditate, keep your mind on things above. You want your enthusiasm, do business with Jesus. And he says, put on "raiment that thou mayest be clothed." Take off the ugly clothes of pride; put on the garments of humility. Take off the apparel of arrogance; put on the cloak of thankfulness. It will give you a warmth in your life and a joy in the service of the Lord.

Then he says, "Put some eye salve on that you might see." Our problem is that we are not looking around us to see what the Lord has done. If you want to know something about the Lord, look at what he's done for you or the way in which he has led you. Look at the pitfalls around which he has brought you. Remember the snares from which he has delivered you. Look around you and see that the Lord is good. He has done great things for us. You will find joy when you remember that the Lord has picked you up and put your feet on a solid rock.

～ 34 ～

LAODICEA, PART III:
THE DOOR OF THE SOUL

Revelation 3:14–22

June 5, 1988

We read at Revelation 3:20, "Behold, I stand at the door and knock: if any man hear my voice, and open the door," as it stands in the King James Version, "I will come in to him, and will sup with him, and he with me." There cannot be any verse of Holy Writ more familiar to this congregation than that verse, because it is our call to worship. But if you look backward a bit, you will realize that the eighteenth and nineteenth verses are very necessary as cushioning between what goes directly before them and our text, "Behold, I stand at the door and knock." Take out the eighteenth and nineteenth verses and we get a kind of resounding collision, a crash, a discontinuity. It is what literary people may call a non sequitur, a sequence that does not follow, a contradiction. If we were to take them out, the sixteenth verse would end with a scathing indictment, a kind of arctic dismissal, "I will spew thee out of my mouth." It would not make sense for this text to follow, "Behold, I stand at the door and knock."

I must not use the word again that I used from the original language and which the King James Version sanitized. Let us not render "spew" its true meaning. I will not use the word for which "spew" stands, because I saw some of you draw up stiffly, and you seemed taken aback. I will not use the word that I used before, but more nicely: "Thou art neither hot nor cold; I will spew you out of my mouth." Kaput, the end, it's over, goodbye. And then, "Behold, I stand at the door and knock." They don't go together. Most copywriters would blue-pencil that and say to

252

you, Fix it; it does not work. "I will spew thee out of my mouth. Behold, I stand at the door and knock."

The eighteenth and nineteenth verses take the shock out of it. What is really happening here, and I am going to have to tell a lie in order to tell the truth, is that we get the negative and positive in God. The lie is that there are no negatives in God. But I use the word *negative* in the sense of the judgment of God, the "thou shalt not." "I will spew thee out of my mouth" — this I call the negative in God, the judgment, sweeping and withering. And in contrast, in the twentieth verse is the so-called positive aspect of God: "Behold, I stand at the door and knock." The positive in God is the mercy in God, tender, pleading, kindly inviting. The mercy and the judgment, united here in the words of Christ: "I will spew thee out. Behold, I stand at the door and knock."

And we had better not play loose with this judgment and mercy in God. Heine, a German philosopher, said with a kind of air of dismissal that God will forgive, that's his business. This approach to God is like someone asking at a grocery counter for a box of raisins: God will forgive; that's his business. We had better not play loose with that. If anybody here dares to feel this is a light matter, you ought to go back to Calvary. You will see first what it cost God to get us on the right track. What it cost him to give us another chance, what it cost him to satisfy his integrity and, at the same time, to express his love. This is an awful combination, keeping One's honor and showing One's love. That can be an awful conflict. Seeing it in God at Calvary, we gasp.

That master expositor Alexander Maclaren has pointed out to us that there at Calvary there were two thieves. Yes, by all means, Christ is able to save to the uttermost. One thief out on the very edge of hell, hanging over that bottomless abyss of endless nothingness, is saved! "Today thou shalt be with me in paradise." But only one! Do not play with it. Christ was there. One was saved; the other went out into endless darkness. And so we get here the judgment and mercy, "I will spew thee. Behold, I stand at the door and knock."

On some other Sunday I'm going to want to talk about who

is knocking, but today, suffice it to say that he who knocks has done you no harm. He will do you no harm. Nobody who has ever opened that door has ever said that it would have been better if I had kept it closed. Of all the thousands of people across the face of the earth I have preached to — God alone knows how many people in how many churches on how many continents and in how many nations — still, I have never heard a single soul say it was better that I had never opened the door to let Jesus in. I have heard countless times the contrary. Under the most desperate exigencies of life, under the most extreme circumstances and vicissitudes of life, I have heard people say, "Thank you, Jesus."

Today I would not want to talk so much about who it is that is knocking. Let me save that for another day. I rather want to talk about the door that is being knocked on. The door of the heart, your heart, mine, every single one of you. For you are in control of something that not even God, I shudder to say it, can countermand. Did you hear that? God is not in control of your decision about your soul's salvation. You are in command of that. That is not in God's hand. It is not in the hands of any seat of government, of city hall, of the White House. You control that! He says, "Behold, I stand and knock." Why don't we open?

A lad said once to his father when this was being spoken about in the pulpit, "Why don't they open, Father? Why don't they open?" "I do not know," said the father. The little boy said, "Well, maybe they live in the back of the house." And it may be that many of us are living too far in the back of the house.

Perhaps this sermon really should have been entitled "The Doors of the Soul," because the Lord knocks in many ways. There is the door of conscience. When you have done something that you feel all miserable inside about, conscience is that part of us which says you ought or you ought not! Christ comes to us and says not only "you ought." My God, all of the lessons of history, most of the philosophers who have thought deeply about the human spirit, have told us about the "ought." You ought to do this, you ought not to do that, you should have, you should not have. But Christ says not only "you ought," but also "you can." All things are possible, he says, and your sins can be as pure as driven snow. And another prophet says God will, if we will let him, not only remove our sins from us. I hesitate to even say it — the figure is too strong, it is too sweeping. The prophet says that God will put our sins behind his back (Isaiah 38:17).

The door of conscience, the door of the Word of God, the door of memory — God knocks. For does it not come back to you sometimes when you are least true to what is noblest in you, of some day when you did make a vow to the Lord? And do you not remember some purer day in your life when things were not as spotted and confused as they are now? A snatch of a hymn comes back that you have not remembered in many a year, but it comes back to rally you and to strengthen you?

There was a Southern Baptist preacher, George Truett, who as a young man years ago was preaching a revival out on what was almost the frontier of New Mexico. He was told about a certain rancher who was a particularly harsh and unbelieving man. He ventured, but a stripling of a preacher, to go out to talk to this man during the week of the revival. He said the man looked at him gruffly and was ready to dismiss him. Finally Truett said to the man, "Did you have a Christian mother?" The young preacher said he could see the gruffness begin to disappear as that man thought of the years long gone and that woman who had taught him to pray and whom he had heard sing the songs of faith. He said he saw the mist of tears come in that gruff rancher's eyes as he looked back across the long years. He said, "Yes, my mother was a dear Christian woman." Something softened in his heart because sometimes the Lord knocks on the door of our memory and we rush back across the years.

Just this week I talked with a young man, rising in industry and in the corporate life of America, who is about to marry the daughter of one of the most prominent of our black citizens in this land. He said to me, "I was spiritually bankrupt." He said that he happened to be in church, it happened to be this church, it might have been any church, but he said he saw the deacons stand, and then he heard a hymn his grandmother used to sing.

This is not just sentimentality. This is the way the Lord gets at us. He says his grandmother's face came back before him, because the Lord knocks on the door of memory. And, yes, you young people, on the door of the mind. Religion is not all feeling. Christ makes sense to the mind! You need some philosophy of life. You need something to give meaning to your years.

I was saying in Oberlin the other day, you will never really make it in this life just making money. I'm not saying that wealth cannot bless us. It can. It has blessed us over and over again, but, my God, when the means become the end, you've got nowhere to go! No God, no purpose, no city of desire! And what, who can give meaning to life except Jesus? I heard something that a former secretary of the president of the United States (it's amazing how foolish these people can be) said the other day in the national press. Talking about the matter of the Olympic foundation, this former Secretary of the Treasury of the United States of America said, "I don't deal in philosophy. I deal in reality." Ah, fool! It is what you think about what you do that gives meaning to what you do. Take that away, and reality is what a hog does — a hog stomping around in a trough. I need some purpose behind my actions, something that I believe in so deeply that my actions are at least tempered and somewhat guided and conditioned by my faith. Ah, fool! "I deal in reality. I do not deal in philosophy." In other words, I do not think about what I do; I just do.

Well, that's what dogs do. They just do. People do because they think and because they believe and because they love and because they care. How stupid can people be who are supposed to have some sense? What fools, what idiots, what dumbbells! And they call themselves smart. Fools! Fools! And only Christ can give you a philosophy that will stand up. What does he say? He says there is a Father above. He says we are children. He says we have an elder Brother who "takes up for us." That's the way we used to put it down where I came from, someone who takes our part. He says that this life is probation. He says there is a home of the soul. That is what life is all about. It does not make any sense reading it any other way. He says that there is a homeland and that here we are "strangers and pilgrims" (Hebrews 11:13), and that death, which we so much dread, is our escort home.

God knocks at the door of events. Do not deal loosely, keeping that door closed, because it is dangerous business. Someone before me has said that there comes — and this is a dreadful word — a last knock. It is not for me to say when it occurs, but you will see the sense of it, won't you? There does come a last knock. Your sense will tell you that, won't it? Don't play with it. A Harvard professor said that this of which I speak can happen to nations as well as to individuals. He says that when a nation rises, it wants to protect itself pridefully, and may spread itself too thin. He does not use the name of God, though he was trained in Catholic schools, but I see God's presence protruding from what he said. And thereby, he says, great nations come down. Do not play with this.

Spare me an aside for a moment. I was thrilled at the persistence and the eloquence with which our president pursued the cause of human rights in Russia. Then it came to me that perhaps never in the history of the world has someone spoken so much and so well about a subject so far away from home and so little and so poorly about the same subject at home. But as for individuals, so for nations, let us be careful. God knocks. There is somewhere, sometime, somehow, a last knock. It has to be. Nothing is endless. There's no infinitude in life. So there must be a last knock.

Let me tell you something for which I thank God daily. There are some things in my life about which I feel proud, and there are some things in my life about which I feel very ashamed, and I must carry that shame to my death. But I do thank God that fifty-odd years ago I heard the Lord knocking at my heart's door. And I thank God that I heard it and I answered it. You remember that spiritual, "Somebody's knocking at your door? It knocks like Jesus. Why don't you open? Somebody's knocking at your door."

I have been going in and out before this congregation for forty years now. I would not trifle with you. I declare unto you that you will make no mistake when you let the Lord in. He will bless your life! He will pick you up, set you on a solid rock! He will open doors for you that nobody can close! He will smooth out your pathways! He will bring down mountains, and he will lift up valleys! He will make crooked ways straight and rough places plain! He'll give you friends, and he'll put food on your table! Let him in! Let him in! He'll bless your life; let him in! He'll bring sunshine every day; let him in! He'll brighten every corner; let him in!

I sat in Houston in the pastor's study at Gethsemane Church two weeks ago, waiting for time to preach that night. I happened to thumb through a book, and I came across the description of a woman on her dying bed. Her frame was lean and emaciated, her fingers now scarce anything but bones with a thin, wrinkled parchment of skin over them. I have a member who is at that level, at that stage right now. Her breathing was labored. Her three sons, young men, stood around her bed. She looked to two of them, so the description ran, and she said, "George and Francis," realizing that she probably would not get through the night. "George, Francis, good night." And she turned to her other son and said, "Billy, goodbye." The third son asked, "Mother, why did you say to the other boys 'good night' and you said to me 'goodbye'?" She said, "They're saved, son, and I will see them again. But if you finish as you are now, I'll never see you."

Well, let me tell you something. Forty years here I've wept sometimes and I've laughed sometimes. I do not know how long it will be, of course. Inevitably the day winds to its end. My shadow is already behind me, the sign that the sun is far, far along. Two of my friends, my oldest friends, lie now in hospitals. One with whom I played college football died this week. But I will say to you who have opened the door, when the Lord calls "good night," not "goodbye." I'll see you when the morning comes. Good night! We shall meet on that healthy shore "where sickness and sorrow and pain and death are felt and feared no more!" Good night! I'll see you where God the Son forever reigns and scatters night away. The Lord knocks. Do you hear him?

~ 35 ~

LAODICEA, PART IV:
THE KNOCKER

Revelation 3:14–22

June 19, 1988

I will next Sunday conclude this series in Revelation because we come to the summer months, though I hope all of us will be in our places as I hope to be in mine for a substantial portion of the summer. We will, after next Sunday's sermon, in the providence of God have completed three chapters. And it begins now to look like that this will be my unfinished work at the rate we are going. There are still all of these chapters left, nineteen of them. Perhaps I should have started this earlier.

At any rate, I hope this morning to speak about the knocker whom you will hear whatever your spiritual condition might be. It is, of course, a word poignantly and pointedly addressed to those who have not accepted Christ: "Behold, I stand at the door and knock. If any person hear my voice and open the door, I will come in to him and will sup with him, and he with me." Those of us who are members of a household of faith ought not to forget that that was first addressed to the church. It has a strong evangelistic thrust, but it was first addressed to Christians, for all of us have either untended rooms or sealed rooms that are not open to Jesus Christ. And while I will be speaking next Sunday very likely about Holman Hunt's painting which hangs now in London, the door is not necessarily an outside door. It may be a door inside, where we will not allow him. I hope all of you will hear, and I pray this every Sunday, not my poor voice but the Lord's.

What a startling reversal this passage is from what we customarily think when we think along these lines. In my youth, there was almost universally, among Baptist people certainly, the idea

259

of seeking the Lord. There would be a revival meeting; sometimes they were called protracted meetings. Those who were unsaved would set out in a campaign to seek the Lord as if he was hidden or elusive. Claude Montefiore, the scholar, said that nowhere except in the Bible do we get the idea of a seeking God. Certainly not in any other religion that I know about is there any notion of a seeking God. And in many of us, particularly in earlier times, the idea was not that the Lord seeks us but that we must seek the Lord. Some of you will remember the long, arduous exercises that people went through seeking the Lord.

On this Father's Day I think I ought to stop to say that I am not talking primarily about the absent father, though it is said over and over again that all too many of the fathers among us black people are absent. I say to you young people this morning — whether there is a father in your home or not, find some male model. All of us need male and female attention. If nature is no fool — I won't talk about God — you wouldn't think that nature would have worked out all of this being a fool, would you? Come now. If you did not need both father and mother, you could get here with just one. Do you hear me? The fact that you need both to get here means you need both to grow up right. And if there is no father in your home, find some male model.

When I was coming along, and you know my father died very early, there were in my church at home deacons. They were brickyard workers and handymen in the week, but I looked at those men, Clarence Burgess, Alex Mosby, Andrew Holman, seventy years ago nearly, as role models for me. You find yourselves some models. You need it. And I'll tell you another thing, black people, and perhaps other people also, do not need all of the emphasis on mothers. We have had mothering.

We have had mothering all right. We need male figures now. Truman Capote's biographer has written about how his life was confused from the beginning because he longed for some male figure to whom he might attach himself.

The idea of an absent God is a concept out of which Luther made almost a theological doctrine: the God who hides, who is elusive, who escapes. *Deus absconditus!* said Luther. What a reversal is this passage. "Behold, I stand at the door, and knock." We speak of seeking the Lord, looking for him, trying to find him — as if he's off somewhere. That was our idea. People felt that they must find God. What a sharp contradiction is this passage, "I stand at the door, and knock," at your door, my door. What a sharp shift this is, from what we are accustomed to understanding, even in the Scripture, about the door. The Gospel of John speaks of the door by which the sheep come in and go out, and then Jesus says boldly, "I am the door." The sheep will go in and out and find pasture. "I am the door." What a reversal! Here he says, "I stand at the door, and knock." These are figures of speech, but the Door is now knocking at the door. "Behold." Do you know what that means? It means "listen," "attention," "look here," "listen to this."

You hear the preacher say the Lord stands at the door and knocks, but you do not believe it. I am not sure I believe it as I ought. Old Alexander Maclaren faced his congregation in an earlier generation in Manchester with that very word, that you do not believe it. If you believed that the Lord Jesus was standing at the door of your heart knocking, there would be such excitement in your hearts that you could hardly sit still. Behold! Amazing truth: "I stand at the door and knock." This word is addressed at the outset not only to those who have never accepted the Lord, but it is addressed to Christian people as well.

The Lord stands at your heart's door and mine asking for entrance, and if we have let him in the parlor, he wants to come into the dining room where the food and drink are. He wants to come into the bedroom. "I stand at the door and knock." He wants to come into the playroom where you entertain your friends. "I stand at the door and knock." The lonely Lord, knocking. Knocking.

Next week I want to talk about "hear my voice." Not only does he knock, but also he calls out. If you believed it, if I believed it, I could hardly stand in this place and you could hardly sit in your pew. Do you know who it is who's knocking? Do you know? This is the answer, after many centuries, to a word that was spoken back in the back pasture of Horeb, where God started to say who he was and never finished. Moses stood there, tending his father-in-law's sheep, and the Lord came to him to summon Moses to lead Israel to freedom, saying, "I will send thee unto Pharaoh, that thou must bring forth my people..." (Exodus 3:10).

Moses asked, "Who is signing this decree? Pharaoh is going to ask me what right have I to come tell him about the direction of the affairs of state. When he puts to me the question 'By what authority do you come here to this royal court, telling me what state policy ought to be,' whom shall I say sends me? I shrink," said Moses. "I'm a fugitive already. I have already killed a man, and I've run away from home. Pharaoh won't take my word. I'm from an enslaved people. Whom shall I say?" And God started saying who he was and would not tell Moses all that he was. He said, "I Am." That is not a full sentence, "Just tell him that I am" (Exodus 3:10–14). "Am" what?

God never finished that sentence back there in Horeb. This passage in Revelation completes who God is in history. "I am Jesus who knocks at the door." I Am is knocking. "I am the Good Shepherd knocking." "I am the light of the world." "I am that bread which came down from heaven." "I am the way, I am the truth, I am the light of the world." The great I Am is knocking at your door. "I am from everlasting to everlasting." "I am Alpha and Omega." "I am he who was dead and am alive forevermore." "I am the First and the Last." "I am knocking at your door." Knocking at my heart's door? Oh, my God, how quick we ought to be to answer him. The Lord is knocking!

Do you know who this is who is seeking entrance? This is the end of the prophets knocking at your door. This is the fulfillment of the whole Bible knocking at your door. This is the bringer of the new dispensation. This is God's Good News, no, no, this is God's *best* news, knocking at your door. This is the gospel in the flesh. This is God come down to earth. This is Emmanuel. This is the captain of our salvation. This is our Passover.

"Behold, I stand at the door." This is the Lord talking to you. This is the Savior of the world knocking at your door. This is the one whom Abraham longed to see knocking at your door. This is the One altogether lovely, the Prince of Peace, the Wonderful Counselor, the Mighty God, the Rose of Sharon, the Lily of the Valley, the Bright and Morning Star knocking at my heart's door.

You say to me, preacher, what shall I do? How do I open the door? And I will tell you very simply: trust him. Trust him. He's no robber, to come in to steal whatever you've got. Trust him, open the door. He has a thousand blessings in his hand. Open the door. He will bless your life. Open the door. Trust him. He will make things right in your life. Open the door. Whatever you have tried and it has failed, try Jesus. If you're down, he'll pick you up. If you're wrong, he'll make you right. Open the door. If you've got no friends, he'll be your friend. Open the door. Trust him.

Some foolish soul says, I don't want to spoil my fun. You will never know what fun is really all about until you know Jesus. You will never know what a party is until you are with the Lord. All of this knocking is of no purpose, no avail at all unless you do open the door. He says, "I will come in." He won't wave to you from the street. "I will come in." He won't merely stand at the door and talk to you, and then leave. "I will come in." Christ is saying, "Give me your confusion, and I will give you my peace. Give me your weakness, and I will give you my strength. Give me your darkness, and I will give you my light. Give you my helplessness, and I'll give you my power. I will come in and sit down and stay there and tarry with you and bless your life and open the way for you. And I will make friends for you and put food on your table and clothing on your back and shelter for your head. I'll give you a new song in your life. Let me in," the Savior pleads.

ᐧᐁ 36 ᐅᐣ

LAODICEA, PART V:
A PROMISE AFTER A WELCOME

Revelation 3:14–22

June 26, 1988

As we come today to the end of the third chapter of the Book of Revelation, one scene stands forth clearly and unmistakably at the end of that chapter. It is beyond misunderstanding. It is that the choice for God is completely in your hands. Not his, yours. The choice against God is surely in your hands, not his. If your destination is to be heaven here and hereafter, it is in your hands and mine. If heaven is to be your home, it is in your hands and mine, not God's.

The most famous picture that we have, one of the most famous paintings in all of Christian art and certainly one of the best known, is in St. Paul's Cathedral in London. It attracts thousands of visitors every year along with the tomb of England's best-known soldier, Wellington, which is in the crypt of St. Paul's also. It, as you will remember, pictures the Lord Christ knocking at a door. There is some kind of foliage around the door. You remember the picture. It is nighttime. We know that because the Seeker, the Knocker, the Suppliant, Christ, holds a lantern in his hand. The door is fast closed and barred. There's a crown around the head of the Seeker. You have seen it. A friend of Holman Hunt said to him there was one mistake in the painting. "What is that?" asked the artist. "There is no latch, no knob on the door." And the next time you see that painting, you look to see and you will notice that there is no latch on the outside. Hunt answered, "No, no, this is not a mistake. The door of the human heart opens only from the inside." The absence of a knob was deliberate and intentional. It is a vast word that not even the Lord Christ has a

264

knob, a latch on the outside of your door. He can knock, he can call out, "Behold, I stand at the door and knock." He can call out, "If any one hear my voice." That's as far as he can go.

You say, as I have raised one or two weeks before, what will happen? And remember, as I said last Sunday, that this word is not merely addressed to those who have never declared a part in Jesus Christ. It was originally addressed to the church, to people who are already declared Christians. Because there are, as I said last week, doors still barred in most of our lives against the Lord's entrance. What will happen? Will the house be pillaged and robbed if the Lord comes in? What will happen? We will not be pillaged and robbed. What will happen, you say, if I open the door and let him in? Does the place become rancid, gloomy, filled with a kind of heaviness, grimness? What will happen? He says, "If anyone will open the door, I will come in." And Jesus goes beyond that and says we'll sup with him. It is enough to take the breath away, if we really thought about it. We'll sup with him. Christ becomes our guest. He accepts what we have to offer. I will sup with him. So that no matter how coarse the fare is, no matter how rude and crude what we have on the table might be, he will be our guest and accept what we set before him. Who could ever think that the Lord, who has everything, would need anything of us? This is another side to religion that we do not think about often. We think often about what *we* need. But that the Lord needs from us baffles the imagination — that he is to receive something from our hands. He says, for instance, bring your tithes. We have prayer each Sunday about that. And yet we sing, and rightly, that "the cattle on a thousand hills are his." I had a deacon in New Orleans who used to say, "And the hills, also!" And yet, God says, give me. God says to us, give me. To think that God would need anything of us is enough to set the heart racing and the pulse beating at a very rapid rate.

He says, "I will sup with him. Christ," our guest! When we turn to the Scriptures we see again and again that the One who has everything has placed himself, located himself in such a condition and situation that he needs to receive from us. It would make a world of difference how we look upon this matter if we realize really that the Lord wants, yes, I dare to say it again, needs what you and I are and have. If you look at the life of our Lord Jesus, it is perfectly clear. He needed another's stable in which to be born. He needed another's boat from which to speak his word. He needed another's fish and bread in order to feed the multitudes. He needed another's house in which to have the Last Supper. He needed another's animal on which to ride into Jerusalem. He needed another's tomb in which to be buried.

I have said it over and over again that the Lord will never be in our debt. You let him in. He is our guest, and then he becomes the host. "I will sup with him and he with me." For, as I said the other Sunday, nobody who has ever opened unto the Lord his or her life has ever found anything except great blessing. I dared to repeat two Sundays later that ten thousand times ten thousand times ten thousand people in these many centuries have opened their lives unto Christ, and not a single one has ever said that it was worse after he came in than it was before he came in, not one. "I will sup with him and he with me."

Now let me talk for a moment with these young people. You young people, sitting there before me, are beginning your course in life, so to speak. I talked with a reporter for one of our daily papers for an article on black young people and the church. As she and I talked, it became clearer and clearer how desperately the young, as well as the old, need the Lord. You are going into a society that is ill. It is not the same kind of overt poison that I saw and with which many of us grew up. I remember forty-five years ago Mrs. Taylor taking an examination for a public position in New Orleans. She finished second on the list. She was told quite openly, "This job is not for a black person." You will not encounter that often now. It is more subtle. Perhaps discrimination was easier back then to deal with because now you are never sure what side of the street you're really walking on. You will likely be sometimes, though I pray God not, passed over. Will it be because of your race, or will it be because you are not skillful enough? How will you know which it is? What yardstick can you have for measuring your own capacity and for looking at yourself honestly? What yardstick is reliable, indeed, except Jesus Christ, who lets us look at ourselves as we are and also enables us to see ourselves as we can be. Nobody else is able to expose us to ourselves. This is the great need of so many of our lives, to understand ourselves, who we are, what we are, why we are, where we are, whose we are. He alone has that word, and he alone can show us not only what we are — perhaps others can do that to some extent — but often what we can be.

How will you tell where you are, and how will you direct your passage? By the sea? It changes, and life, like the sea, is never the same. It smiles sometimes. It frowns sometimes. Sometimes it seems totally indifferent to us. I have seen the sea, and life is like that, so raw and so angry that it foams at the mouth and one cannot see ahead in the darkness of the night.

I have been on ships in great seas where the waters were so turbulent and so angry and the billows would rise so high that it would seem as if the ship at the next trough of the waves would go under. I remember a night on the Mediterranean forty years ago in a little Greek ship on a placid sea. So calm the waters were, so still that they seemed like a mirror. I can still see across forty years the moon casting its light on that placid, calm sea as if it were an endless lane of brightness, an endless highway of light. Life is like that. It is sometimes calm. It seems so friendly. Everything seems to be on our side. We seem to move so easily, so effortlessly along. But, then again, and like the sea, almost in the "batting of an eye" (as we say in the South), it changes. It is raw, angry, turbulent. How will you measure, how will you guide yourself on this sea of life? Will you call out to other ships? Well, thank God, one of the joys of being at sea is now and then sighting another vessel, for they're sailing on uncharted waters also. Will you ask them, Where am I? How do they know where you are?

No, if you're going to sail this sea of life, you need some fixed point, and the only fixed point there is the compass, the Eternal Star, Christ Jesus, and he is a compass by which you can steer safely toward port. Ah, it is a difficult world into which our young people go and in which they live. With all of the wiles and terrors and temptations around, how will you manage it, old and young? How will you manage it?

There is but one answer, and here it is. I would have you notice that from the twentieth to the twenty-first verse there is no skip, no interruption, no pause. "Behold, I stand at the door and knock: if any man hear my voice, and open the door, I will come into him, and will sup with him, and he with me." "To him that overcometh." Directly after "I will sup with him, and he with me," it reads "to him that overcometh." If you want to bring your life to triumph, here it is. Let the Lord in. He promises the victory "to him that overcometh." He would not deceive us. He would not fool us that way. He says, "Let me in. I will sup with you and you with me," and consequently, such a one "overcometh." In a world where crack is and where suicide is and where money rules, my God, the promise of victory is for the soul who lets Christ in.

I spoke in Dayton on Thursday evening. On television that night I saw, after the service, a depiction of how sniffing cocaine and smoking crack can take away everything we've got. I wish every young person, I wish every old person, for that matter, could see it. How after many days of sniffing, friends do not want to associate with us any longer. There are not many days of sniffing before the family is separated from us. Not many days of sniffing or smoking before we have lost ourselves. And you know, people do not take drugs because of what drugs are. They take drugs because of who they fear themselves to be — because they feel inadequate. They can't cope, or they feel they can't cope. They feel down, and they need to be picked up. That's why they take drugs, not just because the substance is crack or cocaine or heroin. They're looking for adequacy.

You young people are coming into a generation that is completely money-minded. Of course you need conveniences and comfort, of course you ought to have that, you ought to have all of those things. But as I have said before here and elsewhere, that when the means to something become the end, you have no-where to go. You're on a dead-end street where there is only end. You have come up in a generation which has been saturated with nothing but debt because people are searching for adequacy. It is no accident, I think, that the two most enduring television shows of this decade have dealt with conspicuous consumption, corporate sleaze, and loose family arrangements: *Dallas* and *Dynasty*. It is no accident, I think, that one of the most widely watched television shows in America today is something entitled *The Lifestyles of the Rich and Famous.*

People do not go out just to get things, and their real motive leads to so many things. It leads to corruption in government and in industry. It leads people to steal, to lie, to embezzle, to take shortcuts. They don't go out to do that because it is fun doing it. They go out because they believe security is at the end of it all. And security is not at the end of it. There is no place to find some integration for our souls except in Jesus Christ. That is what drugs are all about. Drugs simulate a sense of feeling right about ourselves. Christ the Lord can really make you feel right about yourself. There is no security except in Jesus Christ, who says "I will come in and sup with him and he with me. To him that overcometh...."

You know, we talk about being masters of our fate and captains of our soul. I recited that bravely to my classmates when I finished seventh grade. It is from "Invictus," the poem by Ernest Henley: "It matters not, how straight the gate, how charged with punishment the scroll, I am the master of my fate, I am the captain of my soul." If you are the master of your fate, your fate is in bad hands. And if you are the captain of your soul, then the army is going down to defeat! Henley's own last days were saddened by the death of his beloved daughter and estrangement from his erstwhile friend, Robert Louis Stevenson. You, too, need another master. You need another captain.

"To him that overcometh." "I will give you the victory. I will put something in you," Jesus says, "so that nobody can stop you and nobody can hold you down and nobody can convince you that you cannot make it." I would to God as I call to you from out here in the evening and to those of you who are in the morning, remember this: Christ alone can build you up, strengthen you for whatever might happen to you, put a spring in your step and courage in your heart and determination in your will, that no matter what happens, you overcome.

I would for the next second or two that you would hear me very carefully. Christ can do that for you. And he will do that for you. I say to myself as well as to you, let us be done with all defeatism. This world is not lost. Christ has died for it. I get often depressed about circumstances, too, but what we are seeing now is not the last word, not the last word at all. Christ is going to win. His cause is going to overcome. God has decreed it. And Christ and his cause and his purpose and those who are committed to him will go forward. All of these things we now pass through will themselves pass away. You will see it. Prejudice, confusion, these things do not have the last word. The victory belongs to Jesus Christ. Join yourselves to him, young people, old people. Hitch your hopes and your dreams to your Lord. He will not fail you. He promises victory and he makes us "more than conquerors" (Romans 8:37).